NEW PRODUCT DEVELOPMENT

What Really Works

George Gruenwald

NTC Business Books
a division of National Textbook Company • Lincolnwood Illinois U.S.A.

1988 Printing

Published by NTC Business Books, an imprint
of National Textbook Company, 4255 West Touhy Avenue,
Lincolnwood, Illinois 60646-1975 U.S.A.
Manufactured in the United States of America.
Library of Congress Catalog Card Number: 83-71075

8 9 0 ML 0 9 8 7 6 5 4 3 2

To Paul

Contents

Acknowledgments

For suggesting that I write this book, Kathryn Sederberg, then director of *Crain Books*, who also served as its insightful editor. For shepherding it along, its former new products and market development manager, Rich Hagle. For managing the logistics, Clara Westerhaus, friend and assistant. For forfeiting our vacation companionship to this project, my wife Corrine. For a continual input of research, my son Paul.

For early encouragement to take on the assignment, Madeline Betsch and Howard Liszt, both of Campbell-Mithun Inc. And for the assistance of others at major marketer companies who helped mightily, including:

- On the margarine case history: Ralph Hofstad, Ev Baldwin,* Karl Larson, and Tom Minogue of Land O'Lakes, Inc., working with Don Ittner, Larry Buntin, Don Gillies, and Howard Liszt of C-M.
- On The Toro Company case history: Ken Melrose and John Szafranski, with special effort by Lynn Matson, then of Campbell-Mithun, now a Toro Co. distributor.
- For The Quaker Oats Company sales analysis: Ken Mason, its former president (now retired), who also suggested the Fisher-Price Toys case history, specially prepared for this book by its general manager Jim Tindall.
- For other expressly prepared materials for this book: Charlie McGill,

*Then an officer of Land O' Lakes, today president of Welch Foods Co.

The Pillsbury Company; Theo Steele, Landor Associates; Dean Randall and Fredrick Klein, Honeywell Inc.

- For preparation of special art and photography: Dick Hane, Greg Page, and the Communications Workshop staff at C-M. For media overview: Earl Herzog. For research input and overview: Len Larson, Tom Thomas, of Campbell-Mithun Inc., and Bert Kohn, of D'Arcy, McManus & Masius.

- For materials personally selected to assist in this book: Ernie Moffet, Robert Ferderer, Bob Gubrud, M. R. Harsha, and T. J. Scheuerman, 3M Company; Sheila Paterson, Joan Rothberg, and Tad van Dusen, Ted Bates Advertising; Dave Hardin, Market Facts, Inc.; Bruce Atwater, General Mills Inc.; Linus Pauling, Linus Pauling Institute of Science and Medicine; Tate Lane, recently retired from Geo. A. Hormel & Co.; Harry Paster, American Association of Advertising Agencies; and Bill Kobin, KCET-TV, Los Angeles.

- For the fine cooperation of many leading organizations and staff: *Ad Forum*'s Lisa Decker; *Advertising Age*'s Marion Elmquist; American Management Association's Eileen Altman and Therese Mausser; Advertising Research Foundation's Michael J. Naples; Boston University's Kevin Clancy and Don Kanter; The Conference Board's David S. Hopkins; Format's Kathy Madison; *Harvard Business Review*'s Caroline Jacobs; A.C. Nielsen's Travis Whitlow; SRI's Dorothy Benjamin; Schrello Associates' Jocelyn Peterson; Sidley & Austin's Quincy White; J. Walter Thompson's Sonia Yuspeh; Vanderbilt University's Joseph P. Blackburn.

Special acknowledgment to the late Don Nathanson, who underwrote one of the first new products companies and had the faith to encourage its risk taking, and to Saul Ben Zeev, Irv White, Dick Feit, Jim Green, Herb Klauber, Bernice Hagberg, Harold Rosenzweig, and others who helped form Pilot Products Inc. in those early days. To Robert Rountree, who was very early to circulate my theories and procedures nationally in his pioneering new products newsletter, *The Rountree Report*; and to Rance Crain, Sid Bernstein, Jack Graham, Nancy Millman, and all of my many friends at *Advertising Age* who have published some of my observations on the subject of this book: new products.

Introduction

For Whom Was This Book Written?

It was written for anyone making decisions affecting new products programs; anyone responsible for judging the process; any practitioner, consultant, student; or anyone just plain interested in how new products are conceived, born, and brought to market.

Why Was This Book Written?

Business needs new products just to survive. This has never been more true than today. The pace quickens. Consumers accept new products faster and reject them faster. Life cycles of products are shorter—except for those that are continually infused with "newness," significant improvements that keep them in the forefront of their category.

The importance of new products is attested to by the fact that products introduced in the past five years account for the majority of sales and profits for many industry leaders.

At the same time, technology kills entire categories, while creating new problems to be solved by new products. Communications must be briefer, more single-minded. Products must have a sharpened reason to exist—computer inventory control soon sorts out undistinguished brands.

Governmental restrictions, consumerist pressures, buyer sophistication, and foreign competition draw tighter parameters, thus increasing the challenge.

Both the private and public sectors need new products and services to keep up with the demands of rising living standards, disposable income, quicker identification of problem areas, and growing venturesomeness.

Two organizational changes in industry have had profound influence on new products and services.

The first was the widespread adoption of the product manager system. Joining the product manager (or brand manager) organization was the profit center system, accountable for its own profits (and losses). This restructuring of management systems led to an emphasis on cost-effectiveness in marketing decision-making—a concern for favorable investment-return ratios—and, with that, a financially oriented marketing philosophy.

The second change was the shift of new product responsibilities—a change that is continuing today. Formerly, most organized new products efforts were centered in research and development (or engineering) departments. Today, they are mostly centered in revenue divisions—marketing groups with profit responsibilities. Additionally, some companies have new products departments, and some have made progress in seeding new-products-only groups, venture teams to open up new areas. Over-all coordination, including acquisitions, is often centered in a growth and development executive.

At the same time, the research and development effort has become more important through better direction: It improves quality control standards, does basic research, and is given better direction, usually product opportunity targets provided by the marketing groups.

A company may organize the management of its new products program along the following lines:

Revenue division: responsible for the existing product line, its customer franchise, and its expansion, by way of appropriate new additions. This development is funded by the established business unit's own revenues.

Capability development: an extension of the company's strengths (whether manufacturing, sourcing of material, technology, distribution, etc.) to seed new divisions.

New enterprises: an extension of company capabilities within its basic industry to achieve new strengths and to develop entirely new businesses. It often identifies acquisitions, joint ventures, licensing opportunities, or outside contract manufacturing candidates. (However, going *outside* the basic industry for new enterprises is a general management function not normally assumed in any aspect of the formalized new products function.)

Long range development: new business program planning, which integrates forecasting of evolving scientific and technology advances; population and industry changes in composition, location and behavior; etc.

How Does This Book Define a New Product?

For the purposes of this book, a new product also means a new service—or a "package" of services or of products and services (e.g., business machines, programs, software, and technical service may be "packaged" as a new product). To simplify presentation, "new products" will represent any or all of these possible ramifications.

As for a definition, the broadest possible description is used. No one definition is precise to every need. Because of the various interpretations of what a new product constitutes, we have widely ranging assessments of new product success and failure rates. In the shelf-stable grocery field, for example, the leading new product successes are usually low-technology products that are slight variations on existing established products. Under such a definition, one would expect low capital risk and relatively high success rates, where success is related to expected performance against financial risk goals. Such successes are *marketing* successes.

An example of the financial commitment to recent marketing successes was cited by William D. Smithburg, president and chief executive officer of the Quaker Oats Company, in reference to their Chewy Granola Bars: "You would be dealing with $2,000,000 or $3,000,000 in research and development, as much as $15,000,000 or $20,000,000 of marketing development, probably $10,000,000 or $15,000,000 capital investment."

In some industries and scientific services, a new product may be almost entirely technologically based, require heavy research investment, and long lead time. Usually, the marketing investment is relatively low in sophisticated industrial technology successes.

With that understood, what *is* a new product?

- To the maker, a new product is something he doesn't make now.
- To the customer, a new product is something he has never heard of.

There are other judges of what defines a new product—from the U.S. Patent Office to the Food and Drug Administration, which may view a new product under its jurisdiction as something that does not have a long and safe use history in this country and/or has not successfully survived a range of carefully controlled testing procedures, and received the agency's approval.

The reader can think of other definitions.

In a broad sense, here is a useful classification of new products:

A. Evolution of existing product
   1. Repositioned product
   2. Recycled product
   3. Appearance/form improvement
   4. Performance improvement
   5. Packaging construction improvement

6. Price/value change
7. Distribution pattern change
8. Combination of several of the above
B. Expansion of a brand/product franchise
1. Line extensions to the brand
2. Flankers to the brand
3. New category for the brand
C. New entry into an established category
D. New category
E. New business

How is This Book Organized?

In an ideal world, perhaps, new product development would proceed in chronological order. As it is, many steps proceed at different paces; unplanned accidents spawn problems—and inspirations; outside factors exercise more control than inside planning.

This book necessarily addresses a disciplined, phased process with predetermined decision points. In fact, the seminal union of concept and practice may be a constantly regenerative process, fissured however with unpredictable divisions, splices, and clones. Effective practitioners will not lose sight of this.

The critical path to new product success is strewn with broken event bubbles. Nonetheless, a program is planned with a sense of order. The order followed by the sections of this book is:

Need leads to *Commitment* leads to *Exploration* leads to *Conception* leads to *Modeling* (the beginning of the product development process) leads to *Marketing* leads to *Market Testing* leads to *Major Introduction* leads to continual commercial viability by keeping the product forever new.

At the end of each section, there is a summary afterword—a highlight outline of guideposts developed in the preceding chapters of the section.

The direction (and style) of this book is that of a new product generalist. Enough is offered to provide all of the guidance needed to design a new products marketing development program. Highly technical computer forecasting models, various research techniques to optimize successful predictability, and specific proprietary programs being offered by outside services are avoided for the most part. Plentiful literature is available in these fields, for those readers with specific special interests.

Many of the examples given are from package goods manfacturers, who are widely visible, heavily chronicled in the trade press, and least esoteric for students of new products development. The procedures, however, are generally applicable to any field.

This Book has a Bias

It is infused with the author's nearly 40 years' experience as a practitioner in the field working with more than 20 Fortune 500 companies, as well as many others—the learning gained both by participating in and by observing failures and successes in the pursuit of new products in a wide range of fields from telecommunications, business machines, and automobiles to consumer appliances, package goods, and financial services, in various roles as a maker and marketer, as a consultant and as an agent, as well as in executive positions with several major advertising agencies distinguished by their success records in new products marketing development in fields ranging across dozens of industrial and service classifications.

Recent research for this book was done in Western Europe, where many new product forms, processes, packaging, and marketing are inspiring U.S. adaptations, and in Southern California, where life-style changes and quick trial of anything new often foretell our nation's consumer and high tech industry trends.

For me, there is nothing more rewarding in business than the satisfaction and excitement of being party to the conception, gestation, birth, and life of a new product. Once born, the product's growing pains to successful maturity and then the constant search for a fountain of youth to keep the offering forever new outshine any other business experience.

The over-all conclusion from these experiences is that the principles and judgments advocated herein are applicable to any new products program, with appropriate adaptation by the funding resource and to the market needs.

G.G.
Rancho Santa Fe, California

Need

Need for Growth and Diversification

There are only two important functions in business: Marketing and innovation; everything else is cost.
—Peter Drucker

Nowhere is Peter Drucker's statement more true than in new product development. In fact, several companies and some entire industries are based on effectiveness in this area. Their success rates have been conditioned by proven systems of procedure and event planning—well in advance of major financial commitment. The payoff, of course, depends upon the ability to *execute*, both with precision and with realistic marketplace flexibility.

Key to Sales Growth

New products are the key to a company's sales growth. According to a Booz Allen & Hamilton 1975 survey: "In the next three years alone, about 75 percent of the nation's growth in sales volume can be expected to come from new products, including new brands." In other words, if you include everything from minor innovations to major new brands, new products are the most vital fuel of our economy.

Some specific examples:

- The multi-billion-dollar 3M (Minnesota Mining and Manufacturing) Company leverages its technological leadership to generate a 25 percent increase each year from new products that didn't exist five years previously, according to an article in the Minneapolis Tribune, May 24, 1981.

- Some companies in new-products-intensive industries, such as toys (on one extreme) and pharmaceuticals (on another) generate more than 60 percent of their income over a similar period. Even the service industries benefit.
- One advertising agency, Campbell-Mithun Inc., estimates that 60 percent of its income has been generated by helping clients introduce $5 billion (factory, not retail, dollars) in new products over a five-year period.

According to a 1980 report from The Conference Board, even when classifying *only major new products* (not mere line extensions), reliance on new products for company growth is important to all classifications of industry. The Conference Board reports that of 148 companies surveyed,

15 percent of their current sales volume is attributable to the sale of major new products introduced by them during the past five years. This average (as measured by the median) dependence on new products is similar for manufacturers of either industrial or consumer products. The range for individual firms goes all the way from zero to more than 50 percent. As might be expected, firms in stable, commodity-type industries tend to be less dependent on new products than those in specialty businesses, where opportunities for innovation are higher or product life cycles shorter.

Looking to the future, two-thirds of the reporting executives expect their companies to have an even greater dependence on new products over the next five years.

Yet another example of the need for new products is that a key consideration of executive recruits in considering new employers is the company's new product record. This is taken to be a sure sign of a manager's growth opportunities.

New Products Sustain Company

Everyone in industry knows that new products are essential for viability: If we do not continue to grow, we die. To do this, a company must continue to learn (research) and to make a difference in its industry (pioneer).

These are not mottos for milking cash cows; the words are prophetic for any enterprise with a long-term goal of financial and psychic rewards for its employees and shareholders.

Here, new products are the key to success.

Business, whether it sells waste management or interstellar communications, janitorial services or gene-splicing, lives through new growth—not through clones of the past.

Diversification Essential

Both growth and diversification are served by a well-articulated new product program. Most companies recognize that there are various means to achieve diversification.

When the need is not within the capability of your company, but fits the corporate charter that guides the activities of the company, then beneficial arrangements can be made with other companies, to joint-venture, contract-supply, license/acquire or, in rare instances, to merge—be acquired by a complementary organization. Pools of expertise can also be acquired by recruiting within the subject industry and by the use of technical and marketing consultants. If your company is not on the leading edge of a new product development—seek outside help. Beware the defensive NIH syndrome—the "not invented here" factor.

Two of the most advanced new products innovators have no such inhibitions, as witness this news item from the Paris edition of the *International Herald Tribune*, Sept. 23, 1981:

Nippon Telegraph & Telephone said it will sign a cross-licensing agreement with International Business Machines. The proposed five-year accord will allow the two firms to use each other's patents on electronic switching systems, computers and terminal equipment free of charge.

Often, different skills and organizations are needed to advance most effectively on more than one front at a time. All of the above can be a part of a growth plan to enhance established capabilities—or to diversify. Most often, it is both.

The most ambitious and dynamic enterprises should carefully consider a multi-pronged organizational approach to every area of growth and diversification. In many cases, *all* should be adopted.

To recognize the consequences of failure to grow and to diversify, you need only to observe those industries locked into a posture controlled by outside events that have not been recognized. Geographic population shifts and changing needs, resources, and marketplace value systems dictate a review of the corporate charter. Media changes also can affect redefinition of the charter. Contemporary computerized techniques for segmentation make available discrete marketing opportunities that may have been previously inefficient and hence unaffordable. Such segmentation suggests new products opportunities, which may be characterized by the commonality of neighborhood social definition, and reached by new ZIP code sorting, by telephone, with two-way cable, or with programmatic precision over 100-channel cable.

Some savants of doom say that the era of new products marketing is fading with an over-saturation of options, efficient mass distribution, generic low-priced parity products, and a glut of inefficient media.

Then along comes the next series of breakthroughs—and all evidence points to the contrary. The corporate charters, the rules of the game, and the means change—but the need for new products not only persists, but is on the increase.

2

Why New Products Fail

Everything seems stupid when it fails.
—*Fyodor Dostoevsky*

Nobody's perfect.
—*Joe E. Brown*, in "Some Like It Hot," 20th Century Fox

There are no reliable overall statistics on new product successes or failures, though there are plenty offered by industry classification. Even here, the numbers are apt to be misleading. One company's failure could be another's success (and vice versa). It depends on the goals. One chief executive of a specialty food company (flavor enhancers) said: "Bring us all those ideas you have that do not meet the large volume goals of your giant clients—we know how to make money from special purpose products." That's true across that entire field, from McCormick-Schilling spices to Wm. Underwood Co. (Ac-'cent) to McIlhenny's Tabasco. In other words, a failure for General Foods could be a smashing success for General Spices. And so it goes in most categories.

The Numbers

If you'd like some numbers, here are some comments and some success/failure scores from a 1980 study by The Conference Board:

For purposes of the present study, a major new product was taken to be a success if it met management's original expectations for it in all important respects. Conversely, a major new product was taken to have been a failure if, in some important respect, it failed to have met management's original expectations for it. Although such a product often continued to be sold, the extreme possibility was that its performance proved so disappointing that it was actually withdrawn from the market.

Half of the companies surveyed had achieved success, as defined above, with at least two-thirds of the major new products that they marketed over the past five years. The other half reported such success with fewer than two-thirds of their new products—and there were some for which each and every one of their new offerings had proved disappointing. These median values for new-product success (i.e., two out of three meeting management's expectations in all important respects) were the same for manufacturers selling either to industrial or consumer markets. [Table 2-1 summarizes these findings.]

Table 2-1
Success Rates for Major New Products in Past Five Years

Successful New Products	Percentage of Companies Selling Primarily to	
	Industrial Markets	Consumer Markets
All succeeded	9	18
90 to 99%	7	4
80 to 89%	16	9
70 to 79%	11	11
60 to 69%	16	12
50 to 59%	15	15
40 to 49%	4	2
30 to 39%	9	9
1 to 29%	5	4
None succeeded	8	16
	100	100

The success rate reported by each company represents the percentage of all major new products introduced to the market by the company during the previous five years which subsequently met management's expectations in all important respects.

Source: The Conference Board

(A similar poll, conducted in 1971, found that the equivalent median values for success with major new products at that time were approximately 80 percent for industrial product firms and 60 percent for consumer product firms. Especially in view of sampling differences, however, probably not too much importance should be attached to differences in the success rate between the 1971 and 1979 surveys.)

(In each of the surveys, most product failures [not having met management's expectations in some important respect] did not result in such disappointing performance as to require actually being withdrawn from the market. In the 1979 survey, the proportion of all major new products marketed by the reporting companies which later proved so disappointing that they had to be removed from the market was about 9 percent for industrial product firms and about 13 percent for consumer product firms.)

Complete success or complete failure is more common among manufacturers catering to consumer markets than among those servicing industrial markets. However, firms falling at either of these extremes include, to an above average extent, a number that launched only relatively few major new products. A firm that sends to market only one or two major new items over a five-year period is perhaps either exceptionally cautious or exceptionally short in new-product experience. In either case, the low number of products at risk increases the chances of total success or total failure.

Nevertheless, reporting firms with a perfect batting average for new products include a large manufacturer of metal components and equipment with over 100 successful new products; a producer of electrical components with 25; a petroleum products company with nine; a paper products company with six; and two drug manufacturers each having a handful or so of consistently successful new items.

Among the firms that went scoreless for five long years are included a large chemicals producer with 20 new-product failures; a small manufacturer of heating equipment with 11; a producer of sports equipment with six; and two firms making office supplies and two others in packaged goods industries, each with several losers and no winners at all.

Management View

How do managements, in general, regard their companies' new-product performances? On the whole, they are reported to be quite well satisfied. More than one-third of the total regard their rate of success with major new products as being highly acceptable, and another half of them as being disappointing, but still acceptable. Only a small minority view their new-product performance as being unacceptably low. [Table 2-2 outlines these views.]

Managements in firms selling to consumer markets seem to be even more pleased with the outcome than are those concerned with industrial markets. And there is a correlation between the degree of management satisfaction and the relative degree of success actually achieved over the past five years. Thus, as many as four out of five managements of companies with success rates well above average (i.e., falling within the top quartile of those surveyed) find this result highly acceptable. In contrast, where success rates were much below average (i.e., falling within the bottom quartile in terms of success), very few managements consider the result highly acceptable. Yet managements are not uniformly discouraged even in these cases. While more than a quarter of them consider the performance unacceptably low, two-thirds view it as disappointing—but still acceptable. . . .

Table 2-2
How Management Views the Acceptability of New-Product Success Rates Achieved

Management Feeling	% of All Reporting Companies	% of Companies Selling Primarily to		% of Companies Whose Past Success Rate Was			
		Industrial Markets	Consumer Markets	Much Above Average	Somewhat Above Average	Somewhat Below Average	Much Below Average
Highly ac- ceptable	37	33	44	79	42	15	5
Disappoint- ing, but still acceptable	52	57	44	21	53	73	67
Unaccept- ably low	11	10	12	—	5	12	28
	100	100	100	100	100	100	100

Source: The Conference Board.

Dissecting the Failure Rate

The median failure rates for new products found in both the 1971 and 1979 surveys by The Conference Board are sharply lower than averages sometimes quoted and repeated by certain other observers of the new-product scene. The statement has been made from time to time, for example, that typically as many as eight or nine out of every ten new products turn out to be failures.

Differences of definition probably account for most such seeming discrepancies. The Board's surveys cover major new products that firms have actually introduced to the market. In contrast, some other observers have apparently referred to new-product ventures that may have been abandoned at a much earlier stage in their development.

Many managements have had the experience of bringing a new product toward the point of launch, perhaps even to test market, and have then had second thoughts and held it back. Possibly some such ventures might have become winners, yet the likelihood is there were sound reasons for management to fear they would have become losers in the marketplace. And obviously behind such near-starters there are often numerous other projects, or mere proposals, that are picked up by R and D or examined by the company's marketing research unit in a preliminary way and soon dropped from further consideration. In general, the farther back along the development process it is decided to set the cut-off point for definition of a new product, the greater might be the expected proportion of failures reported.

Operating in the reverse direction, however, one could take into account "new products" of all kinds—not only major new products covered in the Board's surveys, but also lesser product improvements and line extensions that characteristically have more assurance of success. In that event, the proportion of "winners" to "losers" might be expected to be higher—not lower—than the Board's findings.

Acceptable Risk

The prevailing view is that it is realistic to expect an occasional loser mixed in with the winners. Most of the marketers surveyed consider some element of risk to be inherent—even desirable—in any active program of new-product development.

One executive sums up for many when he declares: "A 100 percent success rate can never be assured in the marketplace, and any company that insists on this will surely see a great number of opportunities pass it by."

Acknowledging that virtually every new product inevitably carries some risk does not, however, preclude attempts to cut such risk to a minimum. The general view is that management should at least insist on maximum effort and aim for the bull's-eye every time. There is, to be sure, a minority view found in certain industrial firms, where so significant an investment is required to bring any new offering to market that no failure whatever can be countenanced.[1]

Importance of New Products

In quoting a Booz, Allen & Hamilton study of the success rate of 13,311 items introduced by 700 companies between 1976 and 1981, *The Wall Street Journal* writes:

Although success rates for new products haven't improved over the past 13 years, marketers are banking on them more than ever for future growth. New products will account for 31 percent of profits over the next five years, compared with 22 percent over the past five. These new products will account for 37 percent of total sales growth, compared with 28 percent in the earlier period.

In contrast, acquisitions are expected to contribute just 9 percent of sales growth over the next five years; 54 percent will come from existing products. Additional evidence of the importance marketers attach to new products: companies expect to bring out a median of 10 products each in the next five years, compared with half that many in the past five years.

The consulting firm's study, one of the most extensive on a much-researched subject, consisted of a mail survey answer by 700 of 2,800 companies. Three-fifths of the survey respondents sell industrial goods, with the rest evenly divided between consumer durables and nondurable products. . . . Success was determined by the company's own criteria.

Although marketers may not be improving their new-product batting average, they are becoming more efficient at developing products. Today only seven ideas need to be seriously evaluated to find one successful product, compared with a 58:1 ratio in a 1968 study. One reason: earlier weeding of ideas that are weak or don't fit a company's over-all strategy.

[1]David S. Hopkins, "New-Product Winners and Losers," Report No. 773, © The Conference Board, Inc., New York. Reprinted by permission.

New-product spending also is more efficient. Today successful entries account for 54 percent of total new-product expenditures, compared with 30 percent in 1968. Capital investment as a percent of total new-product spending has fallen to 26 percent from 46 percent in 1968.

The external factor most likely to inhibit product introductions is the rising cost of capital. It was cited by two-thirds of the respondents. Internal obstacles mentioned by more than 40 percent of those in the survey: current business pressures that reduce attention to new products and corporate emphasis on short-term profitability. The leading stimulus to new products cited by 86 percent of respondents—technological advances.

The *Journal* cited other findings of the Booz Allen study:

One-third of all companies don't formally measure the performance of new products. Those that do most often use sales volume, percentage of sales, profits, or return on investment.

Successful new product companies don't spend more, as a percentage of sales, than unsuccessful ones on research and development and promotion of new products.

Top corporate management devotes 7 percent of its time to new products. Marketing managers spend 21 percent; R&D and engineering managers, 42 percent.

Just 5 percent of companies surveyed pay new-product executives a bonus tied to the performance of their entries.

Each time a company doubles its number of new products, its cost per introduction falls 29 percent. There's no correlation, though, between the number of new products and success rates.

Reasons for Failure

Obviously, money devoted to failures is money that might better have been spent on developing and introducing successes. Knowing causes for failure can help screen-out ill-fated ventures before much time and money has been consumed.

It is instructive to look at how management appraises some of the reasons for success and failure in achievement of new product goals. As would be suspected, the reasons are similar: e.g., predictive/nonpredictive market research, good/poor timing, etc.

Following is a catalog of reasons for failure, as tabulated by a number of leading research firms. (See Table 2-3.) Note how many may have been predictable prior to heavy investment of precious time and money resources. Note how many, if the opposite is stated, become reasons for success.

Poor Planning

It is unfortunately true that poor planning is the single biggest reason for new product failures. Too often, facts and factors that would have been foretold are either overlooked or are ignored.

Here are just a few examples:

Table 2-3
Studies of New Product Failure Rates

Research Company	Year	Firms Studied	Failure Rate (%)
New Products Institute, Inc.[1]	1955	200	81
A.C. Nielsen[2]	1962	103 brands	46
Arthur Gerstenfeld[3]	1969	158	71
A.C. Nielsen[4]	1971	204 brands	53
Mansfield and Wagner[5]	1975	18	68
A.T. Kearney[6]	1976	Unstated	50–95
Booz, Allen & Hamilton[7]	1981	700	35

Sources:
1. Peter M. Kraushar, New Products and Diversification, Brandon Systems Press, 1970
2. "New Product Success Rate," Nielsen Researcher, 1971
3. Arthur Gerstenfeld, Effective Management of Research and Development, Addison-Wesley, 1970
4. "New Product Success Rate," Nielsen Researcher, 1971
5. Edwin Mansfield and Samuel Wagner, "Organization and Strategic Factors Associated with Probabilities of Success in Industrial R&D," Journal of Business, April 1975
6. "The Breakdown of U.S. Innovation," Business Week, February 16, 1976
7. "Despite Mixed Record, Firms Still Pushing New Products," The Wall Street Journal, November 12, 1981

- The product doesn't fit company strategy.
- The product doesn't fit company expertise.
- It doesn't fit company distribution strength/knowledge.
- It doesn't fit company margin, return-on-investment, or return-on-sales requirements.
- The cost of entering the category is an unsurmountable barrier.
- The diffuse category is not vulnerable to a single entry; a line assault is needed.
- The manufacturing, purchasing, and quality control standards are unfamiliar.
- The regulatory complications are unfamiliar.
- There are patent, copyright, or license infringements.
- The market analysis is inadequate.
- Development funds are inadequate.
- The company fails to face up to competitive strengths—*after* launch.
- The product has no phased critical path with clear time, budget, and go/no go decision points.
- There is no preplan guideline checklist.
- The timing is poor—too early, or too late.

Poor Management

Poor planning and poor management are really interlocking failures. Management is responsible for the planning process and for authorizing the planned programs. Although managements identify poor research and poor timing as top failure factors in many surveys, the answer lies closer to home.

Some examples of poor management:

- The product doesn't fit the corporate or division charter guiding such activities.
- There was no management "sponsor."
- The product introduction is an unchecked management "ego trip" (i.e., the "sponsorship" is too powerful).
- There is no management information system to provide two-way communication.
- Management direction and goals are confusing and inconsistent.
- The wrong department leads the introduction program.
- Those who should have been pioneers and risk-takers are unwilling.
- There are budget and time constraints—change of signals—due to an unanticipated course of events.
- There are manufacturing, sales efforts, and communications constraints resulting from the change of signals, due to the unanticipated course of events.
- Management direction is capricious.

Needed is a balance between carefully designed critical path-planning and entrepreneurial risk-taking. Each major step in a phased program should require management to authorize termination, proceed as planned, or proceed with gap jumps or with added steps. The plan should be a living guide, subject to change with new knowledge, outside circumstances, and unforeseen breakthroughs or roadblocks. In fact, more programs tend to be carried along farther than they should be than are terminated too early or when they should be. There often tends to be a management inertia—a career identification with the project and the procedure—which is not justified by the facts. Some project managers admit that they do not want to recommend themselves "out of a job" by killing their program. Rather than fostering this wasteful attitude, management should reward pragmatic recommendations (which, after all, save dollars that may then be applied to future, hopefully successful projects). Because management of an established brand is often the career carrot for a new products manager, a premium is placed on rushing to market.

Reinforcing this view is an indictment from Gerald Schoenfeld, who heads a New York consultancy under his name, as reported by Philip H. Dougherty in the *New York Times* in 1981:

When a brand manager, who learned nothing about new products in business school, is put in charge of a new product venture and has a success, he or she is quickly plucked out of that job and thrown against existing family jewels. That's what pays the rent. A new product guy is a minister without portfolio, a brand manager without a brand.

What is needed, according to Mr. Schoenfeld, is a corporate reorganization that would make the new product team "the Marines and the Green Berets."

As a former new product brand manager, I would like to underscore that different management attitudes (and, perhaps, skills, as well) are needed to be an entrepreneurial innovator than are needed to nurture institutionalized products. Yet the reward system in most companies favors those who manage the more easily forecastable fortunes of the established products—rather than the sowers and tillers of future growth.

Thorough planning requires more than doing it "by the book." No two projects are exactly alike, nor should any two plans be identical. The "real world" has different effects on the planning. The course being charted grows out of varying degrees of foreknowledge. Careful, detailed, imaginative pre-planning cannot be overemphasized. Start every plan with a clean sheet of paper, an open mind—and all the help that can be mustered.

As R. Buckminster Fuller said, in discussing the planning that went into the Apollo project:

The critical path organization of the Apollo Project disclosed some two million tasks that had to be successfully accomplished before the human astronauts were to be returned safely to Spaceship Earth. NASA's Apollo management then put a scientifically and technically competent control group to work to identify all the approximately two million tasks, a million of which required technological performances the design, production, and successful operation of which had never before been undertaken by humans.[2]

The time to cut and run is early, before the investment of too much money, too much time, and too much ego. Countless experiences have shown that a major percentage of failures are predictable at the planning phase. Further, a wise, noninvolved, experienced devil's advocate asking the right questions of senior management (the approvers, not the submitters) can spare later losses. Such an *éminence grise* may be a respected internal executive or an outside consultant given to candid objectivity.

Poor Concept

"Poor concept" is a relative statement. What is meant by "poor" is that the concept itself does not appeal at the time of and/or in the form of execution being evaluated, as determined by the mode of evaluation or test used. Some examples:

[2]R. Buckminster Fuller, *Critical Path*, St. Martin's Press, 1981.

- The product doesn't offer a unique benefit—or one that is unique enough.
- The product offers too many benefits, unique or otherwise.
- It has no *single* strong reason for being.
- It has unique benefit(s), but fulfills little need.
- It has a unique benefit, but a poor price/value relationship.
- It has a unique benefit, but is out of synchronization with the market—in terms of demographic and psychographic realities, trends, fads, and fashion.
- It is too innovative, ahead of the market.
- It fills an unrealized need, about which it is too expensive to educate the prospect.
- The product message is too complicated—too difficult to communicate.
- The margin of benefit is not enough to break use habit, justify expense, change shopping patterns, etc.

Poor Execution

Marshall McLuhan said: "The medium is the message." That's often true. Every new product is a communication in itself. It has a face, a dress, and a personality. It has always been so.

It is even more so now, said Mel Von Smith in a lecture at the University of Chicago's Center for Continuing Education:

It's an age where people are willing to spend money on fun, on pleasure, on me . . . we have had a lot of booms—inflation booms, divorce booms. Now we're entering a *personality boom*—and products with a positive personality are doing the booming.

In an age of "generics" (another boom), *personality* often becomes the point of difference, more important than function or intrinsic benefit. Here are a few executional problems, all related to the over-all perception of the offering's personality and (hence) viability:

- There are product defects.
- There are other technical problems.
- The product is over (under) engineered.
- It is over (under) packaged.
- The development and introduction budget has been underspent or (not as common) overspent.
- There is a higher cost-of-goods than estimated.
- The product is misbranded.
- It is mistargeted.
- It is mistimed for character of market.
- It is mistimed for other reasons—it is contra-seasonal, has come out amid a flurry of other introductions by company, has come out during an

inventory reduction period, has come out during a trade category buying hiatus, there is insufficient purchasing lead time for a class new to manufacturer, etc.

- It is mispriced (over or underpriced).
- It is misplaced (in the trade channel, distribution method, store section, etc.)
- It has weak distribution.
- The company has poor sales operations.
- Product benefits are miscommunicated (to the customer, to intervening trade channels).
- Insufficient and/or inappropriate media are being used.
- The product is mispositioned.
- It has an imprecise image, an indistinct personality.

Poor concept and poor execution are usually intermingled. A good concept poorly executed, a poor concept well executed—both are paths to the new product poorhouse. When the problems are identified at advanced prototype phases, the faults begin to become obvious.

Unfortunately both good and poor concepts poorly communicated at preliminary screening phases can lead to misdirection. Although concepts may originate from any quarter, it is recommended that the concept statement to be communicated to a prospective respondent be devised by a professional communicator, not necessarily an involved inventor or researcher.

The concept statement should hew to the rules, but should be single-minded, clear, concise, and prospect-directed. Further, it should be benefit-oriented, not product-descriptive. An example: One of the most successful hair-care items introduced by Gillette years ago was Dippity-Do Hair Setting Gel. It never would have come out of the lab if this (unfortunately typical) concept statement had gone out to the mail panel: "Now, there's a new clear jelly for setting your hair. Doesn't flake or stain. Dries quickly. Washes out easily. Comes in wide-mouthed jar so its easy to use. Choose pink or green colored gel." Rather, what the prospect wanted to know was how much fun it was to use; how it made messing permissible (thank you Dr, Freud); how it allowed creative styling with fingers, pins, rollers, etc., that was not easy with sprays, perms, or conventional setting agents; how it was pretty, clear, bubbling, jewel-like, etc. Sensory cues were needed to induce trial.

This important fact, the appeal of sensory cues, is often lost in food products, household products, and appliance concept statements. In all of these cases of hands-on ritual, chore, self-indulgence, or prideful preparation, the sensory component is a *fact* about the product, not an embellishment. In most consumer products, this sensory appeal should be built into the product, its design, and its graphics. At the concept sorting phase, it should be *anticipated*, e. g.,:

Now there is a word-processor typewriter that's easy and comfortable to use any place, any time. Smooth, soft-sided, weighs less than one pound—less than many books. Works on any surface—comfortable in your lap. Stores and plays back on any television screen or (with simple key switch) provides audio transcription on any radio (portable or car radio also) and delivers permanent record print-out upon command, ten copies per second.

Here, then, is another intermingling of the concept and the product execution. Perhaps the example is over-engineered. At the concept-sorting stage, however, this may be weeded out. Each concept can (and often should) be stated and tested in several variations. The above hypothetical example, if tested without the radio playback feature, without the multiple copy feature, etc., each at appropriate price points, might reveal appeals to various targets at various price points. If the concept scores well, then the maker can decide to market the model most appropriate to his distribution strength (commercial business machine outlets), can choose a narrower target with high margins, can concentrate on new consumer channels, or can bring out a variety of more and less sophisticated adaptations for all appropriate markets. Prudence would probably dictate starting with strength, then using the income generated to test other models in markets less familiar to the maker.

Poor Use of Research

Marketers often cite faulty market research as one of the most frequent causes of new product failure. Research, properly handled, can be invaluable in launching a new product. Yet, many heavily researched products have gone on to failure, and others have succeeded while apparently flying in the face of negative research findings.

There are many valid, useful applications of marketing and communications research. The problem often lies not in the research itself, but in how it is used. As The Conference Board put it in the report noted earlier:

Marketers cite insufficient or faulty marketing research as the most frequent cause of new product failure. And lack of thoroughness in identifying real needs in the marketplace, or in spotting early signs of competitors girding up to take the offensive, are often the findings of a new product post mortem.

Thus, after a new item has failed to come up to expectations, marketers sometimes confess to a "serious misreading" of customer needs, "too little field testing," or "overly optimistic forecasts of market need and acceptance." All too often, it seems, some managements still fall into the trap described by the marketing vice president of one industrial firm, who says: "Simply stated, we decided what our marketplace wanted in this new product without really asking that market what its priorities were."

Dr. Edward M. Tauber, professor of marketing at the University of Southern California and editor of the *Journal of Advertising Research*, enlarged on this theme in an article in the August 1981 issue of *Ad Forum*. He observed:

The elaborate systems companies have established for screening new products—evaluating every dimension of the product at every stage of development—reflects the strong *risk-averse* attitude of U.S. management . . . Marketing research does not create failures nor will it answer to a greater number of successes.

Present methods of new product screening such as concept testing, product testing, and test market simulators employ as criteria pretrial and posttrial attitudes and purchase expectations of a sample of consumers upon first exposure to the product. Test markets measure trial and repeat behavior for a relatively short time span (6 months to a year) generally covering only the introductory stage of an innovative product's life cycle. Thus, early attitudes and behavior are assumed to be valid predictors of later adoption behavior. The history of truly innovative products contradicts this assumption.

Dr. Tauber cites videodisc, early television, and negative ("who needs it?") findings for other products that were not predictive. He also states that to be a valid screening device for new products, research must measure or simulate the process consumers go through both individually and collectively in adopting new products. He states that the effects of social interaction are not measured by conventional techniques, and offers as evidence the bandwagon effects common in fashion and image items—clothing, cosmetics, beer, wine, cigarets, etc. I have seen sensitive judgments based on experience and instinct fly in the face of negative research to successfully launch fragrances, designer jeans, wave set compounds, toys, etc. Likewise, such well-researched innovations as the Edsel and Polavision did not go on to success.

Dr. Tauber concludes:

We could reduce the failure rate of new products to zero by simply discontinuing to launch any. The need is not a lower failure *rate*; it is a greater number of major new business successes. The challenge of predicting new product performance should not focus on pretest market simulators alone. By then it is too late. No simulators ever turned a dog into a star.

Instead, we need to understand the clues to success much earlier. We need risk-seeking research. We need brave researchers who are willing to tell management when simulators and other current research technology will not work, do not accurately simulate, and can mislead us so that we discard a potential winner. We need research suppliers who refrain from making outrageous claims about near perfect prediction track records. And, finally, all marketers need to step back, examine history and attempt to understand the circumstances, process and requirements for creating a new business success.

The last sentence, of course, summarizes a mission of this book.

Predicting the future is not a certain strength of most research techniques, which are often one-time experiences (or, merely, exposures to unperfected stimulus material out of true selection and use context). Too often, early screening research is so crude as to actually discard the most promising concepts.

Two common techniques are the large-scale mail panel and the mall inter-cept, in both cases providing a gross impression from atypical respondents (atypical in the sense that the large-scale method purports to offer some projectibility). Here, both the stimulus material and the response catalog (questionnaire or imperfect, but in-person, interviewer) generate data for evaluation that is wholly unrelated to the real world.

Another common early screening technique is the group interview. Here, a few people in one or more locations are shown some representation of the concept, and then guided (by a professional interviewer) through a discussion of its pros and cons. It's another atypical set-up with atypical respondents (unless the target audience is composed of people with nothing better to do).

A supposed virtue of these popular screening techniques is low cost. In the first two techniques, fairly large numbers (hence, presumed statistical re-liability) are surveyed at low cost per respondent. In the last instance, "qualitative understanding . . . in depth" is said to be the yield. Unbeliev-ably, even these less precise responses in low numbers are sometimes quan-tified and passed along as research findings, rather than as explorations to uncover unanticipated plusses or minuses as well as the prospects' patois and frame of reference.

The point is to use research with knowledge of its limitations. It is all too obvious that most, if not all, techniques are available (for a price) to all competitors in a category. Given expenditures of equal amounts of money and time to evaluate similar concepts, each should find a similar success rate. It's just not that easy.

Poor Technology

Technical problems in design or production are the second most common cause of reported new product failures, according to The Conference Board. Such problems often occur in commercial scaling-up from R&D laboratory and pilot plant accomplishments to full-scale production. The electronics and the mechanics are often solved. Yet the quality control of materials and throughput, broader specifications for price-competitive components and ingredients, substitute materials, novel improvements, lowering of quality assurance surveillance, poor labor training, early technical obsolescence vs. more sophisticated competition, over-engineering, and over-building are among manifestations of poor technology.

The Conference Board report cited some of the following examples:

We have entered the market with two new products. In both cases, they turned out to be less successful than we had hoped, basically because of inadequate pilot-plant development. In other words, our research was not complete, and, therefore, caused considerable delay in modification of the process in order to produce the product quality necessary. In pilot-plant work, we were capable of producing the desired product, but not in full-scale production. We were eventually able to modify our process sufficiently to manufacture the product needed, and our sales and production since that time have been satisfactory.

Vice president, sales—an industrial chemicals company

With the encouragement of a major fiber company, we introduced a special yarn designed to replace cotton yarns. Despite assurances that the fiber had been evaluated thoroughly and was ready for commercial exploitation, processing the fiber proved more difficult than anticipated, with resultant delays and problems. Our customers became discouraged and turned to other products, leaving the program insufficient in size to justify retention.

We failed to check the claims of the producer thoroughly, yielding instead to their pressure to introduce the product to meet a market trend. We should have confined our program to one or two critical customers who would have been capable of assessing the product's virtues and market potential while affording us the opportunity of evaluating the fiber's processing characteristics in greater detail.

Marketing vice president—a textile company

One of our divisions designed a [new type of wire]. The specifications were very severe and, in a sense, pushed the technology to its outer limits. As a consequence, our product, although generally reliable in laboratory tests, experienced serious difficulties when produced on a quantity basis. After a year of extensive test work and expenditure of considerable sums of money, we are slowly solving the technical problems.

The major lesson to be learned from this incident is to make sure that we understand the limits of the materials and designs with which we are dealing, and that we do not attempt to develop products to meet specifications too rigorous for our manufacturing procedures.

Vice president, technology—a diversified manufacturer

In the not-too-distant painful past, we marketed a product to meet competition in a new area of endeavor. Our market information, return on investment, pricing and packaging were good. Unfortunately, this information caused our product development and R and D people to shortcut the requirements for quality within the product. To meet cost figures they substituted plastics for the bottle enclosure which let the material inside evaporate and thicken. Efforts were made to overcome the product and container weaknesses, but the sales force had been burned. I removed the product from the market rather than continue to push an inferior product. The lessons are obvious.

Vice president, marketing—a commercial supplies manufacturer

A recent new product developed by our company and introduced at our industry's largest international show has turned out to be far below our expected success.

The problem developed while our new product was on exhibit. Many people liked what they saw—with the qualifications that just a few more functional capabilities would enhance its salability. Unfortunately, we listened to too many suggestions and proceeded to adapt additional features to the product. Its original $55,000 selling price became $80,000 as a result of these added features. We found the $80,000 product put us in a more unfavorable competitive position than if we had left it in its $55,000

configuration. The lesson learned was not to over-engineer a product once it is developed for a specific market need.
Senior vice president, marketing—a machinery producer

As stated by one of the preceding respondents, the lessons are obvious.

Poor Timing

The elements and economics in the late 1970s stifled a surge of new product successes by major makers of snowmobiles, snow throwers, and lawn mowers with two successive years of low precipitation and unprecedented soaring interest rates. Business had been so good for the new models the preceding several years that distributors loaded field inventories in anticipation of record sales volume. Instead, two back-to-back years of demand disappearance were generated by virtually snowless winters, dry springs, and tight money. In these instances, the timing was not wholly within the companies' control.

When time and circumstances change, a formerly unfeasible technology may suddenly become attractive. An example reported in the Sept. 23, 1981, *International Herald Tribune*:

Experiments with coal-oil mixtures date back to the 19th century, but it took the OPEC-led spiral in the price of oil beginning in 1973 to force the substantial advance in the technology that has occurred in the United States, Japan, and Western Europe.

The oil industry is working with various mixtures . . . increases in the price of crude oil have lifted the cost of industrial fuel oil for use in boilers well above that of steam coal . . . The use of a coal-oil mixture necessitates only minor modifications for the adaptation of liquid fuel boilers.

Other penalties of poor timing have come from moving too fast or too slow, often because of poor planning, organizational problems, or lack of suitable controls. Moving too fast on a crash project can mean overlooking vital factors. Moving too slow can mean missing a market change. The domestic U.S. auto industry, caught by the gasoline price leap, is a model example. The tattered remains of cut velvet on 7th Avenue are legendary witness to the result of being caught out of fashion.

Bringing the product out of the lab too soon or not soon enough . . . Testing that is short-cut or overdone . . . Environmental factors that change the rules of entry . . . A surprise move by competition . . . Whatever timing is out of the new product maker's control bears careful, continual monitoring from the beginning of the project assignment. It can provide a sure go/no go signal rarely on the PERT chart. (PERT is an acronym for Program Evaluation and Review Technique, which plans the dovetailed activities of various functional groups contributing to a project in proper time sequence—planning that points up those activities that are critical from a time standpoint, those that if not accomplished on schedule may delay other elements of the program and conceivably delay attainment of the program goals.)

Other Reasons

There is an almost endless array of other reasons for new product failures, many related to the quality of management. The most successful companies have few marketplace failures, but lots of conceptual, prototype (or analog) failures at a stage where it doesn't cost so much.

Among some of the other reasons for failure are:

- Inadequate market analysis
- Poor assumptions, or misidentified opportunities
- Overpowering competitive reaction
- Over (under) reaction to competition
- Too many (not enough) gap jumps to market entry
- Low product awareness
- Low trial (albeit hardcore repeaters) due to underpromising or mis-promising
- High trial, but few repeaters due to overpromising and under-delivery
- Regulations (e.g., FDA) that limit sales
- Unpredicted patent, license, copyright infringement by marketer or by competitor
- Foreign competition (better quality, lower price, etc.)
- Unauthorized style or name knock-off (prevalent in fashion industry)

The Flip Side—Reasons for Success

Clues to reasons for failure yield the flip side: reasons for success. Although new product success requires careful execution of research and marketing, there may also be less obvious signs that management considers the new product important. In a survey of five new product consultants, *New Product Development*, a Point Pleasant, NJ, newsletter came up with 20 critical questions to determine if management will support the effort. According to the newsletter: "Fifteen or more affirmative answers mean the product's success is almost assured. Eleven to 14 suggest probable success and eight to 10 indicate a 'coin toss.' "

Here is the quiz.

1. Has the product been in development for a year?
2. Does your company now make a similar product?
3. Does your company now sell to a related customer market?
4. Is research and development at least one-third of the product budget?
5. Will the product be test-marketed for at least six months?
6. Does the person in charge have a private secretary?

7. Will the ad budget be at least 5 percent of anticipated sales?
8. Will a recognized brand name be on the product?
9. Would the company take a loss on it for the first year?
10. Does the company "need" the product more than it "wants" it?
11. Have three samples of advertising copy been developed?
12. Is the product really new, as opposed to improved?
13. Can the decision to buy it be made by only one person?
14. Is the product to be made in fewer than five versions?
15. Will the product not need service and repair?
16. Does the development team have a working code name?
17. Will the company president see the project leader without an appointment?
18. Did the project leader make a go of the last two projects?
19. Will the product be on the market for more than 10 years?
20. Would the project leader quit and take the item with him if the company says it won't back it?

And so it goes. In summary, it is obvious that successful new products programs are a balanced mixture of good planning, good management, appealing concepts, research well employed but used with discretion, good timing, appropriate risk-taking—and a modicum of just plain good luck.

3

The Hierarchy of New Products

The successful company is the one which is first to identify emerging consumer needs and to offer product improvements which satisfy those needs. The successful marketer spots a new trend early, and then leads it.
—*Edward G. Harness, Procter & Gamble*

This book hopes to be helpful in the development of new businesses that fit marketing-oriented companies—rather than those that serve the goals and prime financial orientations of holding companies and conglomerates.

A company is marketing-oriented if its organizing concept is to serve customer needs, albeit with rewards to shareholders and a demonstrated policy of social responsibility.

Earlier, we defined a progression of new business activities, building from those that were close-in slightly new product refinements to far-reaching new businesses. These broad divisions, which will be treated in some detail in this chapter, move from the evolution of existing products through the expansion of an existing brand/product franchise and new entry into an established category to the creation of new categories and new businesses.

But before we get into that, let's take a look at the role of the brand name itself.

Importance of Brand Name

A rose by any other name would smell as sweet.
—*William Shakespeare*

A rose is a rose is a rose.
—*Gertrude Stein*

If cod was rare, it would sell for more money than lobster.
—*New England fisherman*

Perceptions are key in branding. The fisherman is closer to the truth than Shakespeare or Stein.

Every day this truth hits us in the face. The name "Bruno" calls up a different image than does "Roland."

It isn't often a "Smucker" is the exception that proves the rule.

Much care should go into brand name development and, in the case of entirely new product classes, brand descriptors and generic definitions. These alternatives can be sorted in attribute tests, in cluster analysis, and within the context of winning concept statements that are screened with the name being the only variable.

The brand name, if an existing one, should be well-defined and understood. If it is clearly inappropriate to the new product, it should not be used merely because it is broadly known and the alternative of establishing a new brand is costly.

The better known the brand, the tighter the image—which limits its extension, but does often provide an acceptable base for numerous line extensions and flankers close to home. Campbell Soup Company, a perennial winner of new product success scores, is a clear illustration. But, the Colgate brand on food didn't work.

Evolution of Existing Product

Repositioning to Find a New Audience

Betty Crocker Potatoes, a shelf-stable convenience product in such specialties as au gratin, scalloped, creamed, sour cream and chives, hash browns, etc., were once backed by an upscale advertising presentation, in party settings, with fancy food. The product varieties dominated a relatively small market.

After being repositioned to the mass market, as "the plain meat potatoes" for everyday family meals, the entire category took wing, with the brand maintaining its dominant share. The market became so large that it attracted low-priced generic and store-brand imitations. An increased emphasis on the quality reputation of the Betty Crocker brand name was General Mills' counter, while maintaining the successful reposition—a reposition that built an entire business.

Recycling

Arm & Hammer baking soda was a staid standby household product. It could be used for baking and scouring, as a poultice, as a freshening agent, for gargling, for deodorizing laundry and diapers, etc. It was an ingredient with a multi-purpose image.

Then it was firmly recycled for one prime purpose—as a refrigerator deodorizer. To do that job took an entire package, and that package had to be replaced with predictable frequency. No changes were made in the product, just the emphasis on a contemporary benefit—and business boomed!

Appearance or Form Improvement

Probably the most common change that justifies a claim of newness is an improvement in product appearance or form. This encompasses modifications in formula (new, with lemon added); color (new, blue Cheer); texture/flow (from smooth peanut butter to chunky, from regular oatmeal to creamy, from cleansing cream to lotion, from liquid shampoo to creams and gels); graphics (paper towel "prints," designer-signature fabrics, decorated reuseable jelly jars, new postage stamp editions); and shape (Mrs. Butterworth pancake syrup in a bottle shaped like the lady herself, beer in barrel-shaped bottles, children's vitamins shaped like animals, dog biscuits made to look like bones, screw-in light bulbs shaped like flames).

Performance Improvement

The second, and most helpful, form of newness embellishing an established product is a performance improvement. It is often accompanied by improvements in appearance and form.

To stay viable, almost any product should constantly be searching for improvement. Even a commodity such as flour has been changed by various milling methods, by bleaching, by agglomerating (Wondra), by combining with other ingredients to give it special qualities (Bisquick). Now, it is being recycled to its stone-ground, unbleached origins to create other new flour products.

But let us turn to the nation's leading advertiser, generally regarded as one of the premier consumer product marketers, for an analysis of performance improvements as the path to continuing newness leading to continuing success. Here are some excerpts from a talk Edward G. Harness, former chairman of Procter & Gamble, made to the annual marketing meeting of The Conference Board a few years ago.

Tide was introduced broadly in 1947 . . . This product revolutionized washday by giving consumers a significantly cleaner wash than they had been able to obtain before. This is because Tide, with a completely new synthetic detergent formulation, eliminated the problem of soap film, which had long been associated with the use of laundry soaps and soap powders.

This innovation even revolutionized the washing machine industry. Today's modern automatic washing machine would not be possible without products like Tide.

The Tide product which we are selling today is importantly different from the Tide product which we introduced in 1947. It is different in its cleansing performance, sudsing characteristics, aesthetics, physical properties, packaging. In total, there have been 55 significant modifications in this one brand during its lifetime.

After nearly four decades, Tide still enjoys leadership among washday products.

Performance improvements come about through modifications in structure, assembly, and formulation. Often these involve new active additives, new processing techniques, substitute ingredients, and even subtraction of component parts or ingredients.

Flour was improved when the bran was removed. Now it makes news when bran is added back. Air was added to Ivory soap and it floated!—a distinctive point of difference. Cocoa butter, legendary for its emollient properties on the human skin, was added to bath soap and Armour-Dial launched TONE Soap. Spray lacquers were made water-soluable and a spate of soft-holding hair sprays hit the market. P&G added fragrance to its Puffs brand facial tissues and Crown-Zellerbach incorporated skin conditioners in its Chiffon brand tissues. Bristol-Myers buffered its aspirin. Crest was the first toothpaste to include stannous flouride. Typewriters replaced spool ribbons with cartridges, just as tape reels gave way to cassettes and discs.

Packaging Improvement

Package construction improvements add newness by improving convenience of use, attractiveness, reuseability, bulk, weight, portability, and by utilizing the characteristics of new materials and technological changes to modify the package to fit modern processing, use, disposal, and life-style.

An example of the integration of processing and packaging that has brought about change is the retort pouch, a foil-lined bag that acts as a shelf-stable medium for new food processing and filling technology. It replaces the tin can. An adaptation is the vacuum-sealed Tetra Brik envelope first commonly used in Europe for beverages, both fruit and dairy based. In the United States, the canned foods industry was revolutionized by the bi-pack, containing two separately processed recipes (one usually meat-based) marketed in cans that were packed together with an adhesive strip. The components are combined only in the homemaker's heating process before serving, to yield improved taste and texture.

A collapsible filled polybag inside a cardboard box provides a space-saving, easy-dispensing method to store and serve refrigerated wine, which achieved an important share of the popularly priced "jug" wine segment.

Price/Value Change

Price says a lot about how a company values its new products. At introduction, when marketing dollars are apt to be heaviest, it is important to establish an appropriate price point related to value delivered. It is often better to err on the high side, because it is usually easier to lower prices if necessary, than to raise them, given a stable economy. Usually, the more innovative and the more specialized products can sustain the largest margins, reserving price flexibility for later stages of market development.

Such pricing flexibility might include bonus-packs, extra ounces, with little extra price; step-up prices for a premium version of a standard product (perhaps packaged as a gift, a common holiday practice in the liquor industry); banded deals, two or more similar or related products marketed together at a special price (the salt-and-pepper picnic set); introductory deals (free razor with the new blades); limited-time-only introductory price-offs; limited edition up-charges; etc.

Expansion of a Brand or Product Franchise

Line Extensions

To the Brand

Line extensions to the brand itself might include additional sizes, colors, flavors, forms, or additives. Thus, for salt, you might consider iodized salt, ice cream freezer salt, deicing salt, sea salt, kosher salt, rock salt, pickling salt. It could be packaged in boxes, jars, cylinders, shakers, and bags. Additional variations might include garlic salt, lemon salt, herbed salt, curried salt, salt with monosodium glutamate, and other in various packaging forms.

For Different Brands

Similar products can be marketed under different brand names. This is a way to extend a line with new positionings in very large categories. Examples are coffee, cereals, detergents.

Flankers to the Brand

Brand flankers are additional affinity products under the same brand umbrella. Brand name salt spawns flanker pepper—black pepper, white pepper, peppercorns (white, black, green, pink)—which goes on to inspire an ever-lengthening assortment of line-extending spices, seasonings, and flavorings. Even better examples are seen in a stroll through a hardware store's nuts-and-bolts department!

A successful example of both line extensions and flankers is Land O Lakes' entry into the spread market. Sixty-some years ago, the farmer cooperative introduced the first important branded sweet cream butter; then it innovated by portion-packaging it; then it introduced line extensions in unsalted sticks, whipped versions of both lightly salted and unsalted, plus various sizes and various forms (including individual serving pats) for the institutional food service business. In the early '70s, the first true flanker, with its own line extensions, was introduced regionally: Land O Lakes margarine, in regular sticks, corn oil, and whipped (see case history in Appendix 1-A). In 1981, another flanker, Land O Lakes Country Morning Blend (a combination of 40 percent butter and 60 percent corn oil margarine) began its expansion out of test markets, with unsalted and whipped line extensions. (See Figure 3-1.)

Land O Lakes has defined its market as the premium *spread* category, not butter alone—with the resultant development and introduction of a lengthening line of products appropriate to its strong brand franchise. Land O Lakes is

Figure 3-1
Land O'Lakes Spread Extensions

Land O'Lakes successfully extended its basic butter product with unsalted and whipped versions. In the 1970s, it flanked the butters with a line of margarines. In 1981, Land O'Lakes introduced Country Morning Blend, a margarine made with 60 percent corn oil margarine and 40 percent sweet cream butter. Today, Land O'Lakes is the only major company with leading entries in all segments of the spread market.

the largest selling brand of butter. In its regional marketing areas, both margarine and Country Morning Blend are already among the leading sellers.

An example of product line development that grew into an entirely new business development was the programmed introduction and expansion of the Nature Valley line of granola-based products introduced by General Mills in the mid-'70s. As we enter the mid-'80s, it is still being expanded with new product flankers and line extensions from a volume well in excess of $200 million. Nature Valley identified a consumer need for wholesome, all-natural food in a portable form. It has met this desire with a series of carefully segmented snack and confection entries targeted both to a variety of audiences (defined by age and eating habits) and eating sensations (defined by flavors and textures). The line has developed a grocery store presence located adjacent to cereals and toaster snacks and has expanded its trial and distribution through such new channels as vending machines. Throughout the development, Nature Valley has studiously adhered to its charter of always being completely natural, without any artificial flavorings or preservatives or additives. Consumer trust in this commitment has been a strong underpinning for the Nature Valley success. (See Figure 3-2.)

The best known example of flanking and extending is found in the automobile business. General Motors has not just one car, but a line of cars for each of its target market segments. At the top end, there are not only the economic prestige divisions, but the social set definitions. A Cadillac as a Cimmaron seeks a different audience than does the Eldorado, than does the DeVille, than does the Seville. Within each model class, whether for the low-key affluent, the conspicuous consumer, established wealth, or *noveau riche*, there are various trim options and, in some segments, coupe and sedan models. Using the same basic chassis selection, GM has developed different lines for different targets, with slightly different price points for comparable models, and (most importantly) large numbers of entirely different dealer-franchise groups for Cadillac, Oldsmobile, Buick, Pontiac, Chevrolet, and its truck lines. It is the ultimate demonstration of flanking, extending, positioning, and targeting.

New Category

For the Brand

To carry the analogy along: From salt to spices is an easy affinity. A logical new category may be sauces, another may be condiments—still in the same shelf-stable section of the store. Beyond this, tread carefully into other sections, even if it appears brand-appropriate to offer frozen sauce concentrates or refrigerated salad dressings. Consumers see your qualities within a familiar competitive set. Those qualities might not rank as high in other environments where other brand franchises are well established.

Figure 3-2
Nature Valley Line Extensions

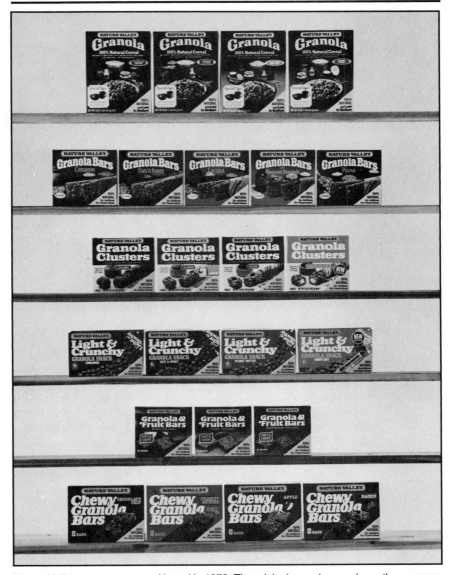

Nature Valley was a new cereal brand in 1972. The original granola cereal was then successively offered as a portable snack bar, a chewy confection bar, and as a light, loose particulate snack . . . with more forms to follow. The Nature Valley Granola line became one of the most successful dry grocery brands introduced in the past ten years.

Combining Different Brands Under a New Category Umbrella

Manufacturers often combine different products with different brand names in a similar category with a unifying use concept. An example is Hormel's line of single-serving entrees, marketed together and positioned as "Short Orders," although branded separately as Hormel Dinty Moore Beef Stew, Mary Kitchen Corned Beef Hash, etc.

New Entry into an Established Category

Even where the product class and the store section may be home ground, an established all-American brand may not comfortably move into foreign territory. Your "Yankee" brand of spices and seasonings might be peculiarly bland and unauthentic on a spaghetti sauce label.

With the technology, materials, and distribution muscle all at hand, do not forestall the entry test. However, consider development of a new, more appropriate brand personality than your present franchise projects. This may encompass a new brand name, position, price point, distribution, and store section. For example, although it was basic in tomatoes and possessed one of the best-known of company names, Campbell Soup Company nonetheless smartly gave its spaghetti sauce an appropriately ethnic label—Prego, not Campbell.

Newness of Brand Name

When entering an established category, consider carefully the necessary brand-name attributes needed. Although a company may have all of the necessary skills and production capacity, it may find that the very strength of its brand inhibits expansion along what may appear to be entirely appropriate lines. In our example above regarding flankers and extensions for a salt company, it might appear that the appropriate reference would be Morton's. Unlikely, however. The Morton brand is so firmly identified wth salt, that its reputation will modify perceptions of anything else the company makes—thus limiting the world of flavorings to those which are necessarily salty (no fruits, no sweets, no citrus, no vegetables).

A lot of baby food is consumed by senior citizens—yet the preeminent name in the field would be disastrously unappealing for a line of Golden Age Meals for our rapidly increasing proportion of over-60 consumers.

It is almost axiomatic that the more explicit and stronger the brand franchise is, the more limited is its capacity to expand into wholly new categories. The very strength that buys a solid core of basic business acts as a ceiling to major expansion.

For this reason alone, it is necessary to periodically assess the meaning of the brand franchise. Entering an established category with a new product calls for an open-minded approach to branding. Remember, it's the product, not the brand name, you want to sell to the consumer.

New Position

To *position* a product is to locate it in relation to something else: another product or other products in the same class, adjunctive to an established regimen, at a point in time, against a specific target, vs. competition, in an entirely new perception from the established tradition. Examples of advertising themes that help establish such positions: "The plain paper copier" (vs. others that use special papers or chemicals); "Nature's answer to candy" (vs. other confections that contain artificial preservatives); "The wake-up beverage" (establishes both its regimen and its benefit); "The Pepsi generation" (ties the product to its target); "It leaves you breathless" (vs. other types of distilled spirits); "Melts in your mouth—won't melt in your hand" (vs. conventional chocolate candies); "A taste of the country" (locates the wholesome source); "The friendly skies of United" (vs. a concern about big, impersonal carriers); "Babies are our business—our only business" (a tight target served by an established specialized authority).

Designer jeans are an example of taking a mundane utilitarian garment and positioning it as high fashion, thereby increasing the manufacturer's and the retailer's margins, while creating an entirely new demand cycle, from an entirely new market segment. This is not *re*positioning, because the designer jeans pioneers were not the basic work clothes makers; they were new to the market.

Pierre Cardin's purposeful purchase of the historic Maxim's restaurant provided his enterprise with a new position from which to market packaged food—not because he wants to be in the restaurant business per se. Maxim's is probably the world's most famous restaurant. It therefore provides a market-entry position that is almost nonpreemptible—and that is highly extendible (e.g., to cookware, tableware, aprons, cookbooks, cooking appliances, tabletop softgoods, kitchen decor, giftware).

Appearance or Form Difference

While a change in texture or form may be sufficient to breathe new life into an established brand—where its performance has already found acceptance, and only a marginal difference is needed to stimulate some retrial or reawaken interest—this is generally *not* an important enough base for a new product entry. The exception, of course, is when the new form is entirely new to the category.

A topical example is Softsoap brand liquid soap in a pump dispenser, introduced internationally by Minnetonka, Inc., which quickly captured a significant share of the toilet soap market by promising a new, non-messy form of soap and no-waste economy when compared with the conventional bar form. Its rise to a 9 percent market share caught the attention of the major soapers, who countered with their own versions.

An earlier example of a small marketer creating a new category that attracted major soapers was Lestoil cleaning agent. It took off dramatically, then was overtaken by the major soapers, e.g., Mr. Clean from P&G and Ajax from Colgate.

This is not to suggest that any new appearance or form difference launched by a nonmajor manufacturer will be overtaken by the entrenched leaders of major categories. It is, however, a consideration that must be taken into account.

While it may be sufficient for the majors to create change in a modest way, supported by major marketing investments, minor marketers need to invade the market with significant appearance and form differences. Examples include Kitchens of Sara Lee, with a new appearance, form, and standard of packaged baked goods quality; and Pearl Drops Tooth Polish from Carter Products, an exclusive special purpose dentifrice in a new form, appearance, and package (squeeze bottle).

Performance Difference

A superior performance that is readily evident—often in a side-by-side comparison—is a powerful appeal to any customer. Examples are all around, from sustained-release medication that meters dosage over time or a choice of sunscreens that let the tanner control the result, to longer-lasting house paint and fertilizers with built-in weed killers.

Most recently, during the first quarter of 1984, Lamaur, Inc., introduced a new product called Perma Soft™, the first shampoo and conditioner system created exclusively for women with permed hair. It is designed to "soften permed hair without relaxing the curl." The market potential is huge. Forty-seven percent of all women with permanent waves shampoo and condition their hair at home. For these women—their numbers are put at 44,000,000—Perma Soft is the first shampoo and conditioner created for their specific hair care needs—it minimizes the dryness caused by the perming while maximizing curl retention.

Packaging Difference

Packaging differences that become the basis for new products are more significant than those packaging improvements that contribute to more convenient product usability or novel appearance.

One packaging change that created entire industries was the aerosol can, which made possible fine mist sprays, instant foams, and controlled-delivery of liquid and lotion streams. New aerosols continue to evolve. Low-pressure, soft-sided packages lightly spray fine powders. The Sepro can has been developed for pressure dispensing where the propellant and the ingredient should not mix. In this instance, it made possible push-button food products (such as cheese spreads) and S.C. Johnson & Son's highly successful Edge Protective Shave.

Resource Difference

A different ingredient, source, and/or location of supply or technology for making a product can be the basis for an entirely new product.

By-products from one process can become a resource for making others. The sludge from paper making becomes charcoal briquets; wood pulp from lumber mills becomes plastic; garbage becomes fuel; minute quantities of silver become antiseptic preservatives.

Labor rates and special economic arrangements in less developed countries make possible new, competitively priced products. Automation of electronic elements makes possible a change in life style, education, and commerce for millions with the introduction of the handheld calculator.

Even newer, as reported in the September 24, 1981, issue of the *International Herald Tribune*:

> McDonnell Douglas Corporation, the aerospace company, and Johnson & Johnson have agreed to put a plant in earth orbit to manufacture drugs in outer space.
>
> The automated factory would take advantage of the weightlessness of space to produce new kinds of medicines that would be extremely difficult to make on the earth's surface . . . Several possible new drugs that might be suited for space manufacture include interferon, the protein used to fight viral infections, and a hormone called erythropoitin, which stimulates the production of red blood cells and might be used to treat anemias.

Although drugs are not new to Johnson & Johnson, the joint venture was initiated by McDonnell Douglas, which innovated the new drug-making process. A positive cash flow is predicted about two years after the NASA-approved space factory goes into production in 1987. In confirming the arrangement, NASA stated that it had identified 500 materials that could be chemically combined in space to create new drugs and stronger, lighter-weight alloys. Fairchild Industries, Inc., will develop the $200 million unmanned space platform for commercial customers, who will pay for shuttle trips at the going rate, according to an article in *USA Today*, September 23, 1983.

Price/Value Difference

A better value, a better price, or both has always been a strong new product introductory position. When this translates to lower price for comparable value, it is difficult to sustain over time, except possibly for basic commodities.

Generic consumables are a present-day example, motivated by the retailer's response to inflation effects on the grocery dollar. Here the trade-offs may be minimum (but acceptable) quality and marketing margins.

Another type of price/value difference is offering the finest quality at its consequent price, both becoming virtues to be considered by the target customer. Hallmark built an industry-dominating business in greeting cards based on the appeal: "When you care enough to give the very best." Outlets were exclusive. Nothing ever cut-price.

From Häagen-Dazs ice cream to the three-star restaurants of France, there is always a market for quality. But once that quality slips, once a maker compromises with a few changes here and there to save a dollar or two, failure follows.

If the price must be high to deliver the quality—make the price a virtue of the new product.

If the quality is compromised to make the price low, make its basic nature an acceptable virtue of the new product.

Sometimes, both high quality and low price are possible. BIC introduced its disposal lighters as the least expensive. They put the cost into the product, stripped away unnecessary features (refillable, replacement flints, etc.) to undercut the market's then prevailing low price point.

Distribution Pattern Difference

Introducing new products through new distribution patterns can often steal a march on competition and provide a point-of-difference customer benefit.

As an example, Control Data and other business systems makers are experimenting with storefront computer hardware and software outlets, convenient to independent retailers, small manufacturers, and other businesses who might ordinarily not be considered prime targets by their sales forces. Just as importantly, these prospects might not normally seek out new data processing assistance because of a fear of the complications, applicability, and price.

In a different area, impelled by the auto fuel crunch, the increase in numbers of working women, and the premium on free time, home grocery delivery has been reintroduced in several areas. Groceries are now ordered by telephone, but two-way cable will soon make possible electronic catalog ordering and billing.

And this ties into other forms of direct response marketing, using inquiry-stimulating print media, telephone, and the mails, which have become newly important to new product introductions. Such methods are best suited to narrow interest categories where selective lists make it cost efficient to solicit the prospect directly. When current experiments with credit card insert into telephone terminals are fully exploited, direct response marketing will really take off!

Other examples:

- Tombstone Pizza was introduced through saloons, then went to groceries as a new form of distribution.
- While most snacks and confections started out as individual servings sold at cashier counters and through vending machines, General Mills began distribution of its Nature Valley granola snacks in multiple-packs through groceries, then added counter and vending distribution for incremental sales and sampling.

USAir—A Case History

Many of these elements were incorporated in the program that yielded a completely new airline in 1979—USAir, sired by Allegheny.

The importance of product personality in parity markets is abundantly evident in the air travel industry, where the airlines themselves are the products. Because airlines fly similar aircraft made by the same manufacturers, offer comparable fares, and service often identical routes, travelers don't perceive much difference between competing companies. A distinctive personality not only sets the airline apart from the competition, it provides a boost to employee morale and motivation, which is reflected in improved passenger service. Personality becomes even more important when an airline introduces a "new product," as Allegheny Airlines did when it unveiled USAir in 1979. A key to USAir's subsequent success lies in the strong identification system that was developed to communicate its new personality.

The new product was radically different in brand name, positioning, appearance, packaging, distribution pattern, and performance and price/value perceptions. The new airline had a dynamic new personality. Here's the story.

Planes are Giant Packages

Air passengers see the company everywhere they look. The planes themselves are giant packages, a kind of permanent media that is already paid for—and offers excellent opportunities for communicating personality. And there are other permanent media that airlines can turn to their advantage—trucks, signs, ticket counters, baggage tags all say something about the company. An intelligently integrated identification system maximizes the impact of the company's message and reinforces its durability.

So says John Diefenbach, president of Landor Associates, the San Francisco-based international marketing design firm that created the successful identity program for USAir.

If an identity program is developed as a mere cosmetic device, it won't work, Diefenbach maintains. It must be developed as a strategic marketing tool. That's why the initial research and positioning are so important. You've got to know the competition and take full advantage of the way target audiences perceive the industry and your place in it.

Plan for Long-Term Positioning

To understand how USAir's distinctive personality was developed, we have to go back to 1974, when its parent company, Allegheny Airlines, embarked on what turned out to be a comprehensive, three-phase, five-year corporate identity program.

In 1974, Allegheny was the nation's sixth largest passenger-carrying airline. Long-range strategic plans included expanded routes and services that would propel the company beyond its regional limitations into national competition.

Research revealed, however, that the public's perception of Allegheny didn't support either the current reality or future objectives. The airline was seen as small and regional. The visual communications lacked vitality. They had an outdated appearance typical of all generic airline design developed in the post-World War II era. They used a color scheme that was very common throughout the industry, featuring a nondistinctive blue stripe with the Allegheny name in red, and an almost generic "flying wedge" symbol. In short, the company wasn't visually communicating any specific personality, either to the general public or to its employees.

Repositioning for Fundamental Change

During design analysis, it emerged that employees would rally enthusiastically behind a new identity program. This helped Allegheny management decide that a complete repositioning was necessary to make the company more competitive in its existing markets, and to position it for future growth and expansion. Research into a name change and a new graphic identity for Allegheny was initiated. USAir was selected as the name because it conveys the personality and stature of a major national airline—Allegheny's ultimate objective.

Reducing Costs of Implementation

But in 1975, when the new identification system for Allegheny was introduced, the company had not yet achieved the geographic expansion it felt was necessary to support and give credibility to the name USAir. The important thing to note is that the new look of the aircraft, ground vehicles, and public spaces implemented for Allegheny that year was designed specifically to support the strong visual personality of USAir whenever Allegheny management judged the time was ripe for the changeover. Since implementing the new graphic design system on hardware such as planes, signs, and trucks represented a substantial investment, this foresight helped reduce the overall costs for the new identification system. (See Figure 3-3.)

Integrating Different Facets of Personality

In the interim, the Allegheny name appeared in a specially designed typeface that communicated a modern, updated image. Distinctive shades of red replaced the former color scheme, creating a more business-oriented and efficient look that set Allegheny apart from the competition. A subsequent ad campaign, by the J. Walter Thompson agency, stressed Allegheny's size, number of flights, number of routes, efficiency, and punctuality—all elements in its new personality.

Identity Extends to Commuter Airline System

Research had revealed that Allegheny's short-haul, frequently scheduled commuter flights were perceived by the traveling public as a great convenience, a marketing plus. Therefore, in 1977, the new Allegheny identity program was adapted to its commuter line. The graphics, featuring red, white, and gold, are compatible with the overall identity system of the airline, but established an individual personality for this special service.

Introducing the New Product

By October 1979, deregulation had made it possible for Allegheny to introduce its "new product"—USAir. Because of the long-term planning that went into this carefully integrated three-phase identity system, all that needed to be changed was the name, with its special logotype.

USAir: Reflecting Change/Positioned for Growth

As communicated through its strong identification system, USAir's distinctive personality is that of a major airline, offering frequent schedules to a wide spectrum of markets, with modern equipment and excellent service at reasonable cost. Reinforced through an aggressive ad campaign, it brought almost immediate benefits in terms of increased passenger traffic and employee morale. The company reported that operating revenues increased by 38 percent for the first seven months of 1980. Equally important, their integrated identification system continues to work for them. As in other parity arenas, distinctive personality helped position this new product for success.

Figure 3-3a & b
Allegheny/US Air I.D. Transition

In 1975, Allegheny's bold new red and white color scheme (top photo) set it apart from competition with a businesslike personality—and paved the way for the new airline name (bottom photo), USAir. This name conveyed the airline's new stature as a major national carrier. Because of careful long-term planning, only the name graphics changed when the switch was made in 1979.

Source: Landor Associates

New Category

When a company enters a new category, it must have a complete business development program, which includes discovering what outside expertise may be necessary. Even when the new category is relatively close, with many common characteristics, this is often necessary.

New Solution to an Old Problem

No-wax flooring was a new solution to an old problem. However, this new product created serious new problems for the industry that had tried to solve the old problem in the old way. S. C. Johnson & Son (to prevent its floor polish from becoming obsolete) soon found ways to enter new household products markets with new products that capitalized on the company's floor polish technology.

In this instance, a move by leaders in the established floor covering category forced another leader in a related category to come up with new solutions to old problems in order to enter yet a third category.

In a related field, 3M Company has applied its technology for making surface protection to the development of a combination carpet cleaner/protector: Scotchgard® Carpet Cleaner + Protector, which not only removes soil but leaves a soil repellent behind that reduces the need for frequent cleaning. This has enabled 3M to enter an entirely new category.

One of the most dramatic examples of a new solution to an old problem is the national introduction in late 1983 of Depend disposable undergarments by Kimberly-Clark Corporation. The old problem is incontinence, chronically or under special circumstances. It affects at least 10 million adult Americans. Until now, only makeshift solutions were available to ambulatory sufferers from this common problem—often tying them down to locations and situations that prevent their active participation in social and other recreational events remote from toilet facilities. Now this old problem has led to a new consumer benefit: disposable products with a patented absorbency system for men and women who need comfortable, discreet, and effective protection from bladder control problems. Kimberly-Clark extended its unique absorbency technology, first developed for other types of personal care products, to create an entirely new consumer market.

Solution to a New Problem

The cost of energy has made business and consumer alike alert to ways to economize. Here, again 3M has identified this "new" problem and come up with a solution that becomes a new category for the company. It is the 3M Energy Savings Center, which carries a broad line of do-it-yourself, easy-to-install barriers against heat and cooling loss.

In a totally different area, smokers' clinics were spawned by the identification of health hazards created by products of another category.

Clairol and Gillette were both dominant factors in beauty aid toiletries, then entered the small electric appliance business with assortments of curlers, hot combs, and dryers. Hair styles and habit changes created new beauty care problems that opened up the new category for exploitation.

Creation of a New Need

Fads and fashion come first to mind. These may relate to life-style, vanity, or the conventional wisdom of the moment.

As an example, many current dietary practices arose in response to newly created needs: for vitamins (natural or otherwise), low cholesterol and polyunsaturated fats, organically grown produce, and fibre-filled cereals. Health-consciousness and social self-consciousness with slimness have created spas, clinics, appliances, and entire lines of food and drug products.

Satisfying the new need for aural gratification on the jog (and, accordingly, shutting-out the rest—perhaps another new need—of the world) are the lightweight, earphone stereo radios, such as the Sony Walkman—one of the hottest new products of the '80s.

Fitness for fitness sake was one thing. Fitness as a fad created a new need. Today, room additions are made to house the Nautilus machine. The rumpus room has given way to the home health club.

Revival of an Outmoded or Dead/Dying Category

In new products, many opportunities come full circle. The herbs, emollients, and potions of folklore became today's newly discovered medicaments. The ancient properties of aloe vera slick the sunning skins on the sands of St. Tropez' Tahiti beach, while jet setters (and the rest of us mere mortals) sip millions of gallons of expensive naturally gaseous mineral water from distinctively shaped pale green bottles. Great-grandfather may have gone to Baden Baden for the waters. Now they are a contemporary chic in the home refrigerator.

Innovation

For new products definition, an innovation is an invented or discovered new use, an adjunctive feature, or a superior sophistication that is part of an already established product or category. For example: The cordless channel-changer for the television set. The automatic transmission for the automobile. The push-button telephone dial. The refrigerator's separate freezer compartment. Disposable diapers. Steel-belted radial tires.

Invention and Discovery

Research breakthroughs build businesses and whole industries. Examples are gene-splicing, space satellite communications, silicon chips, instant photography, and laser discs—the list is almost endless, and is increasing at a geometric rate. Most companies do applied research, putting knowledge together in new ways to innovate and invent. High technology companies do basic research as well, spending billions to unlock the secrets of science.

New Business

Accompanying all the changes in people classification, growing data banks, and computer tracking will be changes in business and industry; in politics, academia and entertainment; in health care, food, shelter, and mores.

This implies defensive strategies to maintain product franchises—and burgeoning opportunities for new products to meet consumer needs. The units of communications—at the point of sale as well as the point of preliminary exploitation—will be of greater range. This necessitates a different approach to product development.

Sheer economics dictate an optimal level of business volume for any product development, merely to sustain the efficiencies of production and the demands of the marketing chain.

Therefore, escalating costs of doing business require a new perspective on product development.

One view is that this will move the emphasis from product development to a broader emphasis on product line development and, in all but the largest categories, to a prime emphasis on new business development and long-range strategic planning. Cost of money, more sophisticated inventory management, escalating media demand and clutter all point to the need for building strong cohesive business franchises, rather than spewing out an unplanned stream of unrelated new products.

As Figure 3-4 shows, improvement of existing products demands the least in time and technology investment, but also probably provides the shortest payout period. As one moves up through product development, line development, and finally business development, each stage requires progressively more input in terms of time and technology, but also holds out the promise of increasingly greater long-term return.

This is not to say that the various aspects of new product development should all give way to long-range business development—but that there should be a balanced program wherein each aspect is given properly proportionate attention, with the shorter range, more mature, established product and category entries funding the longer range business that will assure the future growth of the company.

Figure 3-4
Development Perspective

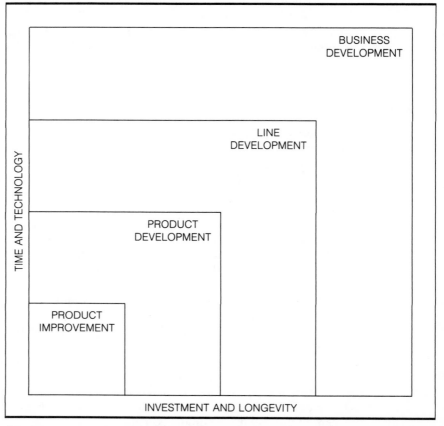

Cost of money, more sophisticated inventory management, escalating media demand, and clutter all point to the need to build strong cohesive business franchises, rather than an unplanned stream of unrelated new products.

Implications are that technology will become more important to those companies with primary marketing skills. Basic research will become more important to those companies with outstanding applied research. Business differentiation will become more important to those companies with product proliferation expertise.

The accelerating net effect is that the corporate persona will be made up of major business units, each with distinctive, well defined personalities. Each will strive for a critical mass in its competitive set. The lesser lights will compete as specialists.

In product development, this suggests a trend to two extremes—away from the middle majority where most of the action is today. On the one hand will be the major newly developed business units based on a combination of superior technology and marketing. On the other hand will be special-purpose, limited-need product development units. Between will be the utilizers of slowly evolving industry standards.

More reliable precommercialization research must emerge to meet the demands of the heavy economic risks of a business-building product development commitment.

As we have seen, there are many ways to be new.

Being new is important. Being different is important.

Being *both* new *and* different is the best start toward new product success.

4

Where Do New Products Come From?*

If you do not think about the future, you cannot have one.
—*John Galsworthy*

The cleverly expressed opposite of any generally accepted idea is worth a fortune to somebody.
—*F. Scott Fitzgerald*

There is a constellation of conventional sources for most new product ideas. These "borrowed" ideas range from bringing foreign successes to the United States (feminine hygiene sprays, enzyme detergents) to going to the institutional trades for consumer products (jarred cheese spread and hair-setting gel) to commercializing developments by industry groups and government agencies.

Then there are outside inventors who shape ideas, but do not identify their commercial roles.

There are other, more blatant borrowings: purchased patents and competitive knock-offs.

And, most importantly, there are your own R&D or R&E, who manipulate their sciences to improve basic materials and compounds.

These represent the vast majority of new product offerings—and successes. They do not, however, represent the methods of the originators of the appropriated inspirations.

How do *they* operate—and is it reproducible?

Leaving out single accidents, but not excluding the driving ambition of a single woman, the truly *new* products require a set of attitudes—which may be identified, but not taught. However, they *can* be organized.

*This chapter contains material edited from *The Rountree Report* series, "Meeting the Challenge of New Products," by George Gruenwald. Copyright 1973–4, Rountree Publishing Company, Inc. Garden City, NY.

To properly channel the attitudes of curiosity, skepticism, disassembly, perseverance, and perfectionism into one champion group (or being) is the requirement. Everyone knows that the venture team needs a marketing generalist, a technical generalist, and probably a financial woman—and the later appurtenances thereto (legal, production, purchasing, etc.). And everyone knows the chronology of procedures.

Why Are Some Companies More Successful?

Why, then, are some companies consistently more successful at developing new products than others?

It starts at the top—where the leader sets the tone, making it clear there is both honor and reward for the disasters of daring needed to come up with the successes.

It continues with a long-range commitment to a system—any system—that places primacy on new products and their management. It is nurtured by recognition of the imaginative champions who have the truest instincts (and viscera) for this highly frustrating field.

Although there is no ready catalog of millionaire chief executives who started as new product managers, Dr. Edward Land fits the attitudinal definition well. If glory alone is enough, take Leonardo da Vinci.

"The Collection Act" and "Seeing Differently"

The most fascinating mental process of the creators of truly new products is what goes on during the "collection acts." These originators seek and store vast quantities of information which they "see" (and hence catalog) in quite different ways than most.

Both Buckminster Fuller and Salvador Dali are able to see a sofa in a pair of lips, and then apply it to a painting or an engineering principle. And they are self-censoring—always rejecting their own creations in search of an ideal.

The mere collection (research) and organization (cataloging) of information are not enough. Nor is the self-fulfilling prophecy of meaning, as Theodore H. White aptly uses in describing one 1972 Presidential candidate:

The mind was like a gravitational field which attracted and rearranged scattered iron shavings of fact about a hidden magnetic polarity within . . . the polarity was always that of Good and Evil.

Between the romantic extremes of white and black lie the subtle shades of success. The complexities of modern marketing do not allow for absolutes.

Taking such illustrations apart leads one to look at matters from many points of view (hence, the basis for techniques such as brainstorming and more disciplined group-think techniques, such as Synectics, developed at fuller length in chapter 14).

With conventional wisdom, packaged goods marketers look at their opportunity targets in terms of arbitrary attributes: Market Share (what if there is no market?); Market Growth (what if the growing one is attracting all the competitive action, and the stable one is a bit sleepy?); Unchallengeable Leaders Dominating a Huge Market (aren't there weaknesses to exploit against those who have so much to lose?); Convenient Product Classifications (the industry may have bar soap divided among beauty, deodorant, and hand soaps, but have you ever seen a triple soap dish?). How about "ethnic" and "gourmet" foods—are those terms really useful?

Barriers to Entry

Then there are the advertising-intensive categories that pose cost barriers to entry for the small advertiser and the price-intensive categories that baffle the large one.

Over all this there is the cloak of industry marketing cliches—consumer sets, overpricing, overpackaging, breaking-the-dollar, odd-number sizing and pricing, push money, co-op funds, traditional trade channels, and the like.

What wonderful challenges these generalizations offer to new-product marketing thinking! What opportunities!

"Inside-Out" and "Outside-In" Approaches

Most marketers seek out targets within industry classifications, trade categories, and store sections—or find gaps in consumer offerings by using a cluster-grid method. This is the "inside-out" approach. The "outside-in" method is to screen consumer use habits and then to elicit responses from stimulus exhibits.

Both methods suffer from the limitations of research—the playback of past and present. Although a seer may divine what is in the future from this data, it is not yet a credible discipline. Therefore, we find the premium on pragmatic risk-takers—those who stimulate future desires.

Sometimes, as Fitzgerald implies in our opening quote, taking the opposite tack from research readings promises the most success. Often, it is both affordable and a good gamble to test a hypothesis that has a champion—even though consumer research is cautionary. Every venture team needs a devil's advocate—because he may turn out to be on the side of the gods.

This book concentrates on a relatively organized approach to new products. The emphasis is on less cautionary risk-taking and on the committed entrepreneurial perspective. It is ideal if "where new products originate" and "who is responsible" are one and the same entity—and backed by corporate commitment. Probably nowhere else in business are there fewer reliable guideposts, more risks, and more Delphic riddles than in new product work. But the payoff, when successful, can be many times greater than the cost of the disasters (which explains why the ratio of failures to successes is so high).

Admitting this admits a lot. Obviously, well-executed procedures alone do not assume success. What then? Beyond the scientific method as applied inside your company, you can look beyond, you can look outside. You can read ahead.

5

Another Path To New Products— Acquisition

Product development and acquisition are methods for achieving strategic results . . . There are situations in which only an acquisition will suffice, such as unique market positioning or proprietary technology.
—*Charles H. McGill,*
  The Pillsbury Company

Although it is the mission of this text to address the process of *internal* new products development in considerable detail, it must not be overlooked that *acquisition* is another path to satisfying the corporation's growth goals. For many corporations, this path has been much more successful than internal new business generation. Of course, the opposite is the more prevalent activity and represents a higher percentage of incremental new product generation for the economy. Other companies have been uniquely successful with a balanced program, addressing each new opportunity area in relationship to corporate strengths and weaknesses—evaluating outside prospects vs. internal abilities.

Even when an acquisition appears to make sense and has been successfully negotiated, its integration may present unanticipated problems in relation to opportunities.

To clearly identify potential pitfalls, it is wise to review Peter Drucker's "Rules for Successful Acquisition," as reported by the *Wall Street Journal,* October 15, 1981.

Peter Drucker's Rules for Successful Acquisition

Drucker says his rules have been followed by all successful acquirers since the days of J. P. Morgan, a century ago. They include:

1. An acquisition will succeed only if the acquiring company thinks through what it can contribute to the business it is buying. Not what the acquired company will contribute to the acquirer, no matter how attractive the expected "synergy" may look.
2. Successful diversification by acquisition, like all successful diversification, requires a common core of unity. The two businesses must have in common either markets or technology, though occasionally a comparable production process has also provided sufficient unity of experience and expertise, as well as a common language, to bring companies together.
3. No acquisition works unless the people in the acquiring company respect the product, the markets, and the customers of the company they acquire. The acquisition must be a "temperamental fit."

Drucker's fourth and fifth rules deal with the integration and cross-promotion of management necessary between the two recently combined companies, important stabilizing and motivating steps, but not the subject of this specific treatment of acquisition process—new products.

Examples where the first three rules were not followed, and where the acquisitions were not successful, as cited by Drucker:

While General Motors has done very well with the diesel businesses it bought, it could and did contribute both technology and management. It got nowhere with the two businesses to which its main contribution was money: heavy earth-moving equipment and aircraft engines . . . None of the big television networks and other entertainment companies has made a go out of the book publishers they bought. Books are not "media."

Another example of a merger not made in heaven is that of RCA Corporation acquiring Banquet Foods Corporation. An electronics and entertainment company didn't understand poultry processing and frozen foods. Subsequently, Banquet was acquired from RCA by ConAgra, a major agribusiness company. Under new ownership and management, Banquet profit margins are growing and bold new marketing efforts are underway.

Now, let's take a closer look at the role of acquisitions in corporate diversification plans. Little has been written on this subject in texts on new products—yet it is of extreme importance to any broad-ranging program of new enterprise development.

The Role of Acquisition in Corporate Diversification Plans*

It is appropriate to consider the option of selected acquisitions as a means of achieving an organization's strategic goals of growth, new market penetration, and diversification. It is not that an acquisition strategy should be used in lieu

*The remainder of this chapter was prepared especially for this book by Charles H. McGill, vice president, mergers and acquisitions, The Pillsbury Company.

of a well-developed and implemented new product strategy, but a coordinated program of new product development and acquisitions can be extremely effective in meeting management's goals for the enterprise.

Following is a brief overview of the acquisition process typical of many major U.S. corporations, as well as a discussion of the specific role of and issues relating to acquisitions as part of corporate diversification.

The Acquisition Organization

The acquisition process in most large corporations typically is controlled at senior levels. Although operating groups and subsidiaries often have their own executives dedicated to finding and evaluating potential acquisitions, the responsibility for executing and frequently for coordinating acquisitions is assigned to a centralized staff function generally regarded as part of senior corporate management. Often the acquisition process reports to the chief financial officer or a senior development officer. Occasionally it reports directly to the chief executive officer. In all cases, an effective acquisition program reflects the participation (and enthusiasm) of the chief executive officer.

The Acquisition Process

The acquisition process itself is a flow of contiguous activities usually progressing sequentially through as many as five major phases:

1. Identification of prospects
2. Courting
3. Deal structuring and negotiations
4. Due diligence and closing
5. Integration

Binding these phases within the acquirer corporation is a constant flow of communications generated by the acquisition team to middle management, senior management, and the corporation's board of directors.

Identification of Prospects

The approaches to prospect identification taken by American corporations are as varied as the nature of the corporations themselves. Generally, where the acquisition process is designed to achieve relatively specific strategic objectives, then the identification of prospects or leads is executed via an active program of establishing concrete, specific criteria; screening industries and industry subsegments for target candidates; and quantitatively ranking these candidates in order of desirability.

On the other hand, where expansion or diversification acquisition criteria are not clearly established, or are expressed qualitatively with little precision, then identification is passive and essentially opportunistic. This "over the transom" type of approach by its very nature can lead to interesting situations for the potential acquirer, yet it is a relatively inefficient and time-consuming way of reaching acquisition objectives.

Regardless of the active or passive nature of the acquisition program, prospects are identified through a broad variety of channels ranging from referrals by investment bankers and business brokers or "finders" to referrals by the candidates themselves to "cold calls" by the corporation to prospects.

Courting

Once a prospect becomes an acquisition candidate, there begins an often elaborate process of courting or romancing with the objective of determining if a suitable "fit" exists between purchaser and seller. During this phase, the specific financial and managerial needs of the seller usually become evident and are compared for compatibility with the specific growth, return on investment, market diversification, and other business objectives of the purchaser.

The buyer's access to the seller's organization varies at this time depending upon (a) possible confidentiality; (b) likely impact on the seller's employees; and (c) the mutually perceived seriousness of discussions thus far.

Far more than a series of lunches, dinners, and other entertainment, this phase sets the groundwork for identification and assessment of the likely satisfaction of unilateral and mutual objectives.

Deal Structuring and Negotiations

Next comes deal structuring. Perceptions and understandings gained in the second phase now are incorporated into a specific financial structure oriented toward meeting the financial and other objectives of both the seller and the buyer.

This is a relatively complex and technical aspect of the acquisition process as it incorporates legal, tax, and often pension considerations as integral parts of a basic business proposition. For example, the desirability/preferability of paying for a transaction with a company's stock as opposed to cash, notes, or a combination thereof impacts significantly on the plans of the seller after the acquisition is completed, i.e., immediate reinvestment of proceeds, estate diversification, long-term decision to hold stock received in the transaction for tax benefits, and similar considerations. Significantly, the price or value of a transaction usually varies depending upon the nature of payment and the attendant tax consequences for both buyer and seller.

When businesses are acquired from entrepreneurs, other, less technical, considerations also are important. The ongoing involvement in the business of the entrepreneur and his management team (occasionally also members of his family) after acquisition is a consideration of financial and egotistical significance and frequently a consideration of paramount importance for a purchaser, which may need the "know-how" of the entrepreneurial team. This relationship is particularly important in cases where the entrepreneur negotiates an "earn-out" or "kicker" whereby he benefits directly, as a significant part of the total consideration, from the future growth and profitability of his business.

Personal considerations make their way into deal structures. It is not uncommon for entrepreneurs selling a business to require that they not be required to move their operations after acquisition from current locations. Similarly, some sellers may require that specific lines (which may be unprofitable at the time of acquisition) may not be discontinued for at least several years.

This phase of the acquisition process involves the traditional "give and take" associated with negotiations. The skills of the negotiator are augmented by lawyers and tax counsel.

The outcome of deal structuring and negotiations is an agreement to agree, i.e., an explicit, written exposition of the structured deal. Known as a "letter of intent" or a "letter of understanding", this legal document usually does not bind either party to perform the obligations recited; however, it typically is not issued when performance is regarded as unlikely.

Due Diligence and Closing

This next phase of the acquisition process is designed to permit the buyer to conduct a thorough review of the business to be acquired, including relevant financial, marketing, operating, and legal records and documents. This process known as "due diligence" is time consuming, but necessary to give the buyer sufficient comfort to proceed toward consummation.

Often the due diligence program is completed via functional teams fielded by the acquiring corporation; occasionally management consultants and auditors are engaged. There may be a human resources team, a marketing team, and teams representing the more narrow corporate functions and specialties, i.e., pensions, insurance, facilities, purchasing, management development, and training.

As due diligence proceeds, so does the drafting and negotiating of a definitive purchase and sale agreement. This purchase and sale agreement will contain all of the key elements of the transaction and serve as a permanent record of the rights and obligations of both parties. Since in many transactions the broad issues have been in effect negotiated through the courting and deal structuring phases, narrower, more technical issues often dominate the purchase and sale agreement negotiations. Not uncommonly, phrases and even words are argued at length if they are perceived to offer either side an advantage—however improbable the likelihood of the advantages being realized.

At the conclusion of due diligence is the closing. In contrast to the often elaborate process that precedes it, the closing is often swift and undramatic, subject occasionally to post closing review and adjustments. The business has now changed hands.

Integration

The final phase of the acquisition process calls for integrating the acquired business into the corporation's structure and environment. In some cases, the corporate acquisition team also is responsible for at least the initial aspects of integration; in all cases the acquirer must ensure a logical and rational transition in order to protect its newly acquired investment.

As with a new product that is being brought on stream once out of the developmental stage, this integration phase is a crucial element to (a) establish appropriate operating and policy guidelines for the newly acquired business; (b) retain and motivate desired key managers; and (c) assess the long-term strategic and tactical factors that will ensure that the acquisition performs at least as well as expected.

Throughout the acquisition process, the acquirer develops quantitative models both for analysis of possible outcomes and eventually as the basis of a three-to-five-year profit plan. The likelihood of achieving the profit plan targets is enhanced significantly with successful integration of the new acquisition.

Why Diversify?

Perhaps the best answer is the retort "why not—everyone else is." In fact, large corporations (and increasingly small and medium-sized public and private companies) see diversification as a critical factor to their success and even survival. For manufacturers, a single product/single market strategy results in a risky no growth situation. Even service firms that are relatively undiversified compared to manufacturers succeed on the basis of new products, new services, and continual repositioning to new markets. A good example is one of the premier service companies, Marriott Corporation, which has successfully diversified from a root beer business to a coffee shop restaurant company to a hotel company and now to a diversified service mix of restaurants, hotels, resorts, airline catering, and other institutional food businesses.

On the manufacturing side, there are many examples of diversification strategies ranging from companies such as Pillsbury, which have diversified within closely related businesses or industries, to the classical conglomerates such as ITT, which have diversified into notably unrelated businesses and industries.

Pillsbury, for example, has successfully diversified its business into several components of the agribusiness cycle. The company is positioned in flour milling, food commodity trading, consumer branded grocery products such as Green Giant vegetables and entrees, Pillsbury branded grocery items, Van de

Kamp's Frozen Foods, Totino's frozen pizza, and American Beauty pasta. Pillsbury also participates in the food-away-from-home market via Burger King, Steak and Ale, Bennigans.*

By contrast, ITT has chosen to diversify with a very broad group of operations including telecommunications equipment, rayon, and pulp and paper milling.

Since diversification is a major element in corporate strategy, diversification moves typically reflect perceived opportunities and weaknesses of the corporation. Among the more common motives for diversification are:

Stimulative—improving an organization's prospects for continued and stepped-up growth in sales and particularly in earnings

Synergistic—extending an organization's strengths to another business. For example, a complementary business that can draw upon distribution and sales strengths established in the acquirer

Strategic—balancing a business portfolio for risk and investment opportunities via acquisition

Reactive—responding to competitive pressures

Supportive—using diversification as a means of retaining and further developing an inplace management team

Coordinated Product Development and Acquisitions

In meeting diversification objectives, a coordinated approach to product development and acquisitions makes sense. Generally, the greater the extent of diversification, the more likely the use of acquisition(s) to reach the goal. There are situations in which only an acquisition will suffice, such as unique market positioning or proprietary technology. Conversely, there may be no opportunity to acquire a business that adequately meets defined criteria, e.g., the business is not for sale or, commonly, does not exist. It is important to recognize that product development and acquisition are methods for achieving strategic results.

The remainder of this section distinguishes between these methods but does so within the broad context of tactical versus strategic diversification. As Figure 5-1 shows, the key variable is not whether the diversification is done via product development or acquisition, but rather if the diversification is basically tactical or strategic in nature.

Tactical Diversification

The strength of product development lies in building upon existing businesses by applying related technology. The heart of tactical product development lies in various line extensions and product proliferations. A

*Since Mr. McGill prepared this material, Pillsbury has also acquired Häagen-Dazs, which participates both in retail distribution of ice cream and food-away-from-home outlets, Azteca Corn Products, Apollo Strudel Leaves and Sedutto Ice Cream.

Figure 5-1
Diversification Approaches

COORDINATED DIVERSIFICATION APPROACHES			
TACTICAL		STRATEGIC	
Product Development	Acquisitions	Acquisitions	Product Development

TACTICAL	STRATEGIC
• New varieties, textures, shapes and sizes • Synergy oriented • Draws on existing management • Utilizes existing sales and distribution systems • Complements existing R&D capability • Easily integrated into the organization • Relatively low risk	• New markets and products • Not synergy oriented • Often requires new management • Often requires new sales and distribution systems, may be totally unrelated • Extends existing R&D capability; may be totally unrelated • Not easily integrated into the organization, may stand alone • Relatively high risk

Source: Charles H. McGill, The Pillsbury Co.

continual stream of new varieties, shapes, and sizes, along with ongoing profit improvement programs represents the bread-and-butter of research and development effort in consumer-oriented companies.

Tactical acquisitions follow logically from the concept of tactical product development. Tactical acquisitions can include acquisition of directly competing products, although more typically acquisitions are likely to center on complementary products that are readily integrated into existing distribution and sales systems. Beatrice Foods' acquisition of Good and Plenty confections is an example of a tactical acquisition, fully complementing Beatrice's position in the candy business. Similarly, the acquisition by Borden's of Morton's Snack Foods and Buckeye Chips fits tactically into Borden's snack/potato chip portfolio.

Tactical diversification is a relatively low-risk, quick way to meet diversification objectives.

Strategic Diversification
The area of strategic product development and acquisitions introduces new dimensions of higher diversification and higher risk.

On the surface, strategic acquisitions are appealing; they may even appear to offer a "quick fit." Such acquisitions permit a corporation to establish a commanding market position, perhaps replete with proprietary technology, overnight. They may offer entry into totally new, profitable businesses.

However, by their nature, strategic acquisitions are relatively risky and typically rely on simultaneous acquisition of a first-class management team. All of this is usually costly, albeit, to the acquirer. It is not uncommon for 30 percent or more of the purchase price to be classified on the balance sheet as "goodwill" written off over 20 to 40 years depending upon accounting interpretations and management's policies.

The acquisition by General Foods of the Oscar Mayer Company is a good example of a strategic acquisition. In short order, General Foods was able not only to enter the processed meats business but also to enter as a market leader. General Foods paid for this privilege with "goodwill," yet in doing so was able to decrease the risk that years of product development and market introductions might not pan out at all. Similarly, Campbell Soups' recent decision to acquire the market leader in the frozen fish portion business, Mrs. Paul's, reflects a judgment by Campbell's that it made more sense to pay for management expertise, brand awareness, and market position than to attempt to build these intangibles over long periods of time.

Occasionally, major diversification objectives simply cannot be met because a business either is not available as an acquisition or simply does not exist. Then, strategic product development is the only way. The advantage of internal development in these circumstances rests with the ability to pinpoint a specific product attribute via technological application. Also, there is no explicit kind of goodwill required with internal product development.

The drawbacks to this approach are significant:

- First, it is difficult to ensure that funds expended will, in fact, have an acceptable pay-back (if any at all). Expensive dry holes are not at all uncommon.
- Second, strategic product development represents a long process of research, product development, test marketing, and refinements. Occasionally, the length of the process offsets some, if not all, of the perceived benefits of the original project.
- Third, there may be a need to develop an entire new management structure around a new product concept and this adds yet another element of risk and effort to the overall project.

Despite these drawbacks, the indisputable benefit of true new strategic product development lies in introducing products that are unique or at least distinctive. The various new shaving products, including Atra introduced by Gillette in recent years, and the currently successful Stove Top Stuffing products and frozen pudding pop products introduced by General Foods speak eloquently to the success of strategic product development. Some companies, such as Procter & Gamble, have long relied on strategic product development as a lifeline to sales and profitability growth.

Coordination: The Final Word

The key word here is coordination. Product development does not usually stand well alone without acquisitions. They complement each other. The successful chief executive is sensitive to this by-play and typically will ensure that both activities are conducted professionally, consistent with over-all corporate goals and objectives.

Section 1
Summary Afterword

New products and services, essential for any company's growth, may be defined as any product or service not now made or marketed by the company, or as any perceived as new by the consumer. Success is determined by goal achievement. Although no reliable over-all success statistics exist, successful companies have high new-product success ratios—that is, a high ratio of successful new products relative to those introduced.

There are many reasons for new product failures, most often related to faulty management and planning. New product information collection and its creative analysis, along with an involved top management, are key determinants of success.

New products are the key to a company's sales growth, both in products and services. This reliance is growing. Comprehensive growth programs utilize both internal and outside sources, and a multi-pronged organization is usually needed to fully address new product needs.

There are no reliable success vs. failure statistics on new products due to the use of variable definitions, survey designs, and evaluation techniques. A failure for one company may be a success for another—and thus not a result of concept failure. Many of the reasons for failure can be reasons for success under other circumstances.

Among the major reasons for failure are:

- Poor planning
- Poor management

- Poor concept
- Poor research
- Poor technology
- Poor timing (often out of manufacturer's control)
- Competitive moves, unanticipated changes not countered

Subsidiary reasons for failure include many that should have been anticipated prior to the program's development:

- Off strategy
- Insufficient technical expertise
- Insufficient distribution
- Insufficient margin, ROS, ROI
- Cost of entry
- Full line needed; only one or a few products entered
- Unfamiliar production
- Regulatory complication
- Patent, license infringement
- Inadequate market analysis
- Development program poorly planned

The hierarchy of new products progresses from the evolution of existing products through the expansion of a brand or product franchise to a new entry into an established category and finally the development of a new category or a new business.

Evolution of an existing product can include repositioning (to find a new audience), recycling (to reintroduce the product for a different use), appearance or form improvement, performance improvement, price/value change, or a combination of any of the preceding. Beyond that, the brand or product franchise can be expanded by adding line extensions and flankers, or by introducing the brand into a new category.

Another type of new product is a new entry into an established category. Factors to consider in this approach are the newness of the brand name, new positioning, appearance or form difference, performance difference, packaging difference, resource difference, price/value difference, and difference in distribution pattern. A look at how Allegheny Airlines evolved into USAir shows how many of these factors can be combined in one "product."

On the other hand, an entirely new category may be created when a new solution is found to an old problem, when a solution is found to a new problem, or when a new need is discovered and filled. Sometimes the revival of an outmoded or dying category may also inspire new products. Other factors to consider in the creation of a new category are innovation and invention and discovery.

At the top of the new product hierarchy is the development of an entirely new business. This is the long-range portion of the plan. It does not replace other new product activities, but should operate in tandem with them.

Where do new products originate? Conventional sources for new products include internal development and R&D, adaptations of foreign developments, allied industry developments, new patents, and competitive knock-offs. What is needed is strong management leadership. Conventional approaches focus on gap analyses of industry and of consumer need fulfillment. The process that goes beyond this includes venture team structures—a means to look at information collection unconventionally.

Another path to new products is via acquisition, which may follow an assessment of opportunity areas accessible through current corporate strengths vs. outside opportunities that are attainable through acquisition.

There are pitfalls to avoid. Three guidelines to follow in acquisition are:

1. The acquiring company must contribute more than money to the acquired company.
2. The merged businesses must have a common core; this may be in markets or technology, or occasionally production.
3. The acquiring company must respect the products, markets, and customers of the acquired company.

The acquisition process includes identification of prospects, courting, deal structuring and negotiation, the due diligence procedure and closing, and integration of the acquired company. The process should be controlled at senior management levels, through a centralized staff function.

The advantages of diversification include the following:

1. Stimulates sales and earnings
2. Synergistically extends strengths to another business
3. Strategically balances the corporate business portfolio for risk and investment opportunities
4. Reacts to competitive pressures
5. Supports the retention and development of in-place management talent

Coordinated product development and acquisition generally takes two forms. The tactical approach complements existing product lines, management, and R&D for synergistic effects. The strategic approach, however, often requires new management, new sales systems, and new or extended R&D capabilities. It does not provide synergy or easy integration, but does offer opportunities for new markets and products. With all this, the strategic form of acquisition entails higher risk than the tactical approach.

Coordination is the key. New product development and acquisition activities complement each other.

Commitment

Corporate Charter

Make it thy business to know thyself, which is the most difficult lesson in the world.
—*Miguel de Cervantes*

Business needs new products just to survive.

While it is instructive to sort out the probable cause of new product failures, it's more important to learn from those high-achiever companies with a consistent new product track record. There appear to be common success characteristics. Among them are:

- Large, definable commitment in money and time—demonstrated by management style, priorities, professional organization, support services, calibre of outside consultants and suppliers, etc.
- Open communication of this commitment within the company, the industry, and to shareholders.
- Career progress of those entrepreneurial and conceptual spirits who are encouraged to stray from the routine paths of procedure into the more risky (and possibly more rewarding) world of new product development.

An environment that encourages commitment is needed at all levels.

Corporate Charter

In the strict legal sense, the corporate charter is an organization's basic starting document—a corporation's Articles of Incorporation, combined with the law, that gives the right to incorporate.

In the larger sense we invoke here, the corporate charter reflects the clearest possible strategic business focus. It is the basis for goal-setting. Many corporations have not specifically defined themselves. Many entrepreneurial and founder-driven corporations depend on the leader's dreams and instincts to guide their growth patterns. Even in such cases, it is advisable that the charter be hammered out in writing—published as a management tool for use in the absence of the instinctual leaders. In all cases, the charter should be periodically revisited—and compared with the corporation's actual performance. One or the other may require revision.

When beginning a new product project, a fundamental question is: Does this fit the corporate charter? The mission's advisability depends on the answer.

Not a hymn to the eternal verities written by a babble of barristers, but a specific, refined—and periodically redefined—corporate charter sets the course. It recognizes the company's strengths and weaknesses in measurable performance comparisons within its industry and in the perceptions of the marketplace. Historically, firms with the most successful new product records stick closely to their areas of expertise and marketplace leverage.

The successful company must stay apace of its technology and customer needs. To be a leader, it must pioneer where both the risks and rewards are greatest (often concomitant).

The forces of change in demography, psychography, and technology require that an enterprise found its evolutionary base on its strongest capabilities. It is critical to recognize these—as well as identifying those areas where the endeavor may be at parity or worse. Nowhere is it written that an enterprise must be first in all things: first in financial leverage, first in science, first in production, first in marketing, first in management.

But *somewhere* it must be written—and posted on the door to corporate headquarters:

This is what we do.

And this is what we do best.

The corporate charter should be strategic. It should not only state, "This is what we are;" it should also state, "This is what we are *not*." It should direct, "This is where we are *not* going."

Every important enterprise does something *best*—best among all the necessary skills, and clearly outstanding within its competitive field.

Bea Arthur, the Tony award-winning actress and star of the CBS television series "Maude," was asked by interviewer Dick Cavett: "Have you ever turned down a part that turned out to be something absolutely great?"

Replied Bea, "I'll tell you what I really feel. Even if you turn down something, whether it's as a director or an actor or whatever and it suddenly becomes an enormous commercial success, it still doesn't mean that *you* should have done it, because if it didn't do something to you originally then you were wrong for it, you know."

Miss Arthur knows *her* corporate charter. She knows what *she* does best.

The shoemaker should stick to his last. That leaves plenty of room to exploit the entire market between galoshes and Guccis. It is rare that a company moves into an entirely new field with a self-generated new product success. A good rule is to proceed with caution into even closely related categories.

Business, a melding of many humans, machines, and processes, may be more complex than an individual actor like Bea Arthur. That's all the more reason why it should articulate—and practice—its corporate charter.

The usual example of what results from a failure to define a corporate charter is the defunct buggy whip company that didn't identify itself as being in the transportation business—and was consequently made obsolete by the automobile. A charter must both be tightly defined and broadly conceived, so as to identify correctly the competitive industry and to be compatible with its trends.

Today, obvious examples of companies with successful corporate charters are found among those members of the petroleum industry that have defined themselves as being in the energy business, rather than as oil refiners and distributors. Today they are already deeply dedicated to coal, nuclear, solar, sea, biological, and even wind-generated energy.

To understand the corporate charter, it is best sometimes to write it—then get management to ratify it. The writing forces the necessary thorough thinking, the necessary development of perspective, the necessary commitment. The stronger the commitment, the more certain it is that successful new products will emerge. The commitment is not only a personal career dedication, but involves support staffing, funding, and psychic investment by both the company and its support resources (e.g., banks, advertising agencies, etc.). The responsibility begins with functional goals. The authority develops for the new product executive through accomplishment.

Other times, there is an existing charter that clearly defines the role of new products in corporate development—anticipating volume increases and expansion targets.

To develop a corporate charter for new products, classify short-range and long-range objectives and place a dollar priority on each of them. Set volume, gross margin, return on investment, and payback goals; trade needs; time frame considerations; as well as defining target markets and product characteristics. Fit those objectives into the life of the marketplace, anticipating your competitors' resources and probable objectives. (One helpful exercise is to define each of your competitor's corporate charters, based on available external evidence. This often reveals attractive opportunities for *your* company.) Define the tools of expansion—which new products will come through internal generation and which by other means.

State the company's or division's image of itself: Is it: "We make air conditioners"—or is it: "We sell comfortable building environments"? Is it: "We process shelf-stable food"—or is it: "We make food quicker and easier to eat [at a given profit]"? The second definition has breadth—the company will consider any form of food and it will consider such functions as manufacturing kitchen equipment, operating restaurants, providing service on air transport, etc.—and a qualifier: convenience. It is consumer-oriented.

To this, add such other qualifiers as: "We will enter a market that generates this return on investment and $xxx in profits, based on a margin goal of xx%"; and/or "We must be the volume leader, with a share in excess of 00%"; or similar objectives.

Conversely: "We will *not* pioneer—but we will out-execute the pioneers in the following areas"; or "We will only enter well-established [mature] market categories, where our captive distribution system provides an edge"; or "We will only market products with life cycles longer than xx years." Be specific.

A specific, refined—and periodically redefined—corporate charter sets the course for a company's commitment to new products. It recognizes the company's strengths and weaknesses within its industry and as perceived by the marketplace. As has been stated, historically companies with the most successful new product records stick closely to their areas of expertise and marketplace leverage; this, of course, with alertness to the changes in resource availability and market needs, as in the petroleum industry example.

Growth Program

Growth goals must be consistent with the corporate charter. Often they are not. Security analyst reports bear witness to the later spin-offs of whole companies as well as product lines that did not "fit" the corporate direction. In all candor, company spokesmen usually identify this as reason for divestiture.

It can be demonstrated that a large percentage of all new product failures were predictable, where the failure relates to the company marketing the product rather than to the validity of the concept. In other words, where the corporate charter is violated (including a violation of the financial guidelines), the risk multiplies. A balanced, well-funded new product growth program nurtures the business by constantly proliferating and upgrading product offerings in value, variety, appropriateness, and availability.

There is also an important portion of the growth program beyond those market maintenance tactics. This critical area of development has the greatest risks, but also the potential of greatest rewards. This is the challenge to build a large, new business base. It requires long lead time, large infusions of money, and a steady hand on the corporate ship to steer an often frustrating course through the shoals of the financial press, shifting government regulations, and the queries of perplexed shareholders. Figure 6-1 illustrates such a total, balanced, growth program—one that looks at proprietary, industry, and break-through opportunities. This schematic represents one approach to managing and monitoring new product programs in line with corporate charter strategic needs. A typical company divides the new product budget

Figure 6-1
New Products Possible Growth Model

EXPERTISE	PROPRIETARY	PROPRIETARY + INDUSTRY	NEW TO INDUSTRY
STRATEGY	*IMPROVE* Maintain and Build Franchise	*INNOVATE* New Franchise in Familiar Trade	*INVENT* New Business Base
TACTICS	Appearance/Form Performance Package Price/Value Distribution Line Extensions Flankers New Category to Brand	New Brand New Entry, Old Category New Category New Solution, Old Problem New Problem Solution Creation of New Need Revive Dying Category Revive Dying Solution	Elements of entire new system for all channels of the making/marketing process
SALES GOAL	From Hold Volume to Major Increases	Major Increases	Largest Volume, Major Corporate Impact
LIFE CYCLE	Continual process needed to stay viable	Continual process needed to stay a leader or to establish it	Long life required to justify program, pay-out
CAPITAL	Funded from existing product revenue base	Short-term added investment	Large, new money
TECHNOLOGY (inc. mfg.)	At hand	Available outside, e.g., contract suppliers, joint ventures, etc.	New knowledge, skills, staff pro-fessionals
DEVELOPMENT TIME	Short	Short to medium	Long
The Bottom Line: CORPORATE COMMITMENT	Routine, within budgets	Normal approvals	Heavy, long-range

between maintenance product changes and development of current markets vs. entrance into new businesses, and determines the optional advantages of contracted R&D, suppliers, joint ventures, licensing, and acquisitions. The company assigns appropriate numerical time and dollar guidelines for return on investment, cost of goods sold, sustaining profits, share of market, rank in category, etc. This approach is a useful discipline for any maker and marketer of goods and services with growth goals beyond those of efficient use of captive resources to increase base line volume and profits.

Business Disciplines

Perspective is key. This is particularly true for the long-term, major-investment ventures. The successful ones are well-conceived at the beginning, thoroughly planned, then professionally executed in a cohesive program. Changing policy guidelines may have other corporate benefits, but they are usually not conducive to the realization of major new business development goals nor are they characteristic of companies with impressive new product success records.

It takes more than a corporate Charter and a growth program to succeed. Companies with impressive new product successes benefit most from well-organized new product policies and procedures—the disciplines of the business.

Opportunity identification, conceptualization, and prototype modeling are the areas where talent, inspiration, insight, and pragmatism count most. Often, too, these are areas where programs run aground. If this is to be, it is less expensive at this stage than later, when plant and marketing commitments escalate costs.

As preventive medicine, use a new products checklist denoting just about every major predictable factor that should be audited at every phase of development—in R&D (or R&E), production, finance, legal, distribution, communications. A useful example is included in Appendix 2A. It lists more than 120 chronologically phased operational considerations—where things can go wrong, as well as right.

Most disastrous is to *not know* when a program is foundering—and to plunge ahead, evading the obvious. It is the obvious (on hindsight) that is usually the cause of failure and—just as often—it is the obvious that is the single most important ingredient of success. *Never overlook the obvious.*

7

Goals—
Deciding Where to Go

The river is a very different shape on a pitch-dark night from what it is on a starlit night. All shores seem to be straight lines, then, and mighty dim ones, too; and you'd run them for straight lines only you know better.
—*Mark Twain*,
  Life on the Mississippi

Now that the corporate charter is understood, it must be executed in strategic new product growth goals to provide direction to managers, impetus to the system, and a trigger to the process.

The corporate charter sheds some light: it tells you where you are; it tells you in general where you want to go. It doesn't take you there, nor prescribe the route.

For this, directional goals must be established.

Product Portfolio Assessment

In an article written for the January–February 1981 issue of the *Harvard Business Review*, Yoram Wind and Vijay Mahajan described how to design a product and business portfolio:

Since its emergence in the early 1970s, the portfolio technique—along with related concepts like the Strategic Business Unit and the experience curve—has become the framework for strategic planning in many diversified companies. Now the art has advanced enough to give a diversified company a variety of approaches when it is considering installing such a system or substituting one that evidently meets its needs better than the current portfolio.

Conceptually, we think, the tailormade approaches are superior because they:

- Permit inclusion of the conceptually desirable dimensions of risk and return, plus any other idiosyncratic elements viewed by management as important.

- Stimulate creativity by forcing management's involvement in developing strategic options.
- Help to gain an advantage over competitors, who are ignorant of the company's portfolio framework and so cannot "read" it with the aim of anticipating the company's strategic moves.
- Can offer explicit guidelines for resource allocation among the portfolio items.

But a tailormade system costs more, mainly in data requirements and management time. Even if top management decides not to implement an idiosyncratic approach (based on cost-benefit analysis), an evaluation of currently used portfolio models . . . should add to the value of the portfolio analysis and the quality of the strategies designed to build a new portfolio.

There are many approaches that can be taken in assessing a company's strategy for new products and its compatibility with the needs, resources, and objectives of the organization. The *Harvard Business Review* article describes nine product profile models that merit study, if only to identify the many variables that must be considered and the need for management to assign (largely judgmental) weights to each element of any model's equation. The nine portfolio models are classified according to degree of adaptability, allocation rules, and dimensions, with appropriate comments. They are:

1. Growth/share matrix
2. Business assessment array
3. Business profile matrix
4. Directional policy matrix
5. Product performance matrix
6. Conjoint analysis-based approach
7. Analytic hierarchy process
8. Risk/return model
9. Stochastic dominance

These models are designed to assess corporate strategies for ongoing businesses as well as to help determine whether the company should add new businesses, and whether these new businesses will be compatible with the needs, resources, and objectives of the organization. Each new product line requires an investment designed to yield a certain return. Top management's role is to determine the products or businesses that will comprise the portfolio and to allot funds to them on some rational basis.

It is clear, in evaluating the various approaches to setting business enterprise development goals, that subjective judgment is the most important aspect in determining success. After all, any and every company presumably can plug into the various business portfolio models. Also, presumably, most of the fact sources will be similar. Therefore, the critical difference in determining the course of action is management judgment.

Because weighing the facts calls for subjective judgment, it is management's responsibility to decide who the evaluators will be and how conflict among them will be resolved. These decisions cannot be left to staff members involved in the construction or implementation of the new product or enterprise development programs.

Establish a New Front

Management must decide where to compete, how to compete, and when to compete. Management must decide whether to follow the generally acceptable strategies of business, or to try to change the rules of the game to obtain a major advantage.

A new front may hit competition where it is strategically weak, it may outflank the field, and it may be the theater in which new weaponry is introduced. Certainly, it gives a timing advantage not available when joining the already identified battle, with its fortresses, entrenchments, and deep logistics. Besides surprise and control of one's own destiny, this approach also often offers the added advantage of creating new entries that are not readily available to the entrenched competition. Among the flanking actions not available to competition are new product standards and tactics, which if adopted by them recognizes obsolescence or improvement of their presumable parity or better lines, new technology that requires costly replacement of existing modes, new sources of supplies not adaptable to present manufacture and assembly, and new forms of distribution, which if adopted would negatively affect support from present distribution factors.

One essence of success in this approach is to upset the static equilibrium in a mature industry. In new, emerging industries still in flux, this approach gives the innovator who has committed a full front advance the ability to establish the rules for the category.

Find a "Sitting Duck"

Where management has the luxury of selecting points of attack, selective evaluation of the practices (and successes) of entrenched competition often reveals a "sitting duck" for new product invasion. In many large, mature fields, the leaders maintain position for historic reasons, and have built up capital-intensive manufacturing with large (often obsolete) plant commitments, unfavorable labor contracts, and dependence on (often captive) sources of raw material or parts supply.

Under such conditions, which are prevalent, the manufacturer can hardly be marketing intensive. The production and transport drain takes up funding that might otherwise go to plant sophistication, R&D, and marketing. Sales operations are likely to be trade intensive, because moving the plant produce at optimum capacity is the first order.

An extreme example of this is the meat packing industry, where it is logistically detrimental to hold large quantities of raw material or, on the other hand, to be undersupplied. No wonder the priorities are clearly spelled out in the motto: "Sell it or smell it." The leaders in this field, incidentally, have deemphasized their fresh meat operations in favor of further-processed products, with raw material needs beyond minimum supplies provided by *other* meat sources. In other words, they are not locked into under-capacity slaughterhouses.

Quick indications of vulnerability are industries where leadership positions have been stable, with little market share change; one-product companies and industries; industries with a high percentage of contract packing; and industries and leader companies that have not adapted to new and more cost-efficient processes utilized by similar makers, and do not use new, cost-saving materials or distribution techniques that will benefit major customers. Opportunistic goals are suggested by protracted price-war battles among industry leaders, which will sap their financial resources and divert their perspectives. Other opportunities are suggested by conservative, entrenched management and by well-investigated changes in ownership and in management.

Framework for Business Planning

Management, then, provides the leadership for risk-taking. Its attitudes will set the tone for the corporation and will largely determine whether the company will be in the forefront of new enterprise development or merely an adequate follower of industry new product practice.

As much as we wish business to be a science, chance forces often prevent this. In fact, Nobel Laureate scientist Sir Francis Crick says: "Chance is the only source of true novelty." True, but there *is* a scientific method—and the investigational and experimental elements of it have been adapted by business, to enhance the odds for success. Professionals do better at games of chance than do amateurs.

Perhaps chance is the reason Roberto Buaron, writing in *Management Review*, refers to his market-entry strategic planning model (Figure 7-1) as "The Strategic Gameboard." The moves are a choice, highly reactive to the competitive set:

1. Do more and better of the same
2. Resegment the market to create a niche
3. Create and pursue a unique advantage
4. Exploit unique advantage industrywide

The scope and mode of competition affects the strategic approach and results.

Before entering any game of chance, however, the possible missions should be reviewed—and the goals established. At this planning stage, management is in control of events. In Figure 7-2, "A Framework for Business Planning,"

Figure 7-1
The Strategic Gameboard

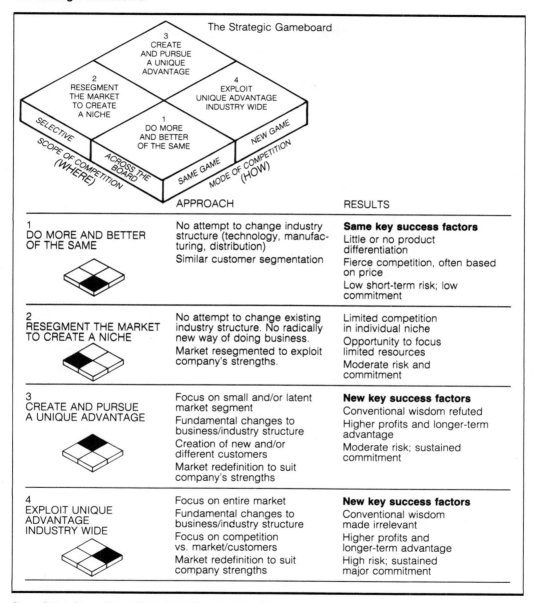

	APPROACH	RESULTS
1 **DO MORE AND BETTER OF THE SAME**	No attempt to change industry structure (technology, manufacturing, distribution)	**Same key success factors**
	Similar customer segmentation	Little or no product differentiation
		Fierce competition, often based on price
		Low short-term risk; low commitment
2 **RESEGMENT THE MARKET TO CREATE A NICHE**	No attempt to change existing industry structure. No radically new way of doing business.	Limited competition in individual niche
	Market resegmented to exploit company's strengths.	Opportunity to focus limited resources
		Moderate risk and commitment
3 **CREATE AND PURSUE A UNIQUE ADVANTAGE**	Focus on small and/or latent market segment	**New key success factors**
	Fundamental changes to business/industry structure	Conventional wisdom refuted
	Creation of new and/or different customers	Higher profits and longer-term advantage
	Market redefinition to suit company's strengths	Moderate risk; sustained commitment
4 **EXPLOIT UNIQUE ADVANTAGE INDUSTRY WIDE**	Focus on entire market	**New key success factors**
	Fundamental changes to business/industry structure	Conventional wisdom made irrelevant
	Focus on competition vs. market/customers	Higher profits and longer-term advantage
	Market redefinition to suit company strengths	High risk; sustained major commitment

Source: Roberto Buaron, "How to Win the Market Share Game? Try Changing the Rules," Management Review, January, 1981, (c) AMACOM, division of American Management Association.

Figure 7-2
A Framework for Business Planning

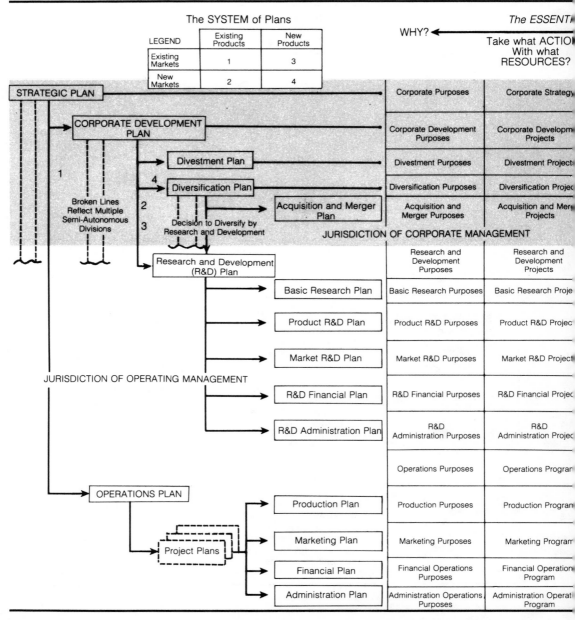

Source: From Long Range Planning Service Report No. 162, SRI International's Business Intelligence Report, SRI International, Menlo Park, California.

ELEMENTS of Each Plan

To ACCOMPLISH what? when?	What CONDITIONS must be met?
Corporate Goals	Forecasts Policy Decision Guidelines
Corporate Development Goals	Forecasts Policy Schedules and Budget
Divestment Goals	Goal Feasibility Criteria for Decision
Diversification Goals	Forecasts Criteria for Decision
Acquisition and Merger Goals	Availability of Candidates Criteria for Decision
Research and Development Goals	Policy Decision Guidelines Schedules and Budgets
Basic Research Goals	Goal Feasibility Criteria for Decision
Product R&D Goals	Technical Feasibility Cost Feasibility Schedules and Budgets
Market R&D Goals	Forecasts Competition Schedules and Budgets
R&D Financial Goals	Technical Feasibility Market Forecasts Cost Performance
R&D Administration Goals	Business Feasibility Managerial Availability Other Resource Availability
Operations Goals	Business Forecasts Organization and Procedures Schedules and Budgets
Production Goals	Workload Forecasts Methods and Standards Schedules and Budgets
Marketing Goals	Sales Forecasts Competition Schedules and Budgets
Financial Operations Goals	Financial Performance Schedules and Budgets
Administration Operations Goals	Managerial Performance

The PROCESS of Creating a Plan

FORMULATE THE TASK

Define its scope
Identify the reasons it is being undertaken
Define the characteristics of the answers sought
Consider alternative methods of procuring answers
Select a method of solution based on cost-value analyses
 and resource availability
List the information required for solution
Specify the action required to develop the information needed

DEVELOP THE INPUTS

Assemble the facts
Forecast or postulate the uncertainties
Develop the alternatives to be considered

Note: Information can be developed by assembling what is known by search and discovery and by creative thought. It is in the development of alternatives for consideration that creativity exerts the greatest influence on the planning process

EVALUATE THE ALTERNATIVE COURSES OF ACTION

Convert alternatives to terms that can be compared
Establish criteria for making a selection
Compare alternatives

Note: Refine the alternatives from the possible to the feasible to the desirable if the evaluation is complex

DECIDE

TRANSLATE THE DECISIONS INTO STATEMENTS OF

Why the action is required

Action and resources involved

Consequences expected and when

Controls for interim measurement of progress by
 Identifying critical forecasts and conditions to be monitored
 Prescribing necessary performance standards
 Prescribing the performance schedule to be met
 Prescribing the budget requirements to be met

SRI International defines the first step in business as "Formulating the Task."
This is management's obligation in setting goals.

SRI defines components of this goal setting as:

1. Define the scope of the task
2. Identify the reasons it is being undertaken
3. Define characteristics of the answers sought
4. Consider alternative methods of procuring answers
5. Select a method of solution based on cost-value analysis and resource availability
6. List the information required for solution
7. Specify the action required to develop the information needed

This is followed by development of the inputs from available sources, evaluation of the alternatives along a continuum of possible-to-feasible-to-desirable—to arrive at the consequential goals.

This generative phase completed, management translates the decision(s) into statements of:

1. Why the action is required
2. Action and resources involved; consequences expected and when
3. Controls for interim measurement of progress, by
   a. Identifying critical forecasts and conditions to be monitored
   b. Prescribing necessary performance standards
   c. Prescribing the performance schedule to be met
   d. Prescribing the budget requirements to be met

For further study by its subscribers, SRI International's Business Intelligence Program, formerly Long Range Planning Service, details this approach in Long Range Planning Service Report No. 162.

Less Risk, More Control

Although entrepreneurial risk-taking in internal development of new products has been emphasized in much that has been written about the subject, the application of narrowly disciplined controls also provides incentives.

Some companies recognize that they are not particularly good at product innovation—but that they are superior at cultivating and harvesting. This logically leads to an emphasis on brand development—and an acquisition strategy. The goal is to acquire well-managed, high-performing companies that are compatible to headquarter controls and ability to provide growth financing for the new subsidiaries.

H. J. Heinz Company is a good example.

Heinz has acquired Star-Kist tuna, Ore-Ida frozen potatoes, Hubinger high-fructose corn-based syrup, Weight Watchers foods and services, Gagliardi Brothers processed frozen meat specialties, and Jerky Treats for dogs. As reported in an article in the *New York Times*, August 2, 1981:

> Heinz's new products have come mainly through such acquisitions—of small companies with few, although highly successful, products—rather than internal development. "The track record of large companies in new product development is chilling," noted Anthony J. F. O'Reilly, chief executive of Heinz. "We've experimented and find that we're not as good at it as the entrepreneur."
>
> Heinz executives recall with a wince, for example, the company's unsuccessful venture in creamed soups, a specialty product line that never made it out of test market.
>
> Within its existing product range, Heinz has concentrated mainly on line extensions. Mr. O'Reilly has stepped up the company's marketing efforts but concentrated on staple products, taken a conservative approach financially and finely focused the company's acquisition program.

The strategy seems to be working, propelling Heinz into the ranks of the top performing food-processing companies.

Different strokes for different folks. General Mills, another top performer (with about 51.8 percent of sales from food products, but nearly all from consumer products) has successfully advanced on many fronts: flankers and line extensions from its strong stable of brands; new brands, new lines; licensing-in and licensing-out; acquisitions; innovative, interally developed technology; and new enterprises. This is an example of a large, multi-divisional corporation whose management has been able to engender entrepreneurial flair in its goal-setting.

Managements, then, are seen to set goals that include an acceptable percentage of failures and limited successes, in order to instill the dynamism necessary to assure both the short-term and long-term future. The "acceptable percentage" differs widely, of course—but no company can expect to be in the new products battle without a willingness to risk failure. The phased programming of each venture, tightly budgeted in advance, provides the controls.

The optimum goal may be to achieve a balanced portfolio of growth opportunities, both from within markets currently represented with company entries and markets new to the company. Within that framework, sales, return on investment, and life cycles are calculated. The smaller the risk (close-in opportunities), the lower the sales and ROI required, with development time and cost at a minimum. At the other end of the scale are developmental needs for new technology and a heavy, extended infusion of capital. Here sales goals and ROI must be high and be sustainable over a lengthy life cycle.

Such goals can be spelled out in measurable terms for the future, and used to audit present and past performance.

Attached to these directions can be some broad goals, such as:

1. Build the basis for a *new brand franchise* with a specific dimension new to the company
2. Build the basis for a *new distribution system,* whether it be through conventional means and staff or one newly employed or contracted
3. Build the basis for *new outlets or store section* penetration
4. Build the basis for a *new preemptive product technology*
5. Build the basis for a *new manufacturing process* that fits the company's present marketing system or the systems employed by the previously stated goals.

Top Management Support

There is nothing more difficult to take in hand, more perilous to conduct, or more uncertain of success, than to take the lead in the introduction of a new order of things.
—*Nicolo Machiavelli*

We don't need more ideas.
We need more champions.
—*Thomas E. Singer,*
The Gillette Co.

The surest motivation for new product success is the attention of top management, not only to the strategic goals but to the evolving details of the business. This requires that management send clear signals of career advancement potential to those entrepreneurial spirits who have the instincts as well as skills to pioneer.

The entire organization must be turned on by the opportunity.

For example, L. W. Lehr, chairman of the board and chief executive officer, 3M Company, writes:

Nothing is more important to 3M Company's continued success than its ability to efficiently develop and market new products which are acceptable to society and profitable to the company . . . A basic 3M philosophy is to encourage all employees of whatever special discipline to participate in the creation of new, profitable products, and for the company to provide an unstructured climate in which to do so . . . While not necessarily part of the prerequisite for a successful new product, an orderly process helps to insure that our new or modified products are compatible with both 3M's profit objectives and the ever-growing demands of society.

The 3M Company's "Guidelines for Planned Product Responsibility" describe the functions of the technical, marketing, manufacturing, and specialized staff services that assist in the successful introduction of new or modified products. The guidelines not only cover the standard developmental phase procedures, but also provide guidance in the areas of product assurance, product safety, and the product's environmental impact. They are detailed in Appendix 2B.

Encouraging Participation

3M is one company that provides broad direction, specific aids, and, most importantly, the atmosphere of management encouragement of brand participation in new product ventures.

In order to innovate, it is up to management to break the mold of tradition, industry cliché, and standard ways of doing business. Most new enterprises follow the guideposts of the industry in which they compete. This follows logically from the industry's public information sources, whether audits of sales or trade channel inputs, and the standard definition of "markets" common to the industry. New divisions of the market drawn along different patterns are conceptually more challenging, but often not as objectively supportable. For these reasons, the rare risk-taking that occurs frequently does not have the opportunity to yield the greater results that the "follow-the-leader" approach routinely sets as objectives.

Gadfly and Catalyst

In a January, 1981, article in *Management Review*, published by AMACOM, a division of American Management Associations, Roberto Buaron wrote:

> It is not surprising, then, that successful new-game strategies are rare. To upset the competitive balance and rewrite the rules of the game for an industry calls not only for exceptionally imaginative entrepreneurial thinking but for uncommonly strong and sustained commitment. Inevitably, both must start with a strong lead from the top.
>
> In the interest of fostering a no-holds-barred approach to strategic thinking, the chief executive will need to get involved early in the planning process as gadfly and catalyst, probing conventional assumptions and proposing novel alternatives to begin breaking down planners' mental barriers to radical change.

Many major companies have delegated the gadfly catalyst roles to outside consultants, who speak with the internally well-publicized knowledge and support of management—but do not have line authority. This allows an experienced perspective to intercede without inordinate time demands on the chief executive, who has an easy-access, informal, off-the-record dialog with his consultant. Such an outside influence, of course, must be chosen with extreme care by the chief executive, as the consultant will also serve as an alter ego and trusted confidant.

Buaron continues:

> To support the necessary level of organizational commitment, the chief executive should take particular care that he is personally sending the right signals to the organization. This means, above all, visibly concentrating his own time and attention

on key strategic functions (such as R&D, marketing) and activities (competitor analysis, for example). It also means encouraging open communication and, in most cases, downplaying rank and protocol by giving special recognition to bright junior executives.

Finally, and by no means least important, he can and should, if necessary, reshape the corporate reward and value system to bring it into line with the desired strategic orientation. Tunnel vision is unavoidable in companies where managers' pay and prospects are consistently tied to short-term earnings growth. Strategic thinking can only flourish in organizations where successful risk-takers and innovators, rather than "solid citizens" who are best at avoiding conspicuous mistakes, are seen to reap the kudos and financial rewards.

Providing Directional Spark—and Support

So, whether a company is in its entrepreneurial phase, or is a highly disciplined, well-established one competing in a mature industry, it is up to management to provide the directional spark—and support—that will yield points-of-entry for new enterprises.

Management must hold high the standards, must flaunt its support for the innovators—to motivate others as well as these essential contributors. Successful top executives who have built companies on outstanding new product track records will never be satisfied with anything short of superiority. Their statements, their actions, their reward systems recognize this. As Somerset Maugham wrote: "It's a funny thing about life, if you refuse to accept anything but the best, you very often get it."

To demand a lot requires giving a lot. To learn, to teach, to make a difference is the role of a leader in the conception of new enterprises.

Management should know the business and human resources of the company, and the technology and practices of the industry. Management should not know as much or more than the supervisors responsible for each aspect. Sufficient knowledge is needed to give a clear direction that can be acted upon: what to do, not how to do it. Not what cannot be done, but what goals and challenges to offer.

Management should know enough—but not too much.

A few examples

Crown Zellerbach

When Harold Reed left the packaged food products industry in the early '70s to join the great West Coast wood products company, Crown Zellerbach, as head of its Consumer Products Business Unit, he set about learning just enough about the conversion of trees into products, spending time with R&D, with quality control, with every plant superintendent. He learned enough—but not too much.

As a consequence, he was able to suggest direction and challenges. If met with reasons why something might not work, he knew just enough to be able to say: "Perhaps you're right—but why not try to do it another way?" The Crown Zellerbach managers responded with remarkable technical breakthroughs, receiving great self-satisfaction in proving their expertise while improving the company's new product superiorities.

Emilio Pucci

Sometimes coming from one discipline to another has its advantages. Mr. Reed is an MBA who left a marketing-intensive industry to join a production-intensive one. An even greater extreme is a member of royalty who studied agriculture and got his master's degree in political and social science from Reed College, Portland, OR. Next, he served as a pilot for the Italian air force. Then, in 1954, after much experimentation he revolutionized an industry.

In an article in the *International Herald Tribune*, October 3–4, 1981, Emilio Pucci told how he felt after World War II, just out of the air force:

Suddenly faced with the unknown, you feel free to try anything, to tackle tasks and experiment with ideas that experts would never consider. To work with women and for women rather than with machines and men was every bit as exciting as flying.

Coming from a highly technical and mechanical field where it takes months to perfect an invention, I loved the idea that I could translate an imaginative thought into a finished product in a matter of hours or minutes by simply using a pair of scissors, a piece of fabric, a needle and thread.

I wanted my things to be in keeping with the colors of nature, especially southern Italy, but to my dismay I discovered that existing chemical colors, developed at the time of the Industrial Revolution, were often at odds with the bright, transparent hues of sea, sky, flowers, and the beauty of nature.

To develop new colors, I decided to start from scratch. I took hundreds of pictures underwater in Capri, at various depths, where water changes from turquoise to blue. I used oils, paints, acrylics to capture the vivid or pastel colors at various hours of the day, from sunrise to sundown in Capri, in Sicily, Calabria, the Tuscan hills, the many splendors of the Alps.

With all this material I arrived in Como, the capital of dyeing and printing, the kingdom of silk, and went to work. When I was told that something was impossible I would not take "no" for an answer, and more and more frequently the "impossible" became a reality.

Finally, some of the colors I had captured from nature came to life on actual fabric. I played with these colors (natural colors, I called them), mixing orange and pink, violet and fuchsia, turquoise and green. Then I started with prints, some geometric, some floral, splashed with bright colors, alive with movement.

Then I faced the problem of motion. Instead of following the complicated prevailing tailoring methods, I started to experiment with simple geometric concepts based on the physical structure of the human body as it changes in movement, trying to liberate rather than hinder, to allow great freedom of action.

As if by miracle, the rigid rules about dressing were shattered, women were finally free to express themselves also with their appearance. A dramatic change, a revolution in fashion had started, while the women's liberation movement gathered momentum: blue jeans, overalls, men's shirts for women spread through the United States at first, then to the rest of the world and even to the Soviet Union.

Support for Risk-Taking

The record bears out that the highest percentage of new product successes are made by those companies who emphasize renewal management—repeating the success pattern over and over. There is nothing wrong with support for "doing what you do best—but doing it better." You need the old pro approach to less risk, albeit quicker but likely less return. The renewal process and the diversification process are more easily quantifiable, because they are based on track record and industry example.

Nonetheless, dynamic leadership also encourages and supports diversification and innovation. Because of the risks involved in innovation, the overall corporate performance from year to year is more likely to affect a consistent commitment to innovation. Net: New products are a need—and therefore—a cost of doing business.

The strongest signal management can send to staff regarding innovation is the development of a new products organization structure that has both high status and high visibility outside the company, as well as internally. This means that forward progress can be made with management blessing and support, but that the organization also has its own independent exploratory budget and charter.

However, the major thrust of the operation must involve top management, to understand its direction, to merit its support—and to gain by the contributions made by responsible executives who have a broad perspective, but are usually not involved in new product disciplines on a day-to-day basis.

Management is looking at the long run. Management is looking for consistent success at a predictable level. Management is also looking for major, breakthrough successes that can carry the company well ahead of planned growth patterns. For this, management will run risks.

A personal aside, to provide an example:

Very early in my career I was exposed to two types of innovative risk-takers, both in the same company. There were the entrepreneurial Harris brothers, who sold their Toni Company to Gillette; and there was Joseph Spang, chairman of the parent company. Mr. Spang made a visit of state to our division, to see how his newly acquired hair care company was integrating with his hair removal company. He was reviewing his troops.

Toni's management arrayed their newly-minted brand managers around the board room table. Each gave his report in turn. Each had glowing words.

Everything we did was a success. Every nationally distributed product was increasing share, we were beating back P&G, Lever, and Colgate at every turn. Every new product being introduced was exceeding test market performance. Every product in test was ahead of program.

We (rather smugly, as I look back at it) completed our reports.

Mr. Spang, dark-serge-vested proper Bostonian, said: "You gentlemen are to be complimented. It appears that everything you are doing is going very well." He paused. "However, I must confess to being disappointed. You see, when everything is going right, it means to me that everything you could be trying isn't being done."

That management support (and attitude) led Gillette into entirely new areas of growth, beyond the logical line extensions and "fighting brands" (to counter competitive new products) that had formerly been the hallmark of the company's success.

What this all means is that top managers must support new product ventures, encourage risk-taking, and find means to cultivate entrepreneurial approaches uncommon to standard business practice—if the company is to be a consistent leader. This encouragement includes financial rewards and, perhaps even more importantly, the psychic reward of recognition that the new product area is most important to the growth of the company.

Organizing for New Products

The selection and development of new products must, in the final analysis, be the responsibility of top management. . . . Of course, top management cannot carry out such a responsibility by itself. The question is how to go about organizing for it.
—*Samuel C. Johnson and Conrad Jones*[1]

Just how does one go about organizing for new product development.

The answer is: it depends.

It depends on the nature of the corporation and its goals. It depends on the existing structural order of things. It depends on the corporation's management style. It depends on the caliber, motivations, and growth potential of the staff in place at the time of installing the new products organization. It depends on past (historic) performance by organizations charged with the responsibility. It depends on the orientation of the corporation, if this is not to change. (Are the present strengths or weaknesses centered in certain areas?)

It depends on patience.

Often, the first structure is not the enduring one. Of all areas, that of new products should be susceptible to new organizations—whether they be flanker organizations (to a new or existing new products department, but charged with a different order of new product innovation), or quite separately conceived organizations, with different reporting paths and budgets, maybe charged with acquisition identification, or with development of entries into industries new to the corporation—or, perhaps, ad hoc committees and venture groups with limited time assignments. Sometimes, a corporation will

[1]Samuel C. Johnson and Conrad Jones, "How to Organize for New Products," *Harvard Business Review*, May–June, 1957. Mr. Johnson is chairman of S. C. Johnson & Son, Inc. Mr. Jones is a group vice president of Booz, Allen & Hamilton, Inc.

"test" various organizational approaches to find the suitable set-up for its specific needs.

It depends on geography.

Some corporations set up their new product organizations in separate quarters from the day-to-day operations. Some locate the new product leaders near the department most important to early development—e.g., if the new product leader is a marketing person, he may office near R&D, and vice versa. Some companies do not change the geography, but create liaison staff positions to integrate one key function with another. For example, a business person might be attached to the laboratories with no lab functions other than to act as facilitator between the lab staff and the new product marketing development department.

Whether accomplished through rearrangement of geography, assignment of a coordinator, or frequently scheduled meetings (including informal ones), it is essential that the marketer and the scientist learn each other's language. When addressing new enterprises where outside expertise is needed, it is critical for the inside scientists as well as the marketers to "go to school" on the communications of the new technology and the new marketing disciplines. Many companies sponsor sufficiently lengthy seminars between parties so that personal rapport as well as a common language is established.

And, it depends on timing.

Proactive and reactive needs are different. For the second need, a strike force with no other priority is an acceptable ad hoc organization. For the first, a venture team is a sometimes solution.

No one type of organization, therefore, is an ideal or even highly practicable organization for any one industry, let alone more than a few companies. Each company will seek its own structure, relying both on its needs and its talent pool.

Defining Goals by New Product Functions

To find the proper new products structure means defining the goals of the organization along lines that can define the functions of such a new products structure.

As an example, let's look at S. C. Johnson & Son, Inc. In setting up its new products department, S. C. Johnson described its needs along the continuums of *increasing technological newness* and of *increasing market newness*. (See Figure 9-1.) The divisions of technology range from "no change" to "improved technology" to "new technology." The divisions of marketing range from "no market change" to "strengthened market" to "new market." Working out the grid shows what type of new product activity is appropriate.

In S. C. Johnson & Son's case, the new products department reports to a top management officer, in order to provide the stature and independence necessary for coordinating interdepartmental programs. The department's

Figure 9-1
Relationship of New Product Responsibilities by Department

PRODUCT EFFECT	NO TECHNOLOGICAL CHANGE	IMPROVED TECHNOLOGY	NEW TECHNOLOGY
NO MARKET CHANGE		REFORMULATION	REPLACEMENT
STRENGTHENED MARKET	REMERCHANDISING	IMPROVED PRODUCT	PRODUCT LINE EXTENSION
NEW MARKET	NEW USE	MARKET EXTENSION	DIVERSIFICATION

Key:

⁄⁄⁄⁄ : R&D   ＼＼＼ : Marketing   ✕✕✕✕ : Joint Responsibility

Source: Adaptation from Exhibit II, "How to Organize for New Products" by Samuel C. Johnson and Conrad Jones, Harvard Business Review, 35 (May–June, 1957, © by the President and Fellows of Harvard College.

director has the staff and freedom to participate in the broad affairs of the top planning committees of the company. The department draws on the various company departments to support its functions: administrative, marketing, technical, and negotiating (external). Several task forces report to the new products director: sponsor groups and product committees.

As defined by S. C. Johnson:

Sponsor groups formulate a proposal and guide its development. Each group is formally charged, after the screening phase, with responsibility for successful development into a realistic product . . . Marketing, R&D, and the new products department are always represented; in addition, there may be one or two individuals drawn from other departments. (This) device discharges its responsibilities in the proposal and development phases. It provides minimum interference with the established departments and maximum reliance on their existing personnel and services.

Product committees are formally organized with regular meetings and agenda, and have a large membership drawn from many departments—but the nucleus of each committee is the sponsor group that developed the product. The product committee is responsible for carrying a product, once developed, through to full-scale commercialization.

The benefits of this organizational approach for S. C. Johnson & Son read like the goals for most companies' new products departments. To summarize, they are:

1. Total product strategy is clarified and scheduled to fit long-range plans.
2. The staff is motivated by the knowledge that the product will be developed and that management knows who worked on it.

3. Sponsor groups and product committees develop broader management skills in participants.
4. Group efforts stimulate more creative ideas.
5. Project profit potential is enhanced by upgraded, controlled selection standards that maximize available resources.
6. A reduction of lost effort and lower product mortality relieves staffing pressures and minimizes personal disappointment.
7. Top management has a complete overview in condensed business terms. Prompt decisions can be made based on complete information.
8. Management is relieved of much supervision and coordination, leaving more time for analysis and judgment.
9. Long-considered as well as new ideas are quickly moved to conclusion, with more new products than before (this approach was applied) moving to market.
10. Ideas are commercialized faster by group anticipation of problems, with solutions devised in advance.
11. Sales features are designed into the product by team thinking before full-scale development, yielding enhanced market success.

Means to Fit the Needs

It is generally wise to consider segregating new product efforts for on-going revenue divisions from the activities of the long-range planning, corporate growth, and new enterprise development functions. An established division or subsidiary or brand franchise or customer segment organization should be responsible for all new product developments that it funds to enhance achievement of its measurable goals. It provides the budget. It must have the responsibility. Under these terms, all appropriate line extensions and flankers belong there.

Not infrequently, a concept is developed by a revenue division that does not automatically fit. In this instance, it can become the basis for that division's redefinition (expansion), can be assigned to another more appropriate channel (another division or an independent new products department), can be sold off to another company—or it can become "lost." To protect against the latter, a company must have an information system among departments and divisions that allows exploration of all activities for "fit," since it may be likely (especially in large companies) that divisions are not fully aware of each other's needs, goals, and plans. Where division charters are exceedingly well defined, they may be so tight that they allow large gaps between divisions, making it ordinarily impossible for the new concept to find a "home," even if it is highly appealing and within the company's expertise to execute. In this instance, a management review of all projects should spot the opportunity and assign it or profitably dispose of it.

As a company moves from the close-in to the far-out opportunities, it has a number of organizational structures to review. The first priority should be to define the *needs*. Then the means may be devised.

No set of boxes and dotted lines will help.

People Are Paramount

A revealing evaluation of the business best-seller, *In Search of Excellence: Lessons from America's Best Run Companies,* appeared in the *Los Angeles Times* on August 28, 1983. Written by Paul W. MacAvoy, professor of economics and dean of the University of Rochester's graduate school of management, the article states:

[The authors] do seem to get closer to knowledge when they find that their exemplary companies practice "almost radical decentralizations and autonomy" in setting up small organizations within the firm, the division, and even the plant within the division. This decentralization is not enough to produce better results alone. There has to be present a product manager able to sustain creative development of new products and services. The Peters-Waterman excellent companies reward the "champion" (project manager), do not strongly penalize the losers, and extend remarkably "complete support systems for champions."

Although this incentive system is found to a degree in other companies as well, this is still a very important insight. The large organizations that make up manufacturing in this country become more efficient and innovative by reproducing within themselves an extremely numerous set of small organizations. They also reproduce within the company the outside public market for progressive and venturesome managers. This involves paying much more to those in the division and even in the plant that are successful in making profit.

The S. C. Johnson & Son, Inc. approach drew all new products responsibilities together into one functional model. MacAvoy seems to be saying that, for other companies, it may be wise to break out new products according to different divisions of interest, investment, and pay-off.

Long-Range Planning

This farthest-out planning role has no line responsibility. It provides a business perspective background for actable decision-making. It surveys and forecasts the effects of change in science, technology, economics, agriculture, legislation, politics, etc.

Two examples:

- If long-range planning had effectively signalled possible impacts of fuel supply changes, the emergence of more efficient new plants and labor practices by overseas competitors, and other changes related to OPEC and post-World War II reindustrialization, this may well have been translated into earlier new product strategies by the U.S. auto industry.

- In the data processing field, the monolithic leader's long-range planning process correctly predicted the explosive growth of the market for small personal and business computers. IBM made unusual strategic moves to quickly enter the market with machines utilizing components, programs, and distribution systems from outside sources—tactics formed and executed by a separate and unconventional division set up to achieve market leadership in segments of the business new to IBM.

Growth and Development

Growth and development articulates the perspective of long-range planning by establishing corporate missions for new market entry areas, acquisition of new resources and technology, and other opportunities in character with the corporate charter. From these missions (or goals), growth and development establishes strategies and preliminary budgets categorized in logical, timely authorization phases.

This operation is responsible for the search, both within the company and outside, to determine the best way to proceed to meet the goals. It may be determined that building up certain internal resources is the best way to move or that, on the other hand, there are enough differences in the new market components to require arrangements for external generation of the new entry.

Proliferation

Proliferation is the extension of existing expertise and facilities along various continuums. For example:

Existing product lines may be extended with different types of the same products. Easy examples would be more automobile and truck types, body styles, carrying capacities, etc.

Existing brands may be extended with new models. Again using the auto industry, examples are the Chevrolet Impala, Chevette, etc.

Existing markets that lend themselves to the expertise of the manufacturer may be reached by easy proliferation from a base of both factory and sales performance. Staying with the automotive model, Honda has broadened from automobiles to motorcycles to power equipment for lawn care—gasoline-driven, service-intensive, relatively high-ticket hard goods all leveraging the same corporate expertise.

While growth and development and separate proliferation activities, under certain circumstances, may fit together, it is often better for them to be separated, with different channels of funding and accountability. Certainly, in all but the very largest corporate environments, the different organizations will draw upon common staff services, thus preventing uneconomic duplication. Growth and development most likely is funded from the corporate treasury, while proliferation is usually funded from a division or brand's own revenue generation.

Example: Dun & Bradstreet Corporation

"Our goal is to be in a state of continuous transition so we can always accommodate the changing environment of our clients," insists Harrington "Duke" Drake, chairman and chief executive of Dun & Bradstreet Corporation. "Instead of concentrating on new ways to package and sell information we happen to have on hand, we are beginning to look at the changing needs of the marketplace and to devise ways to fill those needs," he told *Business Week* in an interview published November 16, 1981.

D&B has carved out many freestanding profit centers that encourage managers to be entrepreneurial in their operations. The company coupled its new market-oriented mission and its vast computerization program to provide the main tool for the new strategy. CEO Drake is bringing managers together to develop interdisciplinary cooperation that could lead to new products. And he has mobilized outside consultants, NCSS staffers, and D&B trainers to teach D&B's staff of 25,000 to view new electronic equipment as vehicles to help create those products. As he described it to *Business Week*:

> There is an influx of new talent throughout the company. Its once meager strategic planning staff is now second only to its financial department in size. Divisions once filled almost exclusively with salespeople and operating specialists are now salted with computer experts and market researchers—some of whom are specially trained to debrief salespeople on customer comments that might indicate a new-product need.

Interdepartmental communications have become the driving force behind D&B's management approach. An example described by *Business Week*:

> Last year, for the first time in the company's history, 140 senior managers (met) to brainstorm about the company's new market thrust. Financial officers, data processing managers, and other functional specialists are pooling ideas at their own interdisciplinary meetings. "Most of the ideas you need to grow a business are in somebody's lower right-hand desk drawer," explains Charles W. Moritz, president and chief operating officer. "We didn't want to miss a new product because divisions can't get together."

> So far, D&B has avoided any backlash from managers who might miss the simpler life of the product-driven days. "The process of change has been revolutionary in its impact, but evolutionary in its development," Moritz explains.

Some Different Approaches

One approach commonly used is to have a new products department that is responsible for enhancement of a company's chief strengths through utilization of internal technology and production, and appropriate established outside sources. This department brings the company no new businesses.

Rather, it has the task of keeping the company in the forefront of its industry through the conceptualization and development of easily commercialized new products, beyond those relatively routine line extensions and flankers launched by the revenue divisions. Within each revenue division, an executive (a new products manager) is assigned to supervise this latter task, utilizing the resources (and budget) of the division.

Separately funded, on a par organizationally with upper middle-management, and reporting directly to top management may be an additional entity assigned the task of diversification into allied new businesses (as opposed to entirely unrelated businesses, such as those making up conglomerates attracted primarily by financial leverage opportunities). These businesses probably are identified in the corporation's long-range growth plans as new enterprises appropriate for the company's future development. Common titles for this department are New Enterprises, New Business, or Growth and Development.

Beyond this, of course, are growth plans unrelated to new products, but rather related to improved efficiencies (vertical integration can be an example), broader distribution (made feasible by additional plant sites, warehouses), overseas expansion, licensing, etc.

The Human Equations

In earlier chapters, it has been stressed that new products must have highly visible, actual support from top management. There are other human equations necessary to the success of the staffing of a new products organization.

When a business is established and going along reasonably well it needs careful managing. There is plentiful information input available. Many of the business circumstances are controllable. The competitors become well known and, to a degree, predictable. The company knows how to buy parts and material, how to make and assemble, how to sell and distribute, how to advertise and promote, how to fund, and how to profit.

This takes a certain kind of professional manager. This person deals with many understood facts on which to base judgments. He or she has a trained organization.

For new products, different situations exist.

A new products manager must have an entrepreneurial ability, be a risk taker, be flexible, be very open-minded—in addition to being a sound strategist, negotiator, and salesperson. Ideas are fragile. Well-nurtured, they become concepts. Dismissed out-of-hand, they die before they are rounded out for expert evaluation. A new products manager must be a protector of the ideation process and its produce. The manager must encourage the innovators and inventors, serving as mentor, sponsor, and, when absolutely necessary, protector from the demands of the system or the uninvolved critics. The manager should champion the ideation process and its participants, then make judgments that bring the concept into the more objective screening process. In short, it takes a different kind of leadership to run a new products program.

The new products manager calls on help from within his department, usually built around R&D and marketing, and from within the company. He uses corporate staff services; advertising, promotion, market research, sales administration, finance, etc. And he forms teams, for over-all direction and to deal with explicit problems.

He may get the corporation to underwrite a venture group, a free-standing adjunct to his charter, but with a separate budget and the entrepreneurial freedom to conduct broad creative exploration. Once the group isolates and embellishes the new enterprise to a point where it is suitable for inclusion within the new products department activities, it goes on to other free-wheeling new development assignments or is disbanded.

On an on-going basis, the new products manager may establish a review committee that includes interested representatives from each staff department, as well as the sponsor member of the new products staff. Sub-committees are established for particularly complicated issues. The committee aids the manager in evaluating the various projects, in providing the direction to their staffs in development of the necessary information and support programming, and in reviewing the department's management clearance recommendations. The department itself, of course, is responsible for initiating action and for the direction of approved new product programs.

Use of Outside Resources

Often, a new products organization is not wholly self-contained and needs outside help beyond corporate resources.

Except for close-in new product evolutions, the use of outside resources enables an organization to job out product development to selected professionals who bring new expertise that does not fit the table of organization until after the company is on stream in the new enterprise. Outside resources make it possible to hire on a part-time basis experts otherwise unavailable within the company or, in some cases, in the employment market. Outside resources can often play a key role in new product development.

Types of Outside Resources

Outside resources are of different varieties.

Suppliers of processing and assembly machinery, original equipment, processed ingredients and parts, laboratory and engineering components, and materials, etc., often make available experts at a gratis or nominal charge, depending on the degree of involvement and commitment from the contracting company. Sometimes these suppliers have free-lance sources on a consultancy basis to whom they may refer.

Developmental research firms exist in all disciplines, from far-out futurist specialists looking beyond basic research to close-in technologists. In between are the bulk of large, well-established R&D expert firms. Beyond the technical development and production aspects, outside experts in packaging engineering and design, sales, distribution, marketing and communications research, and communications also abound. Specialist legal firms in the patent and copyright areas should also be available to the corporate staff and its outside law services. Rather than having them "go to school" as involved participants in the project, let them audit the practices of the experienced experts.

Where companies have very active new product programs or are thin in internal management staffing, using outside services to provide executional controls is also merited. There are specialist firms in this field, primarily concentrated in marketing-oriented product categories. Additionally, there are some advertising agencies with exceptional expertise and success patterns in new product development programs. The use of such resources can help accomplish a number of objectives, including:

1. Acting as an extension of the company's existing new products department or division.
2. Acting as an additional, long-range exploratory new products resource
3. Providing a coordinated new product creative resource on a continuing basis, without disturbing regular company operations/programming
4. Acting as a study group or task force in a specialized area on a limited time basis—without requiring the addition of costly internal staffing
5. Acting as a partner with a company venture team
6. Acting to reduce internal resource loads
7. Acting to get more projects moving faster

One of the benefits of assigning one or more of these roles to a properly qualified advertising agency is that there is an on-going established relationship and a familiarity with the general business style and its participants.

However, this can be a trap.

One of the advantages of an outside resource is its presumed lack of inhibitions. A long, close relationship with an outside source sometimes takes on the same set of inhibitions as the inside staff. Therefore, before assigning a major conceptual and developmental role to an established supplier, be certain that the new product relationship, ground rules, and contractual signals all support independence of thought and candor of comment.

Role of the Advertising Agency

Because a product or a service or a business or a corporation is a communication in itself, early involvement of the advertising agency is advisable. However, as with any other resource, management must be certain that the advertising agency is qualified in the new product consultancy and development role beyond the areas of paid advertising, where the agency is an expert professional that can be held accountable for its performance.

There is no artists and writers school for new product practitioners. Writing a television commercial or a sonnet is not the same as creating a new product idea. A copywriter may describe it better, and that is very important. Equally, the ability to visualize does not automatically carry with it a new product speciality—although it often can convey an idea faster, or reveal a flaw in a product concept. Likewise, an advanced degree in the management sciences may expedite the plotting of the critical path—but promises no special hope for what may start down that path.

Understanding this is important to the assessment of the role of your advertising agency in dealing with new products marketing development. It is a different field than advertising development—although many similar skills and tools are employed.

Often a special type of agency team—an agency venture team—is necessary to best fulfill the needs of a new product assignment. That same team will not necessarily carry through its successfully launched product.

But why should an advertising agency be considered for the assignment in the first place?

First and foremost, because of the increasing inseparability of the product from its image, no one communication alone moves the new product to success. The audience identification, the empathetic message, the appropriate package (for the audience, for the shelf, for the advertising medium and its message) all meld together to form either an integrated or fractionated personality. An important part of that personality building occurs at birth, heavily influenced by the parents—who are hopefully bright, contemporary, strong, mutually reinforcing, and (it helps a lot) successful.

Therefore, the early perspective of how the agency views the eventual communication of the product image should play a highly influential role in the shaping of the product itself. It is often easier for the product to succeed when the partners that conceived it also bring it to the world.

The need for agency flexibility is extreme—inasmuch as the differences among client needs, as reflected in their facilities and staffing, tend to vary more widely in the new product area than in advertising services. The company's advertising policy is established, has an operational pattern, and a common trade language. This is less likely to be so with new product practices.

The advertising agency's role, then, is to mesh with client capability; to be a fellow explorer; to provide an outside objectivity and perspective; to act as an intermediary in negotiations; to provide a synergistic effect in the creative process beyond the provision of optional concepts; to mobilize its special resources for program advancement; and, of course, to develop communication of the new product concepts themselves as well as their advertising messages.

Because a casual oversight, misjudgment, or lack of long-view perspective can create irretrievably disastrous results in the development of new products, there is a special demand for hardy candor, finicky nit-picking, devil's advocacy, and educated skepticism. The most fundamental new products revolutions have come from hard taskmasters, enthusiastic perfectionists: the marketer and the agency must both provide such courageous members to the new products team.

Sometimes it is the role of the company's advertising agency to "sell" the team's program to the top management of the corporation. It is often most effective to communicate a new product concept to top management as it would be done to a customer. The corporate top management expects that before the new product team comes to them, all the proper steps have been taken. Management can always ask questions and dig into details. But first, the team must get this attention.

There is no surer way to do this than by portraying the new product concept in a realistic consumer communications form—both the advertising and the product itself. If it needs further explanation, then there is something missing in the prototype communication. Preparation of prototypical exhibits, especially in package goods, fits the resources of the advertising agency. (Incidentally, studies show that consumer products companies tend to overemphasize and industrial products companies tend to underemphasize the importance of the customer communication.)

Selecting Outside Resources

It is perhaps more difficult to select a new product specialist source than almost any other type of supplier or consultant.

Once a company is satisfied with the professional qualifications, then the key matters often boil down to:

1. *Communications.* Do they understand what I mean? Do I understand what they mean?
2. *Enthusiasm.* Do they not only understand the goal, but do they already have in mind an easily understood program to meet it—and, perhaps, some contributory inspirations that demonstrate both their understanding and enthusiasm?
3. *Rapport.* Do I respect them and do they respect me? Will they be easy to work with, wear well, and justify my respect?
4. *Leadership.* Will they provide leadership for the program, not be merely contributors?
5. *Track Record and Methods.* Do their accomplishments appear valid and are their methods rational and sophisticated? (Check references.)

6. *Compensation Arrangement.* Is it fair and equitable? (Do not base a decision on the amount quoted. Equal expertise earns equal dollars. Low prices generally provide insufficient service or later additions. High prices generally provide the supplier with insurance against the unpredictable and the financial freedom to do wide-ranging explorations. Find out if these factors are the explanation.)

Establish accounting practices up front. Occasionally, some services are appealed to by incentive arrangements, working at cost or cost-plus with a later addition for success. Even royalty arrangements are made, on top of a fixed fee. (Appendices 2D and 2E cover these arrangements in more detail.)

No matter how comprehensive your company's new products organization structure is, by all means use outside services. We all need all the help we can get.

10

A Program to Address
New Product Goals

No great thing is created suddenly, any more than a bunch of grapes or a fig. If you tell me that you desire a fig, I answer you that there must be time. Let it first blossom, then bear fruit, then ripen.
—*Epictetus*

The more the marble wastes, the more the statue grows.
—*Michelangelo*

The need for new business, for new products, has been established. The risks—and rewards—have been weighed. Your company has decided to hew to its charter or to break new ground (and, hence, revise the charter). An organized program of development is needed.

Before all of the elements of the critical path become event bubbles, a blueprint for action must be devised. It must proceed from the general to the specific, from an assortment of many options to a plan for introducing a few, from small financial commitment across an assortment of considerations to much larger commitments to major opportunities that have been identified in the development process.

The favored mode is to risk little in preliminary exploration, increasing the investment as knowledge is gained and the opportunity refined. Each stage in the development has a Go/No Go gate. Here it is decided to stop the program, retrace the route for further information and evalution, or to proceed through the gate along the next path toward further refinement.

There are many acceptable structures for moving from the wide mouth of the exploration funnel to the narrow spout of new products output. The rest of the chapter outlines one that has well served many industries. Its general pattern will be the structure of succeeding sections of this book.

Phase 1: The Search for Opportunity—Compilation of Available Data

Market identification and opportunity targeting is the initiating phase necessary to determine whether a particular market area should be given major pursuit. Often, much of this determination has been made in the corporate charter and the goals it contains.

Knowing the industry, the sales volume and trends, the basic technology, the target consumer, the competition—all factors that help shape the development of a fact book and a plan—are necessary first steps. In some industry categories, there are readily obtainable information sources generally recognized as accurate by all participants. In others, original research, experienced judgments, and reasonable guesses may be required.

Recognizing this, the mission is to reduce the subjective factors and to assemble reasonably acceptable *facts*, on which the first cut at opportunity identification will depend. Because these are mostly quantifiable—whether by demographics, spending, plant utilization rates, etc.—the needed areas of investigation may be quickly listed.

Industry Analysis

All exploratory searches start with an analysis of the industry under consideration for a new product entry. Among the categories of information to consider are sales volume and trends, basic technology, the nature of the competition, and customer definition. These may be detailed as follows, and are explored at greater length in a later section:

Sales volume and trends
- By dollar volume and unit sales
- By specific manufacturer/marketer
- By specific product
- By geographic region
- By population density
- By economic index (per capita consumption, buying power, etc.)
- By media efficiency (if applicable)
- By customer use pattern (user defined by frequency of purchase, use occasion)
- By marketing expenditure as percent of sales, per prospect potential, etc.
- By sales, distribution, and pricing practice

Basic technology
- State of the art
- By component parts, raw materials, labor resources
- By process, assembly, packaging, etc., equipment and subcontract resources

- By patent barriers, opportunities
- By license opportunities
- By purchasing
- By transport

Competition

- By trade practices
- By product specifications
- By product reliability (including warranty practices, service, reputation)
- By product sales volume and trends, broken out from evaluations, estimates, and projections above
- By advertising/promotion spending
- By media patterns
- By selling themes, major claims, image dimensions
- By share trends
- By share of marketing expenditures (and gross impressions) pattern
- By end-user and by trade channel marketing expenditure ratios
- By sales efficiency related to industry average, leading competitors, and trendlines

Customer definition

- By customer use pattern (by frequency of purchase, use occasion)
- By demographic characteristics
- By psychographic characteristics
- By awareness of category, competitive factors
- By attitude toward industry, competitive factors
- By alternative and substitute products (are products first choices, are brands first choices, is it an important decision, etc.?)
- By pricing effects (inelastic, elastic, responsive to small, large, frequent, etc., price adjustments)
- By regional and seasonal purchase, use patterns by individual products, marketers

Other factors, as available

- Outside affecting influences (foreign trade, regulatory restrictions, general consumption changes, ecological conditions, economic situation, etc.)
- Forecasts for the industry and its major elements (growth, diversification, replacement, various changes)

Opportunity Identification

Once the industry analysis has been performed, appropriate opportunities can be identified. The process includes:

- Define targets
- Forecast rough volume and share
- Perform a risk-ratio analysis

- Conduct a preliminary feasibility study using secondary data and professional expert opinion—not prototypes or trial runs
- Study a war-game assessment of competitive reactions, exclusivity, regulatory constraints or protection
- Look at exceptional technical hurdles
- Consider legal and policy issues

Decision

Proposal: Decide to abort, extend, or embellish Phase 1 investigation or to proceed to Phase 2.
(Go/No Go)

Phase 2: Conception

This phase translates market facts into product concepts and customer positioning communications, prior to extensive research and development. The objective is to create and to refine a variety of appropriate product concepts in the form of consumer communications, which may then be screened down to a workable number of the most appealing ones that may be carried forward into the prototype modeling phase.

Input Research

This is a backgrounding step, often required where "hands-on" experience, technical education, patent and literature review, as well as special consultant professionals, are needed for complete understanding of the opportunity area.

This input area also employs many diverse outside influences, from production equipment manufacturers to examination of foreign market trends, etc.

Ideation

Ideation is the generation of large quantities of unconstrained possibilities, utilizing a variety of stimulus techniques. Judgmental expert(s) screen concepts for technical viability. Some are also eliminated for legal, cost, or policy reasons.

Ideaforms

This is the shaping of concepts into single-minded, clear communications. Often a concept may be stated several discretely different ways to appeal to various market segments. As necessary, concepts are illustrated in semi-comprehensive form. The goal is a clear communication that neither goes beyond nor falls short of a real-world summary statement of each concept.

Pre-screening Concepts

Broad-brush selection methods are applied to eliminate or improve concepts that are difficult to communicate or clearly off-target in a very major sense. All others, some changed by this process, move into the next step.

Customer Communications

This is the preparation of customer communications of each concept, together with suitable representations of the product-in-use.

Screening Research

Using the above materials, an extensive face-to-face (or in some instances, a telephone or mail panel) consumer study evaluates the concepts on various dimensions. The techniques can rate many concepts rapidly—individually and in relationship to each other. Again, the aim is to improve the concept and its communications language, and to eliminate from consideration only those that are grossly inadequate.

Decision

Proposal: Decide to abort, extend, or embellish Phase 2 investigation or to proceed to Phase 3.
(Go/No Go)

Phase 3: Modeling (Prototypes)

At this phase, preliminary concepts have survived several selection steps. Now it is necessary to bring the narrowed number of proposed new products closer to reality in the form of prototype products and prototype communications (sometimes called "protocepts"). While the laboratory or engineering department may have satisfactory experimental evidence—even blind test comparisons of bench models—the target customer prospect must see the concept "in the round," as closely as is timely and economically feasible. Modeling accomplishes the development of such stimulus materials.

Descriptors

This step involves classifying the product category and preliminary brand name development.

The category should be classified in the language of the prospect to communicate quickly and simply the product class, the product's difference from others in the class, and (if separate from that) its benefit.

Preliminary brand name development should include brand names that are already in-house as well as newly devised ones. The ideal is a brand name that is reinforced by a descriptor, is distinctive from the competition, has only one or a few words, has one or only a few syllables, and has a graphic appearance that is not generic and can be registered as a trademark. Unless the product is a line extension, a flanker, or it is otherwise necessarily appropriate to use a well-known house brand, hundreds of alternatives can be generated. These are given a preliminary trade name clearance search. Survivors are screened for suitability to all dimensions of the proposed brand franchise.

Prototypes

These cover all aspects of the product and its communications. Included are:

Product, service, system
This is rendered in quickly recognizable form—in appearance when that is sufficient, as a working model when necessary, or both when possible. The model should be suitably finished for photography, if not for actual use. Comprehensive art is rendered if necessary.

Package
This is rendered in true representational relative dimensions, colors, and graphics. Where the package plays an operational role in the product, the prototype should be able to represent this also (e.g., a child-proof cap on a drug product).

Brand name and descriptor
One or several apparently final choices are depicted.

Communications themes development
Brief benefit descriptions in the context of a single major appeal are stated in separate communications themes, which differ by emphasis, nature, and the degree of the support statement, etc. These are screened by prospects for comprehension and to help devise a finally developed single communications selling theme.

Prototype of major communication
This is rendered in a semi-finished state, encompassing product claims, representing product personality equity, and in a format that is reproducible in actual media (i.e., no more words nor pictures than can be accommodated, legally supportable, within policy guidelines).

Prototype testing
The goal is to test the product prototype representation within the context of the communications prototype and among representative target prospects.

Decision

Proposal: Decide to abort, extend, or embellish Phase 3 investigation or to proceed to Phase 4.
(Go/No Go)

Phase 4: Research and Development

This phase of product development encompasses a number of different activities, including *in vitro/in vivo* trials, checking outside scientific resources, pilot plant production, analyzing the factors necessary to scale up from pilot plant production to full-scale commercialization, war game exercises, controlled tests, and feasibility studies.

In Vitro/In Vivo Trials

These are test tube (*in vitro*) and real world living trials (*in vivo*).

Outside Science

Study other disciplines to be certain nothing has been overlooked that might be employed to optimize the R&D project. Ordinarily, this results in a doublecheck that sustains internal R&D direction. This step includes an outside patent search and process choices.

Pilot Plant

This involves a small-scale replication of mass production. It helps to debug the system and devise production controls, systems, and equipment design. It is basic to determining on-stream cost estimates.

Scaling Up (For Commercialization)

Before moving from pilot plant production to full-scale commercial manufacturing, it is necessary to carefully analyze the following factors.

- Manufacturing needs in resources—material, labor, factory, location, procurement, capacity, parts production, assembly, integration
- Marketing factors—pricing, marketing budget (consumer, trade advertising, and promotion), sales force
- Distribution channels—inventory, warehousing, transport, integration
- Service—pricing, speed terms/warranty, factory-controlled or independent
- Financial
- Legal—any plant location regulations relative to pollution controls, sewage disposal, zoning, etc.

War Game Exercises

These are exercises to foretell possible consequences of competitive reactions, counter strategies, etc. The variables are processed through computer models.

Controlled Tests

These are tightly controlled trial and retrial purchase tests to determine sales velocity, usage rate, cut-in on sales of competitive and house brands, promotional variations, etc. The manufacturer controls the distribution, so that the variables are in the product itself and its marketing communications.

Feasibility Studies

Now's the time to take another look at feasibility at a point where there is an abundance of research data, experience, and cost forecasts.

Decision

Proposal: Decide to abort, extend, or embellish Phase 4 investigation or to proceed to Phase 5.
(Go/No Go)

Phase 5: Marketing Plan

The marketing plan should include the following elements:

- Prototype plan
- Test simulation and test market selection
- Sales and distribution trade practices and terms
- Creative strategy (communications of new products)
- Media plan
- Consumer promotion plan
- Trade promotion plan
- Merchandising plan
- Public relations plan
- Payout plan
- Start-up plan
- Test market tracking plan
- Assessment plan
- Expansion plan
- Finance and production plans

Decision

Proposal: Decide to abort, extend, or embellish Phase 5 development or proceed to Phase 6?
(Go/No Go)

Phase 6: Market Testing

Market testing includes evaluation of the following factors:

- Test market execution
- Awareness, attitude, usage
- Distribution penetration
- Sales, share
- Assessment
- Follow-up plan

Decision

Proposal: Decide to abort, extend, embellish, repeat, readdress with major changes, or proceed to Phase 7.
(Go/No Go)

Phase 7: Major Introduction

Finally comes the moment of truth—the major introduction. This is accompanied by a continual monitoring of the market environment, and adjusting the plan accordingly. Expanding from the original test market involves the following considerations:

- Trying additional test areas or an enlarged test area
- Expanding into regional distribution
- Using a phased roll-out
- Completing expansion to the entire sales territory
- Continuing to track the original test areas
- Planning to keep the product refreshed, continually "new"
- Close monitoring of performance vs. plan criteria
- Evaluating line extension and flanker opportunities
- Undertaking a remedial plan, if necessitated by the monitoring of performance

Program Summary

The program to address new products goals is simply an organized, step-by-step method that allows a company to take small risks in evaluating many alternatives in the early phases and take potentially larger, but better informed, risks in the later phases of development. Companies that have followed this process have a high record of failure in the early phases, as may be expected, and a very low record of failure in the later phases. The decision considerations that must be addressed after the new products of a business have been defined are:

1. Is there latent demand?
2. Can a product be made that will satisfy the market?
3. Can the company be competitive with the product and within the field?
4. Will the entry be profitable and satisfy the corporate charter, as well as other company objectives.

A helpful extrapolation of these decision considerations, prepared by Schrello Associates, Inc., of Long Beach, CA, appears in Appendix 2F.

Section 2
Summary Afterword

A well-articulated, specific corporate charter is the starting gate for an effective new products operation. It is the foundation for the strategic direction needed to accomplish the company's goals. Top management must take the lead in visibly recognizing the importance of the program, and in encouraging entrepreneurial risk-taking. An organized approach to staffing and to the process is needed to establish accountability and program the decision points leading to predictable performance.

The corporate charter recognizes the company's strengths and weaknesses in measurable terms. It defines the corporation's purpose in a way that will provide growth goal direction, and thus yields both short- and long-range objectives. This, then, sets the stage for developing new products, new enterprises, and new business development programs.

The formalization of goals—of deciding where to go—sets the strategic direction of the company. The corporate portfolio is first evaluated to determine how to implement options that are compatible with and will enhance the corporate objectives. Next, various methods, or models, are discussed for the evaluation of a corporate new products strategy. Opportunistic competitive gaps within the industry are isolated in the search for exploitable vulnerabilities, and the company determines where, how, and when to compete—whether by upsetting equilibrium in a mature industry, setting the rules in a newly emerging industry, or searching out other opportunities.

The task of formulating a business plan may be defined to include:

- Outlining the scope of the plan
- Stating the reason for being
- Determining the characteristics of needed information
- Looking for alternative methods of obtaining amswers
- Analyzing cost-value and resource availability
- Listing the information required for a solution
- Specifying the action needed to develop information

Such a plan should state why an action is required, what actions and resources are involved, what the expected consequences are and when, what controls are needed for an interim audit of progress, what performance standards are prescribed, and what the recommended schedule and budget are.

The company must determine whether it wants to achieve less risk and more control through downgrading innovation in favor of cultivating and harvesting current product lines; or whether it wants to proceed on many fronts, including internal and external development goals, licensing, acquisitions, or new technology. This is the risk ratio—to gain big success, there must be a willingness to accept failure, on a planned, projected basis.

It is also possible to attach other (implementary) goals to add new dimensions—e.g., by building a new brand franchise, building a new type of distribution system, building sales penetration in new trade categories, developing preemptive product technology, or developing a new production process.

Top management support is key. Top management not only directs strategy, but demonstrates the importance of the new products area by visible involvement. This is done by providing career advancement for entrepreneurial skills, encouraging broad employee participation, giving clear direction on what to do (*not* how to do it), and making a long-term, highly visible commitment to new products—thus encouraging risk.

There is no one way to organize for new products development. A needs assessment will help lead to the most appropriate organizational approach. Many corporate factors affect the new products organization, from corporate style to location, from history to timing. Among the factors that may be taken into consideration are:

- Correlating the degree of technological newness needed with the degree of marketing newness
- Studying the new products spin-off mode of a going business, in which a revenue division supports line extensions and flankers
- Determining what to do with misfit developments—those that do not easily fit into any existing revenue division
- Providing support for new product champions
- Motivating small organizations as parts of a large one

The structure of new products organization is related to:

1. Long-range planning
2. Growth and development (strategy, search, internal/external generation)
3. Proliferation (existing expertise, facilities, product lines, brands, markets)

The new products operation may be organized in several different ways, including a new products department, new product activity under existing revenue divisions, or a new enterprise (or alternatively, a new business or growth and development) department.

The skills and interpersonal motivation characteristics required of new product management are different from those required for established product management. In addition, the new products manager requires assistance from both within and without the company. Internal aids include support services within the department, the ability to draw on company staff operations, the establishment of venture groups, review committees, and so forth. Outside resources can provide expertise not available within the company, but they must be carefully selected.

The following outlines a program to address new product goals:

I. Search for opportunity
   A. Industry analysis
      1. Sales volume and trends
      2. Basic technology
      3. Competition
      4. Customer definition
   B. Opportunity identification
      1. Targets
      2. Volume forecast
      3. Risk
      4. Feasibility study (preliminary)
      5. War game exercises
      6. Exceptional technological hurdles
      7. Legal and policy issues
II. Conception
   A. Input research
   B. Ideation
   C. Prescreening concepts
   D. Screening research
III. Modeling (prototypes)
   A. Descriptors
   B. Prototypes
IV. Research and development
   A. Inside/outside science
   B. Pilot plant

      C. Scale up
      D. Controlled testing
      E. Feasibility
  V. Marketing plan
 VI. Market testing
      A. Execution
      B. Assessment
      C. Follow-up
VII. Major introduction
      A. Monitor environment
      B. Adjust plan
      C. Expand from test market

Exploration

11

The Search for Opportunity—
Industry Analysis

Attempt the end, and never stand to doubt;
Nothing's so hard but search will find it out.
—*Robert Herrick*
(who also said: "Gather ye rosebuds while ye may")

The corporate charter, long-range plans, and strategic goals of the company set the stage for opportunity identification. Except where proliferation through the same trade channels and corporate resources is involved, new opportunity areas should begin with an investigation of the industry. Often, an opportunity looks appealing from without, when one is not acquainted with the complications from within. It is the obligation of the industry investigation to get *inside*.

An outside look is the first step. Maybe this will be sufficient to either abort the interest, or to reveal some unexpected opportunities.

Sales

Sales volume, size, and trends are important. While your own sales figures are helpful, industry and leading competitor numbers may be even more useful. These are usually expressed in units or sales dollars, which can be translated into roughly comparable numbers to your own sales figures, using conventional trade margins, performance discounts, yielding an estimate of gross manufacturer sales, or factory dollars.

If the industry is a relatively new one, then the growth figures may be difficult to project, especially if they do not relate to population trends, etc. A probability range will have to suffice. If there are only one or two dominant factors in the industry, growth and seasonality may be determined by the practices (or happenstances) peculiar to these companies.

The same figures should be evaluated in terms of the national, regional, and emerging (possibly geographically expanding) factors in the industry. If new entries are being test marketed, these too should be tracked.

Because no company has similarly efficient performance everywhere at the same time, it is important to isolate the extremes, as well as the norms. Why is it doing so well here— and so poorly there? Is it a consequence of geography, regional season length, population density, ethnic origin, economic index, media efficiency or media mix difference, special localized competitive forces, recent or long-established market penetration, abnormal media and/or promotional and merchandising spending patterns against the trade or prospect, special distribution situations and pricing practices, high or low purchase frequency of the category in particular areas, etc.? Or is it the result of a unique sales force performance, historic trade relations, particularly strong/weak local competition, etc.?

The answers to these questions will help determine your company's interest in the category, as well as isolate special circumstances, competitive vulnerabilities, etc. It may even be that there are clusters of competitive vulnerabilities, within a major factor, or within one or several analysis divisions and across several major factors.

For example, maybe the South is rising—but the big national competitors have been slow to recognize this, while entrenched regional manufacturers have continued their historic hold. This could represent a two-fold opportunity. On the one hand, the big national companies don't do well in the South. On the other hand, the local factors have grown fat and complacent, satisfied with their profitable expansion carried along by the region's increasing prosperity. Interest in the category is enhanced by identification of this special regional situation. It will also have later effects on pretest operations and test market selection.

On yet another hand, it may be that the products marketed by the major competitors in the South are the same as they market everywhere else—yet Southern needs are different. That difference may be small enough to leave room for local businesses to market conventional products or may be necessarily addressed by the local marketers with product adaptations. Perhaps these special adaptations are not of interest to the opportunistic outsider.

Where you identify a sales performance difference that is peculiar to one market, you may find special trade circumstances, competitive activity, unidentified (till now) product performance failure, or an overlooked local holiday or habit of culture. If so, is the rest of the market still interesting, assuming the South is written off as not being of major importance to the category?

The numbers have to be looked at very closely. Sometimes each of the areas that are aberrations from the norm should be visited. Perhaps a seasonal influx of migrant workers is not accounted for, a new labor situation not reflected in last year's statistics, etc. Don't simply accept all differences as being necessary to make up an average—instead, investigate. Not everything is reported in secondary data, especially if the data are developed along standard norms or are part of surveys that are national in scope, with limited representation in each segment and/or sub-segment of the sample.

If on-the-scene investigation indicates a different situation than the accepted data, either make a judgmental adjustment—or commission an expanded survey of the situation. In other words, for every major difference from the expected performance there should be an understandable reason. Discover this reason either from secondary data, observation, original research, or judgment. Where the difference may not be actable, then make a judgment. Where the difference may be actable, but the cost to determine the reasons is prohibitive at the investigation stage (although perhaps mandatory later), arrive at a consensus judgment through an experienced company team of involved associates from sales, market research, etc. as applicable.

Competition

Look hard at the competition, for they make the market you are considering entering.

Are the general trade practices compatible with your company's—from operational, philosophical, or even legal aspects?

Study the array of product specifications. Can you upgrade them? Are there too many adaptations in the leading lines—many models, for example, with but a few dominating the sales. By simplification and sophistication of specifications will you have an advantage both with the trade and with the customer? Perhaps by reducing the number of stocking units (SKUs) you will reduce your warehousing parts, and assembly costs; increase sales emphasis on your most attractive items; and more clearly direct the consumer's attention to a more focused set of choices.

How reliable is the performance of the competitive products? Perhaps the industry is at an almost commodity stage, where parity products are the rule and positioning ploys and marketing muscle make the share differences. Here may be an opportunity to upgrade product reliability or performance, or both. Or, conversely, there may be an opportunity to slightly downgrade performance to achieve a major price/value advantage. This type of trade-off is difficult for an entrenched leader to follow, since it tends to undercut the established product franchise. Another tactic is to change the rules of the game, make a new and important component for a product in the category to carry, a certain feature that is inconsistent with the leader product's reason-for-being. The stronger and more well-developed the competition's customer franchise is, the more the competitor is locked into an easily identifiable product line position. Under this circumstance, the new entry company knows where the major competition is and thus the gaps become more easily identifiable.

One example is the soft drink battles, where the leading cola brand was hesitant in meeting the assaults of its sugar-free and caffeine-free competition—because by responding under its most famous brand name with a like product change it both cannibalized its parent franchise and admitted to its frailties. On the other hand, the new entry colas had little to lose, and much to gain.

Are there product servicing or warranty term vulnerabilities the new entry company can afford to exploit? For example, a new appliance company may market solely through service outlets—and thus can both promote them and underscore reliability with a speed of repair and/or length of warranty coverage claim, not deliverable by competitors selling through conventional channels.

But first, a clear understanding of the customer franchise of each major national, regional, and to the degree of important significance, local and emerging factor must be determined. A semantic differential study, a cluster analysis based on a factor survey, educated judgment, or secondary research can isolate this.

Various research methods may be employed, if published data do not exist. For example, a branded product can be assessed by customers and prospects in comparison to alternatives, on a feature-by-feature basis and in an over-all sense related to occasion, time, and appropriateness of use. Various psychological probes are sometimes useful, soliciting reactions to various general descriptions on a scale ranging from very approving to highly disapproving. Sometimes, a list of personal characteristics is offered for selection after asking the question: "What kind of person would I be if I owned a (name of product)?"

Besides obtaining an understanding of the consumer perceptions of competitive entries, there are many additional dimensions of each established marketer that need to be identified and evaluated, such as the major selling theme (usually a user benefit expressed in memorable terms), as well as supporting claims.

Especially telling is the consistency over time of these aspects of communications. Is it a characteristic of the category for each leader to chase the other, changing its communications frequently? Is it a characteristic of some competitors to react quickly to competitive tactics and sales slumps with important copy changes, media adjustments up or down, different trade and consumer tactics? Is it the custom of the entrenched leaders to hew to the same line and style in their communications, dealing with competitive attacks with short-term tactics relating to media blitzes and price promotions, rather than adjusting image or major copy themes? How do advertising impressions and expenditures against the target market, as well as the total market, compare? What about the frequency of trade, consumer and advertising delivery from period to period? How does this marketing spending compare with share-of-market performance? How do share-of-voice expenditures track with share-of-market? How does the marketing dollar divide among media, promotion against the trade, and prospect cultivation? How does sales efficiency relate to the industry average, to leading competitors and trend-lines? What does this tell the new entry company about the differences in this new field—and how will it affect entry strategy?

Customers

In order to connect the variable performance of the industry and its major players from area to area, season to season, and over time, it is necessary to understand both the present and past state of the customer prospects. This will help project the future both for the industry and for the new entrant.

The prospects may be businesses and they may be people. In nearly every instance, they are both. People tend to influence businesses more than the other way around. Many whole industries have been sent foundering when not recognizing this.

Therefore, a look at the demographics of the prospects—how they have changed and are changing—helps direct thinking in the development of new opportunities.

Who one's parents are, where one has lived, been educated, when one was born, whether the prospect is a he or a she—all of the demographic facts of life join with many measurable, unmeasurable, and unexplained influences to help determine life-styles and personalities, intertwined to create one's psychographic makeup. The activities of the largest population segments affect the products and services offered, which in turn affect the life-styles of the other segments. These mainstreams provide further opportunities for emerging secondary markets, characterized by new fulfillment needs (designer jeans, expensive imported cars, macrame, and ferns all over the house) and segmented by location both in society and geographically, as well as style of living and value systems. Every change yields both problems and opportunities. The new entrant should be in the best position to capitalize not only on the prevalent mainstream, but to position the entry for adaptation by foreseeable waves of change.

For example, the newest retooled American cars are from Chrysler, which has elected to bring back much of the style that vanished with the OPEC scare that created down-sizing, cars stripped of ornamentation, and ones bereft of much reserve power. Chrysler has invested in new machines that can be made more hedonistic as the times demand. Commenting on the important role new products have played in Chrysler's turnaround, *The New York Times* wrote in July 1983:

The only area that was sacrosanct was the one developing new products, such as the compact K-cars . . . Those and other new products helped Chrysler to raise its share of market from a low of about 7 percent to the current level of more than 10 percent.

The category and the industry may have a high level of recognition and respect. On the other hand, it may be out of sight for most prospects, or actually have attitudinal barriers to overcome. This must be discovered. How—and how well—are the industry, the category, and the various competing factors regarded by customers and potential prospects?

What is the awareness level? What are the attitudes? How loyal are customers to a category, to a product type, to a brand? Are there easy substitutes? Is it easy to forego the brand, product, or category? Which items tend to be first choices? What role do they fulfill? What, if anything, do they substitute for? If they were unavailable, what, if anything, would be the first substitute selection? How important to the prospect is the decision to select one vs. another offering within the category? What role does price play? Is it elastic or inelastic? Are there major differences in the answers to these questions in the demographic and psychographic breakouts? What is the customer use pattern, frequency of purchase and use, and use occasion? What does this mean to the entry marketer?

Basic Technology

A thorough technology review precedes commitment to research and development (and engineering) of pilot prototypes and, in most instances, comes before concepts are developed for review by management and the hoped for sales prospects. This is to determine manufacturing feasibility—how much ready technology is at hand, or must be acquired, and at what cost.

Although the product offerings of the category may have many characteristics similar to those your company now markets, the art and science of the field may be radically different from what you now do. The source and state of raw materials or parts may be affected by different processing, packaging, and assembly requirements. Different regulatory requirements, different types of transportation needs, different procurement practices and seasonal pricing, different patent and licensing restrictions may be present.

Assuming the technology is adaptable and applied rather than having to rely on basic research, there may be marginal or major opportunities presented simply because your company is a new entry into a mature category. This will allow you to use the most advanced plant application of the technology at the full commercialization phase. Although subcontractors may be utilized in the testing and early marketing phase, at short-term cost penalties, the long-term benefits of a utilized state-of-the-art process may be just enough to provide the new product with both a customer benefit competitive edge and a manufacturer cost benefit.

Early on, however, the company will need to adapt its own scientific resources to the new technology, either by buying expert staff additions or by buying outside consultant and bench-research services, or, most likely, all three.

Technology Review

Very important to many programs is the technology review, which not only assesses the industry and its resources within the planned making and marketing territory, but also thoroughly investigates foreign industry and technology resource developments. Frequently, there are advances here from less mature but more sophisticated technologies that can be easily adapted or moved into place.

In the light of the present economy and the shortage of long-term investment capital, Robert Rothberg, associate professor of marketing in the graduate school of business administration, Rutgers University, writes:

> Business will probably try to minimize the investment required to develop promising new products, and to seek greater assurance that acceptable levels of profit can be achieved. This would seem to imply two things: a heavier reliance on proprietary product technology and proven marketing strengths and a more deliberate pace through the process of product-market expansion.
>
> A greater reliance on proprietary technology and proven marketing strengths means that companies will tend to concentrate on what they do best and try to minimize their weaknesses by working more closely with and through other firms. Colgate-Palmolive, for example, considers itself to be a strong selling organization but recognizes its limitations insofar as the development of new product technology is concerned. This company has tried to maximize its strengths and minimize its weaknesses by entering into a variety of exclusive sales agreements with firms possessing complementary capabilities such as Wilkinson Sword (razor blades), Mobil Oil (Baggies), and Weetabix (Alpen cereal).
>
> Consider also Corning Glass Works. It is a leader in a variety of technologies, but it appreciates its weaknesses in the marketing area. It has long been willing to enter into licensing agreements and joint ventures of various kinds in order to obtain the marketing strengths it lacks.
>
> The point to be made here is that new products frequently require a sizable investment in new product technology or marketing capabilities. These investment requirements can be reduced by working with and through other firms with complementary strengths and weaknesses.

Patent Search

Part of the technology investigation is a patent search. Questions to consider include: Are there many significant patents that impede the development? Are there ways to improve on the technology by licensing patent rights or by working around the patents—or are there opportunities implied by the company's approach to the technology that will allow for its own patent protection? And should such patents be applied for—and when?

On this subject, R. Buckminster Fuller wrote:

The worth of a patent, however, is not established by the merit of the invention but by the expertness with which its claims of invention are written . . . While a U.S.A. patent can be obtained for less than $200, a patent that the great corporations' patent attorneys see no way of circumventing requires expensively expert professional services.

But Mr. Fuller's use of patents may be for a different purpose than a corporation's. He goes on to say:

Now that I have proven that an individual can be world-effective while eschewing either money or political advantage-making, I do my best to discourage others from taking patents, which almost never "pay off" to the inventor. My patent-taking was to effect a "bridgehead" accreditation to more effective employment of humanity's potentials.

Indeed, an article in the May 11, 1981, issue of *Business Week* suggests that patents may be expiring as a spur to innovation.

The most technologically fertile sectors of industry do not rely on patents as a way of really protecting their inventions. Research in bioengineering boomed well before the Supreme Court ruled last year that living organisms can be patented. The rapidly changing electronics industry continues to build arsenals of patents but uses them as tools of competition—"bargaining chips"—while relying on secrecy to protect innovation.

Patents are like "having a gun in a crowded bar" where 25 people are similarly armed, says Jean C. Chognard, vice president for patents and licenses at Hewlett-Packard Co. Adds Roger S. Borovoy, vice president and chief counsel for Intel Corp.: "In the electronics industry, patents are of no value whatsoever in spurring research and development. We use them because we have to. You can't be the only holdout against the angry hordes or else you pay everyone."

Where patents have had an important role in the career and reputation of Buckminster Fuller, for many corporations the view is different. Writing in *The Times (London)*, Clive Cookson says:

Recent evidence suggests that patents may be losing the central role in technological progress which old-fashioned economic theory assigns to them. Companies are putting less reliance on patents as protection for their inventions.

Particularly in industries where progress is most rapid, such as microelectronics and biotechnology, secrecy and a fast-moving research and development program seem more reliable defenses against would-be imitators.

. . . Recent surveys in the United States suggest that if patent protection were suddenly abolished, the pace of innovation in most industries would not be affected all that much.

Professor Edwin Mansfield of the University of Pennsylvania, who analysed 48 inventions in several fields, found that the existence of patent added only 11 percent on average to a competitor's cost of copying the innovation. Some 60 percent of patents have been circumvented legally within four years and Professor Mansfield estimated that at least three-quarters of the patented inventions did not need patent protection . . . However, there is an exception to the general rule: the pharmaceutical industry. The development of drugs really does rely on patents. . . .

Even companies that produce spectacular technological developments have had trouble defending their patents. A classic case is EMI, which had to spend more than $1 million in legal fees, asserting its patent for the CAT body scanner against infringement by American imitators. . . .

Whatever the academic researchers may say about the overall irrelevance of patents for technological progress, there are too many clear cases of innovations, such as the Xerox photocopier, which have benefitted by the system.

A satisfactory alternative to patents has never been proposed, and no one would want to establish secrecy as the only protection for innovation.

Sometimes secrecy is merited prior to commercialization, especially where there is a long development period. In the case of design patents (as opposed to the molecular structure patents involved in chemistry), which may be more easily circumscribed (with noteworthy exceptions such as Mr. Fuller's structural geometry), this is especially true. During this period, however, the innovator must keep constant track of all published applications, to intercept any potential encroachments.

Other Factors

Other factors influence the industry analysis. They include foreign encroachment or vulnerability; general consumption changes; political, economic, or ecological influences on source labor, materials, and shipping; changes in the character of the industry and its leaders; and identifying growth sources whether from new demand, replacement, diversification of offerings, whether they are important or negligible.

Sales, customer behavior patterns, demographics and psychographics, competition, technology, and other factors will help shape the company's interest in the marketing opportunity. If interested, how will the prospective entrant define the most profitable target?—That's the next question.

On the other hand, if the investigation of the industry and these other factors raise too many problems to confront as an alternative to other available opportunities, the company should elect either to give the situation further (perhaps deferred) study—or to drop the project. Then the investigative resources may be directed toward other areas of possibly greater potential interest.

12

Targeting—Other Perspectives

Slight not what is near through aiming at what's far.
—*Euripedes*

The search for opportunity has taken us through an analysis of the industry, its competitive factors, its technology—and its consumers. That was the *traditional* outward look.

But this is not enough to identify and prioritize targets.

Most essential is the inward look.

Much is to be gained by a new product program that shores up a company's strongest segments, by leveraging corporate expertise. New products can correct real and predictable vulnerabilities to protect the main line business—or to hedge it against future developments. The market is always changing—and new products are one consequence.

One example: For more than 60 years, Land O'Lakes has meant butter. It commands the leading share, ever increasing, with its premium-priced, premium-quality product—the only major advertised brand of butter. Land O'Lakes means butter. Only one problem—the market has changed radically over the years.

While per capita consumption of fats and oils has remained fairly steady, butter's share has consistently fallen and margarine's share has risen. Margarine's quality claim is that it tastes like butter. Who better to protect its franchise with a margarine entry than the leading butter brand? When Land O'Lakes says its margarine tastes like butter, there is no other authority to challenge. When Land O'Lakes introduces a new margarine, who has more to lose if its margarine is not of the highest quality? And which brand has the most concern about trading butter volume for margarine volume? Land O'Lakes, of course.

As a consequence, the giant farmer cooperative approached its margarine introduction with a very high R&D standard and a very sensitive marketing development program (see the case history in Appendix 1A). Says Ralph Hofstad, President, Land O'Lakes, Inc.:

Our successful entry into the marketing-intensive field of margarine illustrates that the strong Land O'Lakes consumer franchise can be leveraged by continued dedication to the highest quality, effective positioning and a consistent program of consumer communications.

The Inward Look

The inward look, as a dimension of new products targeting, should direct a company to rethink its approach to technology and to marketing. Are both of the activities advancing ahead of the industry? How can new product challenges meet the mutual goals of sales success and increased internal expertise sophistication?

Take marketing as an example. Hanes hosiery brought innovative packaging, new distribution channels, new store fixtures, new sales and detailing operations to the hosiery business when they introduced L'eggs brand hosiery (and later spawned a stream of imitators). Hanes success was largely due to its recognition of how a change in consumer shopping habits could be leveraged by a new marketing concept for their industry. (Their earlier contract manufacturing of hosiery for supermarket controlled labels provided a lesson well learned.)

Looking inward, reevaluate the company's product mix and its sales emphasis. Look not only at financial contribution, but also analyze the mix as a reflection of present practices and for compatibility with coming change. Perhaps heretofore underachiever products and related categories should be readdressed in the light of regional population differences and shifts, demographic trends, as well as changing consumer habits and trade practices.

Perhaps a company's competitors have not met some potential needs. Perhaps one of the company's leading products still fails to make the desired market penetration. New products in these markets are important targets also.

An example of such an attempt is offered by a leader in the canned chili category. A new product opportunity was needed for further penetration—or to expand the size of the market. A new entrant was designed to attract those consumers not satisfied with canned chili. Consumer research indicated that 75 percent of all U.S. housewives make homemade chili for their families. Therefore, it was presumed that there was potentially a large, new market ready to be served.

In product tests, 74 percent of the women trying the prototype improved chili product liked it "extremely" or "very much"; 57 percent preferred it "strongly" over the current brand, and 56 percent said they would "definitely" buy it. Based on these results, the new product, formulated with "homemade" style ingredients, went through test markets successfully and began its market expansion—set both to enhance the marketer's share and to expand the market for canned chili.

In the beginning, a small number of chili aficionados were so impressed with the quality of the new chili that they bought it by the case. Unfortunately, too few were that enthusiastic. The marketer simply was not able to get enough of the upscale chili users interested in the canned product. Perhaps the image of the package form or the cooking habits of the target chili chefs were barriers to high volume acceptance.

Nonetheless, an upscale version of the basic product or line is often an appropriate business-building strategy—as Campbell proved with its Chunky Soups.

In doing a risk-ratio analysis of new product opportunities, give an edge to those ventures that shore up the going business, protect the corporate charter, and invade competitive territory to preempt logical flanker categories from pioneering competitive advances. In general, it is less expensive and more essential to reduce the risks on close-in, known areas than on far-out explorations. If those basic business elements are not protected, there will not be sufficient earnings available to underwrite the next generation of new business. The far-out exploration programs are planned developments with the expenses increasing with feasibility assurance, hence as the risks decrease.

The Outward Look

Simple matrix approaches reveal gaps that a company may advantageously address. Try this: Take population characteristics. Overlay present and predicted (time-frame defined by industry development pace) grids with customer characteristics—now and as forecast.

You can make up any appropriate grid. For snacks, a grid could range from sweet to salty on one axis, from hard to soft on another, and from young to old on a third dimension. Each block in the grid would be filled in with mature and newly offered brands and dollar volume estimates. This would give a graphic view of whether emerging areas were being equally addressed, whether there were gaps, whether there were blocks filled only with old and perhaps tired offerings. This type of matrix is one quick way to possibly identify an opportunity.

There are many revealing questions that can point to opportunities:

- Is the company on the leading edge?
- How can a targeted new product program effect change, to bring this about? This analysis can help target goals. In this way, the new product

program is not only aimed at short-term business increments but also enhances future success.

- What is going on outside the business that may have inside effects? What is going on outside the business that will have inside effects *only if the company takes the lead.*

Some examples:

An insulation materials company decides that the building shells to which its products are applied can be completely replaced by insulation materials alone. Of course, the materials must be adapted. Habits (and building codes) must be changed, etc.,—but the timing is right. Energy conservation concerns tied to advanced technology in inert materials make it possible for the materials to not only replace the shell, but—by molding and boring—to replace the ducts, vents, plumbing pipes, applied decorative molding, and other decorative effects.

A baby food manufacturer, eyeing the shift in population trends, sees an opportunity at both ends of the spectrum. How to make baby food (already surreptitiously consumed by many elderly) under a new guise, position, and brand, a socially acceptable convenience product for the growing older-age market?

A lawn sprinkler maker, capitalizing on the concern for water conservation, adapts technology from agribusiness and puts ground moisture sensor rods into its sprinklers—so they sprinkle only on a *need* basis, rather than by routine (whether automically timed or not).

Financial service institutions redefine their businesses as retailing of financial product packages. Hence, the mergers, acquisitions, and conglomerations of banks with brokers with insurance underwriters with real estate sellers with credit card instruments, etc., to form money supermarkets.

New combinations of services make new products and new businesses. The new businesses, in turn, will spawn yet other new businesses, possibly to include many service packages now undertaken by government and transport agencies. The computer hookup of the retail service supermarket can direct the electronic satellite distribution system to sort and deliver mail, trigger warehouse withdrawals around the world, etc. The financial retailers tie universal product codes to the consumer's personal code card to coordinate financial transactions, prepare and validate tax returns, channel routine investments, etc. Technology and point-of-view make the difference. Adaptive marketing skills and consumer familiarity and trust determine the speed of acceptance.

More examples abound—but these are sufficient to the point.

As discussed in the preceding chapter, many targeting advantages lie in strategic reconstruction of the industry's trends, and of major competitors' corporate charters. Often, more is to be gained by imaginative interpretation of the industry's numerical reports than by merely following the forecasts that are projections of an established format. A company creates new hypotheses, establishing original formats—and hence new projections that may best serve the overall corporate goals. There is room for much intuition, much art in the translation of always meager information into major new product opportunities.

Section 3
Summary Afterword

Creative assembly and interpretation of data are the most important contributions a new products executive can make to the exploration of opportunities. This requires qualitative, subjective, and objective recasting of large quantities of information from the entire range of affecting influences, as well as from the standard category reports on the status quo. While the corporate charter defines general boundaries, and the long-range plans and strategic goals point to general direction, it is the mission of the exploration phase to both qualify and quantify specific targets.

In the exploration phase—the search for opportunity—the first step is the industry analysis. This includes analyzing sales, competition, customers, technology, and patents. Other factors to be investigated include foreign developments, the political and economic situation, consumption patterns, ecology implications, labor, materials, shipping, replacement, diversification, and the industry leaders.

In targeting new product opportunities, the analysis of industry opportunities can be used to determine whether to enhance, defend, or enlarge corporate strengths. Such an inward look directs the rethinking of technology and marketing for immediate and long-term new product success. Looking outward also provides clues about how change can be effected through new product development and marketing.

Conception

13

Input Research

Discovery has led to invention, invention to technique and practice; and the shape of our world has changed its day-to-day character almost as much as our knowledge.
—*Robert Oppenheimer*

The creative process is based on a selective assembly of information. It's not a mere playback; its execution communicates something. In fine art, it may express the creator's own self. In the commercial world, it must express and fulfill a latent or at least a perceptually real desire.

It is based on knowledge.

The knowledge that leads to new products ideation comes from diverse sources. It is organized through reassembly, through simplification, through a penetrating grasp of the obvious—which has escaped the recorder.

Some examples:

- An office boy revolutionized the sewing machine industry by suggesting that the hole be placed at the point of the needle rather than at the opposite end.
- Celluloid was invented to make a better billiard ball—but it also made the movies possible (perhaps a more important use).
- In the beginning, Coca-Cola was only a soda fountain drink in which the syrup had to be mixed with carbonated water just before serving. Then someone suggested, "Bottle it."
- Years later, the wife of a very wealthy inventor inspired the packaging form which is revolutionizing shelf-stable retort packaging of food, the Tetra-Brik Pak, by observing that the objective could be accomplished by applying the principles she used in packing ground meat into sausage

casing without trapping air. Today, beverages have another delivery form.

Problems Are Greatest Input Source

Problems are the greatest single source of new product input. Every problem is an opportunity. The new product solution results from a blend of the art and the science of problem solving. Problems may be real or perceived—it almost comes to the same—and may revolve around issues that are economically, biologically, demographically, psychographically, or ecologically important now and in the future.

The energies motivating problem solving are corporate charter commitments to growth areas, competitive pressures, unused production capacity, new and often proprietary R&D technology, the threat of technology, the threat of product obsolescence, government-agency technology, changes in regulations, synergistic corporate mergers, or new organizational structures. There are other outside influences—such as naturalism, consumerism, the energy crunch, the economy, a shut off of raw materials due to foreign events, and changes in leading-edge products, services, and life-styles.

Such rapid changes explain why a high percentage of corporate growth is attributable to new products that were not marketed a few years ago. Identification of just such problems may be the most productive place for new products ideation to start.

Go for the easy one first. The most rapidly developing problems are the easiest to identify—and to solve.

As Buckminster Fuller said in an interview with the *Los Angeles Times*,

In the world of electronics, where invisible electromagnetic waves move at 186,000 miles per second, there is only a two-year lag between invention and its industrial use. In aeronautics, where you move about 1,000 miles per hour, there is a five-year lag. . . . We can see the second hand on the clock moving, but we can't see the minute hand move. When you can't see something move, you don't get out of the way. The faster a thing moves, the more chances you have to see what is wrong. So we find that in a single-family dwelling, there is at least a 50-year lag because of the least visibility of motion.

Example—Waste By-Products

One fast-moving problem is industrial waste and its potential for pollution. Yet, much of this waste may be salvageable if it is attacked as a new product opportunity. Examples: Garbage to alcohol. Monosodium glutamate residue used as a protein source. Cheesemakers' whey turned to a protein beverage, then to wine. Fat runoff from pre-cooked meat used as an energy source to drive the oven. Paper sludge to charcoal briquets and cat litter. Must (the finely crushed grapes) from the winemaking process distilled into brandy, then the cellulose left behind made an important source of vegetable fibre.

These are cheap ingredients. The disposal problem is handled at a profit. And the resultant products fulfill genuine needs.

The Manufacturing Process

Sometimes there is something going on in manufacturing that no one at headquarters knows about, understands, or fully appreciates the significance of.

Get a lot of input from the factory.
Ask dumb questions.
Factory tours can yield dividends.

A "nonionic surfactant combined with a debonding agent," was being used in a facial tissue-making process to help line up the cellulose fibres for a smoother sheet. An advertising man asked about its chemical properties— and a familiar bell rang. By following up with the supplier, he learned that the identical compound was used for making skin conditioners—thereby suggesting an exclusive new product advantage *already* built into the product.

Trooping through a brand new margarine plant, several marketers noticed that fresh skimmed milk was being added. "Is that the way everyone else does it?" was asked. "No, we think it makes ours better," the plant superintendent answered. Another strong competitive claim to newness with a difference was born.

While visiting a small brewery on an informal tour, a writer was told: "Unless you want to see where we store the stuff, that's about it for the tour." Out of courtesy, the writer said he'd enjoy seeing the entire process—yes, let's see the storage bins. "Well, we age it over there in those limestone caves—they're naturally cool, so we save on refrigeration and, of course, we didn't have to build a warehouse." It doesn't take an Ernest Hemingway to know that there was a powerful, new, exclusive claim and an evocative image in that casual revelation.

No matter how the feet may hurt after that long tramp through the production lines—look for product ideas and inspiration right under your nose. They may be happening while no one knows it.

Contract Packers

Contract packers are manufacturing companies who will make products for any company under any brand. They'll make products to specification or make them to their own standard, with cosmetic differences for the contracting company.

There are other companies who are not in this business, but might be, if asked—or persuaded. They have good facilities, but they are not optimally occupied. Hook up with them and you might help both of your bottom lines.

In any event, you may well learn more about your new area of product interest.

Get to know them. Ask them: "What else can you make on this equipment? What else is this packaging line used for? How flexible is it?" Then suggest some opportunities. "Would it be a big deal if you made blankets instead of rugs on those looms? Can you extrude corn meal dough through those pasta dies?"

Sometimes, you can put a couple of packers together—or you can fabricate one part, while they make and assemble the rest. And so on. Do not overlook the input and idea-generation value of becoming familiar with what is going on in the factories.

Associated Trades

Your products may be designed to go directly to the consumer. Another division of your company—or even a competitor's—may make different formulations of similar products for different distribution classes or as sub-assemblies for further processing. Even more simply, they may pack out special versions for the service trades, such as restaurants or beauty shops. Often, these products can lead to mass-marketed consumer products.

Examples abound: Kraft's successful processed food spread Cheez-Wiz began as a food service item designed to speed up preparation of cheese-topped dishes. Gillette's Dippity-Do hair-setting gel was inspired by a beauty supply item used by hair dressers, and its Deep Magic line of skin care products by an expensive treatment line of cosmetics marketed by Max Factor.

Inventors and Patents

Patent searches can stimulate ideation. Furthermore, relatively inactive patents properly positioned may lead to new product breakthroughs—with a lot of protection from early competition.

Inventors can sometimes lead to new product opportunities, both with their own inventions—and through the original, outside viewpoints they bring to a project. Because of the legal sensitivities involved, a company should be wary of who reviews inventions (a designated party or department) and under what conditions. A tightly worded protective release must be signed before any invention may be reviewed. One of the outstanding new products companies is 3M. Their invention release process and format is shown in Appendix 2C.

Licensing

One crucial element of new product management is licensing, an effective means of exploiting technology. "Licensing agreements can open up new markets and new lines of business, and provide opportunities to increase corporate revenues," writes Linn Grieb in a professional report published by the University of Texas at Austin.

Licensing-in, where you license a product or name from another company, can be used to gain a faster start, to save internal development cost, and, in some instances, to also capture the stature of a licensor's reputation in trade and consumer marketing.

Licensing-out, where another company licenses a product from you, can help underwrite a company's own R&D costs, add volume to the manufacturing operation, help spread the reputation of a newly developed entity, spread the marketing cost across more items, and, in the case of consumer appeal items, increase the media reach and frequency behind an exclusive concept.

Little technology went into the development of a greeting card character named "Strawberry Shortcake," but American Greeting Card's creation has been licensed-out to become a doll, a cereal, and hosts of other associated items—all advertised to the benefit of each other, providing a synergistic impact that American Greeting could not have afforded in launching its creation alone.

Pierre Cardin has made hundreds of millions of dollars in licensing-out his name and designs for everything from airplanes to zoot suits, and licensing-in the name and reputation of the famous Parisian Maxim's restaurant (which he has since largely acquired). Cardin's Maxim's already has more than 500 food product outlets in France alone, plus a school for hoteliers and restaurateurs. As for licensing-out, according to an article in the *New York Times* (September 6, 1981): "The initial marketing strategy was to sell the maximum number of licenses. . . . Cardin has agents in 25 countries keeping an eye on licensees." Manufacturers pay a minimum guarantee for the right to produce goods under the Cardin label (e.g., 7 to 10 percent for clothing, with a percentage of sales above a guaranteed base.)

Getting Out and About

Men and Machines

There are always contract technologies and innovative new machinery. Make it a point to learn from these resources.

Some of the most advanced technologies suffer from want of cash to scale up, to do definitive testing, to fund the research protocol acceptable to governing agencies. Consider a technology joint-venture, or contract it. Buy in, if it looks promising. At any rate, investigate and learn. That's an important part of the input process.

The big trade fairs display the latest in machinery. All of the established companies already have machinery, but most of it is not state of the art. A company interested in a new area can gain an advantage through the acquisition of advanced machinery. With a big enough order, the company may be able to arrange for a significant lead time over incumbent competition. At the same time, learn as much as you can about more efficient factory layouts, materials handling, automation, etc. It's all part of the input. And may be a critical advantage.

Example: A visit to a trade fair exhibit by ex-Kitchens of Sara Lee executives Walter Friedman and David Tittle resulted in their being granted the U.S. franchise for Yoplait yogurt (since granted to General Mills, Inc.). Friedman brought the trademark and process to the United States from Sodima S.A., after seeing their exhibit at the S.I.A.L. biennial food fair in Paris. Yoplait has since become No. 1 or No. 2 in every U.S. market where it is sold.

Trade Schools

Good trade schools look to the future. Audit a few classes related to your interest. Befriend the profs. Give a guest lecture, if they ask. Spot the top students. Ask a lot of questions. You're in school—so *learn*.

Other Trades

What is good for Peter may well be good for Paul.

But Paul may never have thought of it.

Find some parallel trades and see how they do it. Maybe you can exchange some ideas with the management. Cosmetics were bubble-packed before tools, but the techniques and benefits are the same.

One far afield example is borrowing chemistry from a wholly unrelated category, as with the Olin Mathieson zinc omadine fungicide marketed to orchard growers to treat peach blight. It was licensed to Vanderbuilt Chemical, which brought it to the attention of several toiletries manufacturers as a possible hair shampoo additive. One turned it down because of possible toxicology concerns. Another leading company, however, gave it more elaborate investigation, proved the ingredient acceptable to the Food and Drug Administration, and introduced a highly successful shampoo. This not only strengthened the marketer's dominance of the large business segment where it already had several successful entries, but also established an entire new category of home dermatological treatment for dandruff.

Other Places

It used to be that we were ahead of the world in almost everything—or thought we were. Today, neither is true. There's a lot to learn beyond our boundaries.

It depends on how you define boundaries.

For some companies, their boundaries are limited to the headquarters city; for others, to the area of distribution; for others, to the immediate competitive industry.

Determine what your boundaries are, and then look abroad. The smartest new products practitioners look to the most dynamic marketing areas in their field—whether they have distribution there or not. They look to the coasts, especially West, for consumer product trends. They look to Europe for new technologies and new packaging. They know which countries have the most liberal laws for authorizing the marketing of new products. They find a sugar-based product in Australia that prevents cavities. They find a carotene pill in France that gives the user a beautiful suntan. They find soft-sided plastic aerosol packages. They find shelf-stable food that tastes almost fresh. They discover single-lens-reflex photography (Pentax) in Japan. (See Figure 13-1.)

Figure13-1
Photographing Shelf Set-ups in France

Seeing what competitors and others in similar fields are doing may inspire helpful insights. Here a new products investigator is photographing shelf set-ups at Casino Supermarché in Cannes, France.

And they look into the most advanced marketing outlets for merchandise—and merchandising—trends. The sharpest retailers are bellwethers for their field. Listen to them; get input from the buyers and the merchandisers. Here, too, looking beyond the immediate geographic region of interest may pay dividends. The hypermarkets started in Europe. So did generics. Look and learn.

Have a system.

One company requires that all of its well-travelled executives allow time to make at least one store, or factory, or other learning-experience call on each trip made away from headquarters. The procedure is orchestrated by the company travel department. If the company or a competitor has a test market in the area, specific directions and information retrieval sheets are provided. If the area is a raw material source, factory, or trade association location for the industry—it is suggested that contacts be made here also. Trips are optimized to hype the learning curve.

Get Up Off Your (er) Chair

Too many new product planners are tied to their computer consoles. All those teach is the product of a rapidly assembled feedback of data and assumptions fed by other armchair generals.

Get out into the field.

If all the forecasting programs worked so well, every company would have a market share in direct relationship to its investment in the programs and in its product marketing. Fortunately, it is not that simple.

The leaders not only cause change, they are alert to it. They not only read the numbers, but they buy the competitive products. While the laboratories are analyzing them, they try them—meticulously following the instructions. They have "hands on" experience. This sharpens their understanding of the research reports and deepens the questioning search for knowledge.

Research

Listen to Your Spouse

It is a standing joke around some offices that the boss has to check everything out with his or her spouse. Let him or her. Chances are the spouse has a good grasp of the business, its competitive set, and a deep interest in the product area . . . and is no security risk. There's also an about equal chance that the spouse is a shrewd business person in his or her own right. And more candid with the boss than most around. Occasionally, this is the best input of all. Don't miss a bet. (And don't forget the offspring, either.)

R&D and Marketing

These are among the most important inputs. Experiments. Simulations. Industry audits. Blind tests. Surveys. Monitoring systems. Panels. Stitch it all together in a cogent fact book that covers all the bases, from available sources, to syndicated, library, proprietary, and basic, fundamental research.

Then ask all the questions still unanswered. Then decide what it is worth to find out more answers. If the missing information is critical, do not spare the expense. Research "on the cheap" is not as trustworthy as the informed judgment of professionals in the chosen field of interest. Despite the cost, sometimes that is a quicker, more economical, and better choice.

Gurus and Geniuses

These are not necessarily the same. But neither is to be ignored. The former may symbolize a trend; the latter may presage the next important break-through. No matter how skeptical the professional societies may look upon these highly publicized mavericks, pay them heed. The gurus have affected the tide of civilization, as have the geniuses. The creative geniuses of science possess conceptual abilities far beyond entire graduating classes from the most prestigious universities. They may be ahead of their time. They may be pilloried and unfashionable. But listen to them.

Albert Szent-Györgyi, one of the world's most honored scientists, winner of the 1937 Nobel Prize for Physiology and Medicine (he discovered Vitamin C), tells this story in a letter published in *Executive Health*:

> If Pasteur would rise from his grave and would want to work on cancer, he would have very little chance to get a grant. I can imagine him ringing the bell at the gates of the National Institute of Health, and the following conversation taking place:
>
> Pasteur: I would like to work on cancer and need a grant.
>
> NIH: You have only to write down what you will do and why.
>
> Pasteur: Research is going out into the unknown and I don't know what I will find and do there.
>
> NIH: How do you expect us to waste money on you if you do not know yourself what you will do? We are responsible for the taxpayers' money and have to know what will be done with it.
>
> Pasteur: Thank you. I left my grave open and am going back.

General Observation

The world is changing rapidly. The population mix and its movement—the level of information being disseminated and absorbed—the meaning of special affinities unrelated to old demographic understandings—the tissue fabric of new fads obscuring strong strains of old ideals—all of this and more should be considered in new product planning, *any* new product planning that has less than an immediate payout and expects a reasonably long life in the marketplace.

There are new needs. There are opportunities for substitutions. There are new perceptions and new life-styles. Just as factories yield byproducts, so do the changing patterns of trade and consumer behavior.

All of this, in the end, has to be synthesized into a workable body of knowledge, quickly grasped input that can initiate the ideation of new product concepts.

Force-fit a one page summary—no matter how giant the appendix. This discipline requires the tough-minded thinking that produces clean direction.

Then, it is time to generate ideas to improve, to innovate, to invent.

14

Ideation

When I examined myself and my methods of thought, I came to the conclusion that the gift of fantasy has meant more to me than my talent for absorbing positive knowledge.
—*Albert Einstein*

Albert Einstein had both of the essentials:

1. The ability to collect and to absorb positive knowledge
2. The gift of fantasy

That fairly sums up the ideation process.

How do we stimulate this process to yield the most productive results?

We discussed "input" in the preceding chapter. Now, *output* is the goal.

Ideation is based on many factors.

Between fantasy and routine solutions lie the beginning ideas for new product concepts. Both areas must be explored, for in apparently irrelevant wishes will be found seemingly impossible goals, while in precise possible solutions will be found the ways and means to the beginnings of innovation. When the dreamer and the scientist sit down together, wonders can and do happen. Schematically, the range of ideation application to new products is shown in Figure 14-1.

Lateral Thinking

Dr. Edward de Bono, a psychologist and professor of investigative medicine at Cambridge University, England, has assembled a set of simple skills for improving thinking. His system has been adopted by corporate executives, has been taught in schools, and has been studied by government officials from a score of nations.

Figure 14-1
Ideation

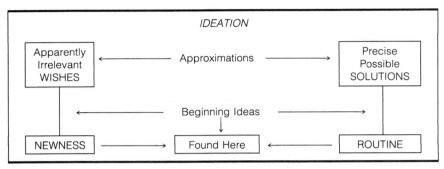

Dr. de Bono espouses a number of basic tools for better thinking, including broadmindedness; consideration of all factors; consideration of consequences and their sequels; assembly of aims, goals, and objectives; evaluation by setting top priorities; looking at all possible alternatives and choices; and turning to others for other points of view (the ideation sharing common to brainstorming).

As helpful as these approaches are to new product conceptualization, they are not new. De Bono himself asserts that yesterday's idioms don't work as well as they used to.

Today, he is advocating a notion he calls "lateral thinking," an unconventional way to think creatively.

Lateral thinking (an entry in the *Oxford English Dictionary*, as de Bono is quick to point out) is the opposite of vertical thinking. Quoted in the December 20, 1982, *Forbes* magazine, he says that vertical thinking is a process by which one solves a problem by going from one logical step to the next, moving toward one correct solution. The lateral thinker essentially shuns the expected approach to a problem by playing games with the data he has to work with.

Thinking laterally involves scrambling the patterns into which your brain automatically arranges all received information. One type of lateral thinking is that in which a problem is posed and only outrageous solutions are suggested. From one of these a principle can be extracted and used to solve the original problem. An example, cited in *Forbes*: How to invent a new advertising medium? Solution: Bring back the town crier. The working principle behind the idea is that the town crier is the ultimate advertising medium. He cannot be shut off.

Applied to reality, the principle yields the following possibility for an ad medium: a telephone booth in which local calls are made for free and paid for by an advertiser. Twenty seconds into each call the speaker at either end hears a recorded message that cannot be shut off.

The object of lateral thinking is not to arrive at workable solutions to problems each time at bat, but to train the mind to bring something extra to the raw facts of a situation to get more out of it.

Rearrangement of Information

Members of most industries look at their businesses according to trade styles, reporting-source categories, arbitrary research classifications, and governmental census and other statistical indices—in other words, convenient groupings of data that can be compared over time for trends and at any one time to assess share of market, share of mind, absolute volume, target audience, etc. Thus, there is yielded the "over 50 (years of age)" market, the A & B county market, the "under 500 employees" business target, the seasonal bulge, the geographic bias, etc.

But, there is another way of looking at information.

Rearrange it. Look at it differently, to discover new opportunities.

Some examples from the food industry:

1. One manufacturer used to base its products aimed at youngsters on the accepted premise that young people like bland food, don't like mixtures of flavors. That had been the tradition—sometimes explained by the evolution from baby food, which had these characteristics (obviously built into them by adults!). Then it was pointed out that young people liked pizza, sloppy joes, hotdogs with mustard, etc. Interviews were conducted with school cafeteria supervisors and with youngsters—and it was found out that they liked spicy food, but not strange nor subtly spiced food; that they liked mixtures all right, just so that they could see each item in the mixtures—see the big chunks discretely identifiable, not all mushed together. This led the company down a new (and successful) new product path.

2. Still another food manufacturer used to classify its cost comparisons on a per-serving basis. When it was suggested that changing life-styles and smaller family units might yield an opportunity to market individual or two-pack serving sizes of their products, a logical barrier was confronted. Because of packaging and distribution costs, the cost per serving would rise dramatically—with an assumed loss of appeal. By rearranging the information, it was shown that the cost-per-leftover for users of the current product produced its own barrier to frequent and broad consumption. Research revealed that users would prefer to pay a per-serving premium in exchange for not "wasting" unconsumed food, eating too heartily, or eating warmed-over processed food. Thus a new product was born—a line extension that fit the changing needs of the consumer.

3. The industry called the category "all natural cereals," so (naturally!) that is what the first national brands called themselves. But consumers

called them "granola," so that is what General Mills called its later (and successful) entry. It smartly preempted the generic descriptor and made it an identifiable brand: Nature Valley Granola Cereal.

But that was just the beginning. Looking at a production line differently can pay off also. Here's an example from the nation's Number 1 new products company, General Mills. Here's how F. Caleb Blodgett, its vice chairman for consumer foods, saw the obvious in 1974, as quoted in a January, 1981, article in *Fortune*: "He watched as 6-by-300-foot sheets of granola came rolling out of an oven, only to be crumbled. 'Let's cut that into bars,' he said. A new product was born: Nature Valley Granola Bars." This helped spawn the most successful new dry grocery product line introduced in many years. Now, besides the cereal and bars, there are Nature Valley Granola Clusters, Light & Crunchy Snacks, Granola and Fruit Bars, Chewy Granola Bars, and more.

Mr. Blodgett's ability to see new products while viewing a production line calls to mind an illustrative aside. "Seeing differently" has been the inspiration of the world's greatest artistic creators from Leonardo to Picasso. In Vallauris, France (where this chapter was first drafted), Picasso saw a bullring crowd on the surface of a pitcher, a dove in a porringer, a goat in bicycle handlebars. So inventive was Picasso that he created whole new schools of art, each influenced by his "periods" of different directions in art and artifacts.

It is the genius of true creativity to see in the signals of everyday experience what later becomes obvious to the vicarious appreciators. The interpretation of the random assemblages of the invention process is crucial to selection of concepts for research sorting. Countless rearrangements are suggested by the array of life-style trends, industrial clichés, or manufacturing process. I once participated in a problem-solving session that achieved a dramatic lowering of costs by changing the manufacturing technique for making nonwoven fabric garments. A production expert was on hand to explain the problem and the conventional techniques, but unencumbered amateurs were able to see original, non-traditional solutions. As a result, automated spray gluing on balloon forms was substituted for piece-work sewing on Union Special machines. Similarly, new recreational equipment for playgrounds was invented for Game Time Incorporated by outside imaginative minds, working with young children. Park board officials and school district experts were involved to explain the problems, safety regulations, etc.

Other rearrangements are suggested by the array of industry information. Wherever the industry has a pronounced seasonal skew—and *all* of the major brands participate in that skew—there is an implied opportunity for a contra-seasonal new product.

The same is true of market size, geographic area, ethnic skew—there's usually an opportunity.

The same is true of a large, rapidly growing new market—one a company may be late in entering. There is usually a *better* opportunity offered by an understanding of the factors that have made the category take off, than by directly jumping into the fray of competitors with a late entry that has only a slight differential. Unfortunately the latter is too often the case.

On the other side of the coin, there may be opportunities in the so-called unattractive mature markets—those barely keeping up with population growth. Usually, these markets are characterized by having several major leaders who have held a stable share of market over a considerable period of time. One may assume that a lot of the dynamism has gone, that the trade style has become a cliché, and that reaction time is slow. The consumer is ripe for some excitement and it may be that rapid share gains are available to an aggressive new product line.

Similarly, the so-called parity/commodity categories that are so unattractive to most go-go marketers offer new product opportunities. These commodity producers tend to be manufacturing-oriented, not marketing-oriented. A sharp marketing company can often find ripe opportunity for slightly differentiated, but smartly marketed, new products.

Fisher Nut Company, for example, quickly latched onto the concern about salt intake and brought out salt-free peanuts, low-sodium peanuts (half the salt of ordinary salted peanuts), and other low-sodium snack nut lines. Consumer needs were met with smart line extensions that did not inhibit the established varieties, but did steal a march on the commodity snack nut competition.

Seeing the Category Differently

How do you get into a frame of mind to see the category differently?

Most products are based on old technologies. They improve by evolution, not revolution. But if a company is not beset with the old technology and the old state of mind—but *is* interested in the marketplace—it has conceptual advantages in thinking about product entries.

A company entering an established market could choose several perspectives:

1. How to make a better one
    This would result in optimizing the status quo. The incumbents are probably ahead here.
2. How to invent the first one
    This would result in applying all of the latest technologies, without the preconceived notions implied by the existing products. This process has yielded successes in many fields, from cameras to catamenial devices.

Thinking Outside-In

Another way to circumvent the evolutionary approach is to start thinking outside-in, instead of inside-out.

Most companies try to leverage their production engineering, or their distribution, or both. This is the inside-out point-of-view, and it is most prevalently, most successfully, employed in new product marketing development. However, there are many successes coming the other way, coming from the perspective of the end-user rather than that of the maker. A good example of the latter is the L'eggs recognition that supermarket distribution of panty hose would be a great time saver for consumers, and that inventory display maintenance provided both the problems and the opportunities. It was not the way Hanes or its competitors marketed products via the inside-out tradition. Solving the new distribution channel problems (including the trade resistance) built a giant business for Hanes, which has since been extended into additional profitable lines. Outside-in thinking—and action.

Another more recent (introduced in 1983) example comes from Jockey International. Long the leader in fitted, 100 percent cotton men's underwear, Jockey realized that the 100 percent cotton knitted underwear offered advantages for women as well. The absorbency of cotton, its breathability, its easy laundering, its form-fitting style, all offered benefits for female consumers. What's more, the vast majority of Jockey shorts for men were purchased for male family members by women. They were familiar with its excellent qualities. Hence, a line of fitted panties (from bikini to briefs), with a variety of colors and designs has been successfully introduced. Although inside-out thinking may have indicated that Jockey is for men only—a fresh perspective has created Jockey for Her.

Most product development lays out a program in phases from today to tomorrow, with optimization steps along the way. Instead, start with the end result—and build back from that, to arrive at the development program. This shift in point-of-view allows for greater scope in thinking.

That's a shift in time cycle perspective. Another shift is to think of making a new product, or an innovated product, or an improved product, differently also. The usual way is to *add* a feature, an extra function, an extra ingredient, an added appearance trim.

What happens if you think outside-in, think *subtraction*?

One company, Beech-Nut Foods Corporation, found that mothers had been avoiding or minimizing the use of prepared baby foods because of concern over additives. So, in 1977, it pioneered by removing all salt from all of its products and sugar from most (the exceptions being tart and/or acidic fruits). Beech-Nut ads featured such headlines as: "NEW Beech-Nut—131 baby foods with no added salt, preservatives, artificial flavors, or colors." Here's another: "In a recent national survey, 9 out of 10 pediatricians prefer baby foods with no sugar added." Two years later (in 1979), ads continued to stress the pediatrician preference, stressing, "Beech-Nut took over 5½ pounds of sugar and salt *out* of baby's first year." There are many, many other examples of positive subtraction, from stripped-down energy-efficient automobiles to the light (less calories) beer and wine (less alcohol).

Sometimes, as Ludwig Mies Van der Rohe said: "Less is more."

Peer Group

Gather together experts from different companies but related to the same area of interest. Tell them in advance that you are seeking their help in order to quickly get up-to-speed in an area of your interest, that they will not be asked to reveal any proprietary information, and that a transcript of the session(s) will be provided to each of them. (This is best arranged by a third-party consultant.)

The yield is a grouping of experienced professionals eager to share experiences and perceptions of the category with their peers—with much of this colored positively by their extensive work and research in the field. Inject into the discussion broad but specific areas of new product interest, to stimulate ideation. Usually, this will be practical, experiential ideation—not flights of fancy. However, if an excursion into fantasy seems appropriate to the group, it sometimes can be productive.

Delphi

Because grouping experts together can cause such side effects as status-jockeying and compromise instead of consensus decisions, the Rand Corporation devised the Delphi technique. In an article in the April 1976 issue of *Business Horizons*, Richard Tersine and Walter E. Riggs described it as follows:

It is a method to systematically solicit, collect, evaluate, and tabulate independent opinion without group discussion. [It] replaces direct debate with a carefully designed program of individual interrogations, usually conducted by a series of questionnaires. The control of interaction among respondents is a deliberate attempt to avoid the disadvantages of the more conventional use of experts via round table discussions, committees, and conferences. The experts are not identified to each other in any way, and there is usually a greater flow of ideas, fuller participation, and increased evidence of problem closure.

Appropriate input questions can utilize Delphi as an ideation tool in new products invention. It also is a way of overcoming geographic and time availability problems that may prevent assembly of the experts.

Ideation Incentive Program

Dun & Bradstreet, Inc., reports in a 1981 AMACOM Management Review:

Our ideas come from senior management, middle management, line management, salesmen, our credit reporters, and consultants. By encouraging the flow of ideas . . . we have been able to examine . . . more than 150 ideas in the last two years. We currently receive most of our new ideas from field personnel through our $5,000 Club—a new idea incentive program. Any eligible Dun & Bradstreet employee can receive $5,000 for suggesting an idea that reaches . . . nationwide introduction. Our

CEO supports this program and ideas are sent *directly* [italics ours] to the director of product planning and research. This avoids any problems with the chain of command.

Consumer Mail

Many companies carefully classify and analyze customer complaints—and suggestions—as a means of tapping pent-up desires and direction from the marketplace. After all, if a customer makes the effort to applaud, castigate, or question, the subject must be an important one.

Brainstorming

"Brainstorming" is a step up from bull sessions. It involves getting a group together for an informal sharing of ideas, hoping to spark new ones as a result of the group dynamics, rapport, and a nonjudgmental context. It's often a very preliminary, unplanned project beginning. Although the yield may be high in conviviality, it may not be as focused as later developed embellishments may offer. It is sometimes also successfully employed as a follow-up technique to concept development or as an aid in communications developments (e.g., product descriptors, brand names, etc.)

Synectics

Another popular approach is "group think." One disciplined method, Synectics, pioneered by Synectics Inc., Cambridge, Mass., offers the benefit of stimulating uninhibited flights of fancy that can be brought down to earth and become practical concepts or problem solutions. They call it "dynamic group problem solving." It requires a role-playing client, a relatively uninvolved leader, and a small group of participants. (See Figure 14-2.) It is capable of generating large quantities of ideas in a short span of time—a matter of hours or, preferably, a few days. The best sessions often include appropriately expert participants, whether professionally expert or others briefed in advance on the general background and goals. This allows time for appropriate information "simmering."

The benefits of free-wheeling ideation were summed up by E. M. Forster: "Think before you speak is criticism's motto; speak before you think, creation's."

Role Playing

Assemble the participant group as a management body, charged with new product decision-making. Tell them that matters are moving rapidly, and that they will be expected to cope with each change as it is announced: competitive moves, government regulation, raw material shortages or cost rises, legal

Figure 14-2a & b
Synectics

Synectics leader lists "what ifs" in session, where each participant builds on ideas of others—no matter how fanciful. Such group dynamics can often help develop wild ideas into innovations.

constraints, medical discoveries, etc. Brief them on the purpose of meeting: e.g., to build a better mousetrap than the General Mousetrap Corporation, if that's appropriate.

Shortly after the meeting begins, a news bulletin is delivered—it changes all of the briefing signals. The problem must be readdressed. A different new product than was originally being generated now begins to evolve. A long-distance telephone call comes from France, with the announcement that an international patent is being issued covering a critical area of the mechanism being considered. Furthermore, the international company already is beginning pilot plant manufacturing in several countries, including this one. Back to the drawing board. A new technology emerges. Then: a Senate committee staffer leaks word that they are going after the mousetrap industry in major hearings to be announced shortly.

The ground rules shift again, to make use of mousetrap technology for other purposes . . . the scenario goes on, to seek out, to inform, to create an atmosphere where new kinds of ideas are developed.

Roll Playing

Note the spelling. This is different.

Everyone can draw. Some can draw better than they can articulate verbally. Roll playing is named after the use of lengthy rolls of blank paper. Participants group around a small table and draw concepts—adding on to and embellishing each other's sketches. This works particularly well for hard goods conceptualization. (See Figure 14-3.)

Roll playing helps in surface design and structure invention. Many are familiar with the first phases of designing that "dream house." Shift the rooms around, alter the views, decide on the type of roof, etc. Much of this is helpful (and more economical than waiting until later) when the architect is finally selected. The preliminary thinking, the mandatory elements and the rejected elements, have been established.

Much the same process takes place in designing dimensional products. Verbal descriptions simply do not communicate as well. A sketch, no matter how crude, is concrete; others can add to it, redraw it, change it in ways that enhance the creative realization and future direction. When several persons work together to sketch a concept, a mutual dynamic can take place that will enhance the idea. Often, too, one person's idea may have a problem that another person's insight (and drawing pen) may solve. Roll playing is working together with pictures and conversation, not just with words.

Ivory Tower

Not everyone performs best in a group. Some assimilate and ideate best as loners. Thinking time to generate ideas is provided at the participant's chosen place of solitude.

Figure 14-3
Roll-Playing

"Roll Playing" author and freelance designer Paul Kemp ideate non-electric housewares concepts, building on each other's construction sketches on a continuous roll of paper.

Some of the best ideation is done all alone—or by small teams. The designer, Gabrielle "Coco" Chanel said: "Those who create are rare; those who cannot are numerous. Therefore, the latter are stronger." Not to be discouraged, the former make the world go around, are remembered longest, and can be the key to the most productive ideation. Bernice FitzGibbons, the retail advertising whiz, said: "Creativity varies inversely with the number of cooks involved in the broth."

So, don't hesitate to turn over a giant assignment to one or two individuals or teams, while the conventional processes proceed.

Competitive Set

Some highly motivated ideators perform best under the fire of competition. Seek these out, put them together—and get out of the way.

Personification

Know your target. Know your target's role model. Then ask the question: "What kind of [fill in product category] would [fill in name of clearly characterized famous person] use?"

For example:

What kind of razor would Paul Newman use?
What kind of candy would the Harlem Globetrotters eat?
What kind of car would Jane Fonda drive?

Self-Identification

What kind of person am I if I buy [insert new product category]?

Now, here's my problem. I have it in my power to provide the solution. What is it?

Milk has just become extremely costly. What am I going to drink instead? Why?

Personalize the assignment in the most self-interested manner.

Ridiculous to the Sublime

Stretch out. Start by pushing yourself or the group out to the wildest possible fantasies. Locate the company on the planet Gorp, where any element is available just by invention, money is limitless, and there is a market for everything. Then take the tiniest aspects of the assignment and evolve the most elaborate, complicated optimization. Often, out of this comes a thought process that opens up new avenues of product exploration—ones that are really down to earth!

List Making

Start a list, add to a list, have associates add to the list—make it a game. (See Figure 14-4.) See how many ideas, in the form of topic sentences, challenges, names, etc., can be generated. Set a deadline. Give a prize (recognition) for the longest list (not the best, necessarily). Set a time limit. Have fun!

Finding an Equity

Many successful products stem from an equity that already exists. Easy examples are designer jeans, the equity being the fame of the designer's name; the Reggie bar; the partly borrowed and partly invented equities of children's cereals such as Count Chocola and FrankenBerry; the Muppett-spawned toys and games; the created equity, such as the Cabbage Patch doll—or Michael Jackson.

Figure 14-4
List Making

Ingredient	Drugs Proprietary	Toiletries	Soap	Household	Food
Enzyme	X	X	X	X	X
Wine	X	X	X		X
Caffeine	X				X
Cocoa Butter	X	X	X	X	X
Alcohol	X	X	X	X	X
Vitamins	X	X	X		X
Wheat Germ	X				X
Aloevera	X	X	X		
Silica/S. Gel	X	X	X		
Benzocaine	X	X			
Papain	X	X	X		
Anhydrous CO2	X	X	X		X
CO2	X	X			X
Nitrogen	X	X	X		
Glycerine	X	X	X	X	
Rose Water		X	X		
Silicone		X	X	X	
Algae	X	X	X		X
Witch Hazel	X	X	X		
Protein	X	X	X		X
Cactus		X	X		X
Optical Brightener		X	X		
Lemon	X	X	X	X	X
Placenta		X	X		
Queen Bee Jel		X	X		
Hormones		X	X		
Iron	X				X
Avocado		X	X		X
Peach		X	X		X
Almond		X	X	X	X
Laurel (Bay)		X	X		X
Mink Oil		X	X		
Cucumber		X	X		X

Figure 14-4 (*Continued*)

Ingredient	Drugs Proprietary	Toiletries	Soap	Household	Food
Honey	X	X			X
Mango		X	X		X
Milk	X	X	X		X
Papaya		X	X		X
Beer	X	X			X
Vinegar	X	X	X	X	X
Egg		X	X		X
Lanolin	X	X	X	X	
Rum	X	X	X		X
Germicide	X	X	X	X	
Insecticide		X		X	
Soil Repellent		X	X	X	
Soil Release		X	X	X	
Pine	X	X	X	X	
Ammonia	X			X	
Pumice		X	X	X	
Chlorophyll	X	X	X	X	X
Bran	X	X			X
Linoleic acid	X				X
Polypeptides	X	X	X		
Oatmeal		X	X		X
Menthol	X	X	X		
Beauty Grains		X	X		
Bubble Bath		X	X		
Baby Oil		X	X		
Bath Oil		X	X		
Baby Lotion		X	X		
Coconut Milk		X	X		X
Blusher		X	X		
Fruit Fragrance		X	X		
Deep Colors		X	X		
Olive Oil		X	X		X
Lechithin	X	X	X	X	X

Figure 14-4 (*Continued*)

Ingredient	Drugs Proprietary	Toiletries	Soap	Household	Food
Amino Acids	X	X	X		
Caseine		X	X		
APAP		X			
Histamine	X				
Sunscreen	X	X	X		
Ice Melter				X	
Driers		X	X	X	
Stain Resisters				X	
Spun Soy					X
Avicell/CMC		X		X	X
Gel Forms	X	X	X	X	X
Seaweed/Kelp	X	X	X		
Linseed Oil				X	
Iguana Oil		X	X		
Myrhh	X	X	X		
FPC					X
Frankincense		X	X		
Mercaptan				X	

List making leads to clusters of ideas. Shown here are 92 ingredients spun out in an actual list-making session, which yielded 246 opportunities in the five areas of a company's interest. Lab technicians participated in the free flowing session, which stimulated the concept for a successful new beauty soap.

Start the ideation process by identifying equities. Ones existing and not yet applied to your subject category. Ones existing and not yet applied to any category. Old ones, now in the public domain. New ones, which must be licensed. Really new ones, which are invented to suit the subject.

A noteworthy example: Designer Robin Roberts' Clarence House, the created equity that is responsible for selling $20 million in bed gear for Cannon Mills. Fifteen to 20 percent of bed gear carry such designer names as Yves St. Laurent, Calvin Klein, Oscar de la Renta, etc. Underscoring the importance that a bed sheet, like any other product, is a complete communication, Mr. Roberts keeps his designs simple, so that they will reproduce well in catalogs, the source of most sales.

What or Where

Start with a brand—possibly a mythical one; possibly it will become a real one. The brand says "what" you are striving for (to look thin in a bathing suit, hence: Skinny Dip). Or—it may say "where" you are coming from (a carefree uninhibited state, hence: Footloose).

Such words start to shape the new product concept, and get the ideators off and running.

No Holds Barred

It is a rule, in the beginning, that anything that is not immoral or illegal goes. Then, some practical constraints enter. An idea must be conceptually credible to the end-user, even if the scientists don't know how to make it work.

Then, it is an assignment to make the credible practicable.

Then, it is an assignment to make the practicable communicable in some format that may be used to convey the idea to a respondent.

You must know (and understand) what you have wrought. And so must the consumer. Don't be like Mickey Rooney in the burlesque musical "Sugar Babies." He plays a mad inventor of the light bulb. He displays it proudly. Then holds it to the side of his head and tries to place a telephone call.

That's okay in the ideation process, if it gets pointed in the right direction. At that time, the process for visionizing is even more important than the process for analyzing the visions and acting on the analysis.

Sometimes, trying everything at once produces exceptional results. Some years ago, with a goal of conceiving and executing in finished stimulus presentation format literally dozens of new products in the personal care field, ten bright, aware, young members of an advertising agency were assembled and given this challenge:

Think about your personal care problems. What is there about your appearance, your bodily functions, outside effects on your comfort that some kind of product might improve? Bring back your ideas. Experts will tell you which ones are feasible. Then, we'll make prototypes. You will name them. You will put them into any type of presentation form you wish, just so it is simple and demonstrates the product and its benefit.

Individual members of the team, sometimes in groups and sometimes alone, arrived at the ideas by looking into mirrors, talking to boy and girl friends, consulting physicians, synecticizing, baring their souls before the group, dreaming, etc. As I reported in an *Advertising Age* article published Nov. 20, 1972, hundreds of ideas were generated, from very serious, clinically supportable, preventive medical regimens to hair deodorizers to costume jewelry insect repellents to a suntan gel that won't wash off[1] in fresh or salt water (except with soap) to a complete beauty spa home treatment line,[2] etc., etc.

[1]Similar product concept introduced seven years later in 1979 by 3M Company as Mmm—What a Tan.
[2]Similar product concept introduced three years later in 1975 as La Costa, by La Costa Resort Hotel & Spa.

The point of this anecdote is that leaving no stone unturned in the creative process is often rewarding. Although a high percentage of the ideas will be discarded, just having one that survives is worth the stimulating exercise of developing hundreds and hundreds.

A few gentle prods along those lines come from Peter J. Jessen of the International Policy Institute, who concurs with the stress on unencumbered inspirational ideation. In a May 21, 1981, seminar Jessen advocated

turning to dreams and visions, not gurus and oracles; innovating the new, not repeating and duplicating the old; exciting possibilities explored, not tunnel-vision foreclosures; strategic planning and long-term views, not repetitive planning and short-term views; innovating the unthought of, not model building from extrapolations; creative dreaming, not equivocating predictions and prophecies; creative forecasting, not blindly accepting extrapolations.

These are challenges to meet, every one of them. And as new ideas are produced, the spirit and fulfillment of ideation starts all over again. The pipeline is filled with new opportunities—using all three aspects of the mind: thinking, willing, feeling.

15

Ideaforms

Great floods have flown from simple sources.
—*William Shakespeare*
All's Well That Ends Well
Act II, Scene I

The company charter is understood; the goals have been set; the opportunity areas have been defined; the ideation process has been productive. In order to sort out those ideas to be pursued, two elements are needed:

1. A clear communication of the idea
   a. In business terms
   b. In prospect communication terms
2. Methods of reducing the number of candidates for further development

This discussion deals with the *forms* in which ideas are expressed for evaluation.

Communicating the Idea

Business Term Description

A business term description will not spell out the customer benefits of the new product idea. Instead, it will look at the general attractiveness of the product in terms of financial goals (sales, margins, return on investment, cash flow, cost of money, etc.), expected growth potential (relates to maturity of the category and changing industry and population factors), competitive set, industry restructuring (required or ongoing), distribution of risk (related to other corporate activities and guidelines), energy, geography, ecology, regulations, etc. How will these elements perform over time?

Beyond this, you will ask how appropriate is this product to our business? Does it fit our capital structure, marketing strength, manufacturing, technology, raw material and component access, and other skills?

At this point, you can conduct a quick, broad screening of ideas based on their appropriateness to your business interests. Certain factors will immediately delete some ideas from further consideration, while raising the interest in others. Still, the choices are many and varied. To get at these in the rough screening process, assign a numerical value to each business element, on a scale ranging from 0 to 10, which will allow you to array your company strengths, financial considerations, supplier reliability, etc., across each appropriate consideration.

The usefulness of this approach is that it is largely objective, allows for the incorporation of internal expertise in the decision process (R&D, manufacturing, marketing—all participate in assigning values), and provides an early indication of the answers necessary to a "go" decision: What will it cost? How long will it take? What will the volume be?

On the flip side, it will also diagnose some of the idea's failings. This done, you may decide to remedy the failings, if they are few or not major. If they *are* major, but when/if solved the product shows great profit yield for the company over time, and may be protectable by proprietary technology or a special marketing edge, again it may be worthwhile to remedy the failings.

Even with this approach, there may be disagreement over the values assigned to certain business elements. Recast the numbers with the dissenter's figures. If this does not change the total picture, then the process is completed. If recasting the numbers alters the picture significantly you have the option of going to a higher (management) court or (if there are enough other positive elements) moving the idea into the next phase of ideaform development and assessment.

One company uses the in-house expert evaluation format shown in Figure 15-1. Here, as in the 1 to 10 ranking system described above, internal expertise is tapped early in the decision process, prior to any testing, prototype development, etc. Specific questions are posed for comparative purposes and decision weighting. Additional essay-type commentary is encouraged to cover areas that may have been overlooked in the questionnaire design.

Prospect Communications

Prospect communications identify the target and describe the benefit (need fulfillment). If there is more than one benefit, the galaxy of advantages is arrayed and stressed in order of importance.

Here's an example:

Figure 15-1
In-House Evaluation Scoresheet

IN-HOUSE EXPERT EVALUATION

Information to be completed by MARKETING expert | Product Concept #_____ |

1. What do you think the *total* potential market is for this product?

    MOST LIKELY _____ units   LOW _____ units   HIGH _____ units

2. At each of the following points in the first fifteen years of the product's life, what level of annual unit sales do you forecast?

	MOST LIKELY	LOW	HIGH
1 year	units	units	units
5 years	units	units	units
10 years	units	units	units

3. What market share do you expect for this product at the following points in its life cycle?

	MOST LIKELY	LOW	HIGH
1 year	%	%	%
5 years	%	%	%
10 years	%	%	%

4. What do you see as the price for the product at the following points in its life cycle? (excluding inflation)

	MOST LIKELY	LOW	HIGH
1 year	$	$	$
5 years	$	$	$
10 years	$	$	$

5. What level of *introductory* advertising and promotion will be required for this product?

    MOST LIKELY $_____   LOW $_____   HIGH $_____

6. What level of advertising and promotion, as a percentage of sales, will be required to support this product once it is on the market?

    MOST LIKELY _____ %   LOW _____ %   HIGH _____ %

7. What test market costs would be required for this product?

    MOST LIKELY $_____   LOW $_____   HIGH $_____

8. What level of selling costs (salesmen's commissions, dealer support, displays; excluding advertising and promotion), as a percentage of sales, are required for this product?

    MOST LIKELY _____ %   LOW _____ %   HIGH _____ %

Figure 15-1 (*Continued*)

Information to be completed by RESEARCH & DEVELOPMENT expert
1. How many hours of R&D personnel time do you estimate is required to draw up the plans for this concept?

    MOST LIKELY _____ hours   LOW _____ hours   HIGH _____ hours
2. What rate (per hour) applies to R&D personnel? (including mix of management and engineering personnel)

    MOST LIKELY $_____   LOW $_____   HIGH $_____
3. What costs are required to develop a prototype model of this product concept?

    MOST LIKELY $_____   LOW $_____   HIGH $_____

Information to be completed by PRODUCTION EXPERT,
by FINANCIAL EXPERT,
etc.

Automobile owners double their mileage when they add one pint of this new discovery to every tankful of gasoline.

The statement may go on to elaborate:

Approved by Society of Automotive Engineers and all major automobile makers. Nonpoisonous, noncorrosive, made from a by-product of the plastics industry, costs no more than a gallon of gasoline—yet cuts your cost of gasoline almost in half.

The subparagraph of elaboration supports the claim, answers the obvious questions, and provides authoritative endorsement. It also adds credibility to the proposition.

Statements such as these, which describe easily measurable performance and do not have any special visual appeal, may be used in sorting and screening research results, whether they be obtained by mail, telephone, intercept, group, or intensive one-on-one discussions.

An illustration probably would add only a marginal enhancement—and may divert the respondents into the evaluation of (in this case) relatively low priority considerations such as: packaging convenience, handling, material, disposal, etc. Further, an illustration could divert discussion from the chosen generic descriptor to that of the arbitrarily selected (for illustration purposes) container. For these reasons, no brand name or descriptor has been used in the stimulus communication. The attempt is to find out about the idea—*not* about its execution. That will come later.

In other situations, an illustration—no matter how schematic—may be necessary. In others, a very comprehensive illustration is necessary. Where relative size, visible texture, color, graphics, or mechanics are necessary to understanding, illustrations should be employed. Where the end effect has visual impact, as with decorative items and the appetite appeal essential to certain food and beverage items, supportive illustrations should be used in the concept stimulation material. While anyone can visualize a sugar-frosted corn flake, few are likely to be able to accurately imagine how a French-fried spaghetti snack would look. The first needn't be illustrated; the other should be.

For this reason, the selection of a research technique should be based on appropriate stimulus material—rather than stimulus material being developed to fit a predetermined research technique.

At this stage in ideaform development, communications embellishment is to be eschewed. Just state the facts, arranged as a clear communication. You don't need personality, image, enhancing surroundings, or hyperbolic puffery at this point. The ideaform is not the advertising prototype. It is a bare, essential distillation of the concept. Because it is a bare essential, it allows the respondent to feed in information that may become part of the marketing communications blueprint. It seeks to describe a product in such a way as to make it understandable, leaving room for the respondent to embellish it with his or her own experience and language. It is hoped that the respondent will place the product into perspective as to its importance and the place it may play in the routine of the prospect's life or business.

The nature of the idea also helps determine the ideaform communication.

An idea may be able to go in multiple directions, yet one direction must (at least, initially) be selected or rejected prior to prototype development. In choosing among alternatives, a number of ideaform concept statements are prepared and studied. This is not *positioning* selection. That, too, comes later. At this point, you are trying to define the idea in each of the various ways it may be developed as a product, as an options guide to later R&D and/or prototype development.

Writing the Concept Statement

As already established, new products are essential to a company's successful growth. For this reason, top professional skills should be applied at every step of the way. This includes the preparation of ideaforms—the concept stimulus material.

Unfortunately, the concept statement is often written by persons with professional skills in other fields—business management, marketing, engineering, medicine, pharmacy, research—but not in communications. Yet any of these same experts would not think of entrusting finished communications, which will be addressed to the prospect, to any but the finest communicators. The concept champions (especially!) will want the best possible communications to help introduce *their* new product. But often these champions become highly proprietary at the ideaform stage, rather than turning this critical task over to communications experts. Policy should require that professional communicators write the concept statements within prescribed research guidelines. If the research guidelines get in the way, revisit the purpose of the research and the rationale for the guidelines—and revise them if possible and necessary.

The clearest approach to writing a concept statement is to be knowledgeable about the new product and its market environment. Then, state in one clear sentence what you would tell an uninitiated friend about the product, so that he or she would immediately understand and possibly be infected by your enthusiasm. The best guidepost to this kind of writing is journalism—the who, what, when, where, why, and how formula, captured in a headline and lead sentence. Still the best text, for even the most complicated concept communication, is Rudolph Fleisch's *The Art of Plain Talk* (Macmillan, 1962).

(A highly paid professional communicator once told me that his first job was to write repair manuals for complicated data processing machines. "Me, who has never looked under the hood of a car—and can't drive a nail straight!" Undaunted, he set about interviewing the experts—and rigidly followed Rudolph Fleisch's directions. His manuals were so well received that their format, style, and relevant content are still in use to this day. "You know, I never repaired a single machine. I just watched, asked questions, took notes, and wrote the manuals. Even with my excellent instructions, I'd still be afraid to approach those mysterious electronics, tools in hand.")

Concept Statement Preparation

A good communicator must be able to describe a complicated concept so that anyone can understand it—and understand it *accurately*. The first thing the professional does is to make the complicated simple. The second thing is to make the now-simple concept understandably relevant to the needs of the prospect. A well-written concept statement should embrace all of the following factors:

Differentiate
Give a reason to buy—a single one is best, just a few at most. A concept that is all things to all people usually interests none. The ideal concept appeals to selfish interests. It promises more convenience; it is cheaper; it is quicker; etc. A "preventive" concept (such as a vitamin compound) also must be differentiated from similar concepts in terms of form, use routine, accessibility, etc.

Some "Sell," But Not an Ad

Skip the hyperbole, but write the concept with a sale in mind. Position the concept so that the respondent can immediately place it in his or his company's world—can see a possible place where it may be applicable. Make clear who it is for, when and where and how it should be used—and what it may replace (another product, wasted time, wasted space, etc.)

The Pricing Issue

Do not include price unless it is really relevant. If the product category is a known one and if the price of the concept product is within the expected range, do not include it. The respondent will either assume this or (possibly) say: "I'd expect to pay a bit more for this because. . ." or "I'd buy it if it didn't cost more than my regular brand" or "This would have to cost a lot less than X—because it seems less convenient." Lead the consumer into the pricing issue, if it is relevant; if it is not, lead the consumer into the value issue. An example: One of the truths in portable food product concept studies is that if the consumer says "It would be great for camping," you know that this expresses a search to place it somewhere positively—but that there is obviously no broad appeal.

Sometimes, however, the pricing issue is an essential. Sometimes, to price low in a price-sensitive market means a trade-off. In this case, where low price is a virtue but a sacrifice is made to achieve it, it is well to state the trade-off, minimizing the importance of the minor change. If the price is higher, justify the importance of the additional feature(s). Good examples abound in the home entertainment category, where the bells and whistles can be few or many—and usually relate to price points. Nonetheless, unless the only virtue of the new product is price, insert this issue separately in the respondent discussion process.

Other Factors

Accuracy of statement prevents misleading feedback from respondents. Too often, inaccurate statements creep into ideaforms because the author does not have a real-world, hand-on affinity for the use category. The result then becomes "factory talk"—description of the concept from the point-of-view of the maker, rather than its relevance to the user.

Another temptation to resist is telling more than the prospect needs (or *wants*) to know. It is better to err on the side of a well-stated main appeal, with minimal support, than on the side of a fully rounded statement of everything you always wanted to know, but were afraid to ask.

The first approach allows the respondent to understand enough to stimulate questions and comments—which will provide clues to other important elements for consideration. The second approach may lead to unproductive comments and/or misunderstanding. (In the earlier example of the gasoline additive statement, a preliminary office screening of uninvolved respondents revealed that it was necessary to somehow describe the substance and its origin, but not in chemical terms. The industrial by-product allusion provided just enough information to close that information gap, and was added before the statement went into screening.)

The uninvolved office or factory screen should not be overlooked. It can save millions of dollars—and help make millions more.

An example: Years ago, a paper company developed a way to bond fibers together with water-soluble starch. One product suggestion was a sanitary napkin covering that would allow the cellulose fibers to be easily dispersed in the toilet and hence make the napkin readily flushable. The male conceptualizers had been confronted with many office and hotel signs warning against flushing sanitary napkins—and had invented a new product that had overcome the problem. Prototypes were made before any women were involved in concept statement studies. Products were placed in homes for use tests. Meanwhile, the outside new products consultant firm did a small sample office study (100 respondents) and found out a few simple facts that were ignored in a costly development program—but later proved to be correct. The majority of the 100 female respondents said: "I don't worry too much about what I flush down toilets in public office buildings . . . BUT I wouldn't flush *any* sanitary napkin down my *own* toilet. Besides, if the covering will dissolve in the toilet, won't it be a problem for me too?" Despite this, the product was introduced in test market—and failed. This study illustrates the relevance of use-related concept evaluators as early as possible, even if informally involved.

Know the Language Territory

Obviously it is useful to try out feasible concepts on small samples of potential users very early in the process. This informal feedback can be conducted on a conversationally casual basis among possible prospects. Often, it will lead to concept refinement—or raise issues not well addressed or even anticipated. There may be a gap between the inventors and the intended recipients of the innovation.

This may be a language gap, not a gap between the product delivery and the respondent need. Knowing the language of the marketplace can help you sharpen the understandability of the concept statement. What works in the lab may not work in the real world. This is why *in vitro* (test tube) experiments do not necessarily predict *in vivo* (real world) results. It is important that concept statements be clear communications to the customer. The product or conception must be understood. The idea must innoculate a compatible culture. Words alone may not be enough to enliven the prospect's petri dish.

Concept Illustrations

Sometimes a picture or a graph is worth more than a thousand words. It may open a clearer path to understanding when you depict a complicated process with a flow chart, or show a multi-stage or many-featured product with schematic drawings of each component. The aim is understanding—not gloss or embellishment.

Sometimes a concept may be packaged in several alternative formats—although the resultant end-benefit does not change. The benefit description alone, then, is insufficient to promote understanding of the concept in alternative forms. Only an illustration will do the job well. Examples of such illustrations are shown in Figures 15-2, 15-3, and 15-4.

Evidence of the ability of a simple illustration to change comprehension and

---

Figure 15-2a-i
Concept Illustrations

These representative illustrations of new products extensions in the canned meats field, all of which utilize existing production technology and minor capital investment. Packaged product drawings were used to stimulate discussion among manufacturers. Several items from the presentation have since been marketed.

Figure 15-3a & b
Concept Illustrations—Buttery Tasting

New Push-Button Spread with Butter-Like Taste

New push-button discovery instantly spreads itself, as it comes from the handy container—to replace butter knives, butter plates, maybe even butter itself. Spreads its golden, rich butter-like flavor without crumbling crackers, crushing toast, waffles or pancakes. Sandwich making is a cinch, even with softest bread and rolls. Needs no refrigeration—always ready to serve. Made from pure, polyunsaturated vegetable oil. Enjoy the butter-like taste and added convenience.

New Push-Button Topping with Butter-Like Taste

New Push-button flavor topping looks like, acts like and tastes like melted butter. Its golden richness instantly melts into baked potatoes, corn on the cob, disappears into peas, beans, all vegetables. Keep attractive container handy to add buttery flavor to all foods. Needs no refrigeration—always ready to serve. Made from pure, polyunsaturated vegetable oil. Enjoy the butter-like taste and added convenience.

BUTTERY TASTING vegetable oil in a push-button dispenser was readily feasible, but a quick check to determine appeal and use-occasion frequency was handled with comprehensive drawings and descriptive copy before any major lab or communications development were committed. Here are two of the stimulus posters; on left product is positioned primarily as a spread substitute, on right primarily as an ingredient.

interest in a concept is exhibited by many studies where the illustration was revealed after full discussion of the verbal description. The evaluation of written descriptions can change dramatically after visualizations are added.

Reducing the Candidates: Preresearch Screening

In the early stages, a typical interest area may yield hundreds of concepts, each with the possibility of various positionings, stylings, packagings, trade names, features, and even various methods of sales and distribution. By this time in the development process, the major technical feasibility and manufacturing issues should have been addressed. Broad costing guidelines are understood. Yet—the project team must screen down to a workable (and affordable) set of concepts for preliminary screening research. Following are some ways they might do this.

Identifying the Organizing Concept

Is there a single organizing concept—or is the concept statement a string of features, no one of which will justify the concept as a whole? A simple

Figure 15-4a & b
Concept Illustrations—Humidifier and Bubble Bath

NEW INVISIBLE SPACE-SAVER ROOM HUMIDIFIER

Now there's a wall-mounted room humidifier which takes no
floor space. It's mounted between the wall studs -- and can
be painted or papered to fit any decor. Completely automatic
on-off cycle. Easily installed near any standard electrical
outlet. Complete installation instructions and template
included. Room humidifier helps guard against colds, protects
wood furniture from drying and cracking, provides comfortable
atmosphere with less heating energy. Space-Saver Room
Humidifier costs no more than bulky similar-capacity free-
standing floor models.

NEW PUSH-BUTTON BUBBLE BATH

Just attach to the faucet of your tub, turn on the hot water
and push the button once. Tub floods with giant bubbles that
soften and condition the skin. 100 relaxing bubble baths in
each refillable container. (Fits most faucets.)

checklist and rating scale should help determine this. Alternatively, a single statement of the single element of innovation must stand up to judgmental evaluation by the team. No "yes, buts" allowed. If a concept falls down on this basis, it should be dropped from further consideration.

For each case, make a listing of important considerations, then weight them in order of importance. The most promising concepts, then, will be those that focus on the single elements that are determined to be perceived as yielding the greatest benefit to the user. Using such a scale, you can rank the concepts. (In some instances, negative considerations are also listed, creating penalties to consider in the concept evaluation. For example: something may be terrific, but the cost will not justify the benefit.)

The best, the strongest single-statement stoppers say it all in a few words. When the talkies were young, this was enough: "Garbo talks!" Other examples: "How do you spell relief? . . . R-O-L-A-I-D-S." "M&Ms melt in your mouth, not in your hand." "Visine gets the red out."

If the concept is a novel use of a key technique or ingredient that is hoped to be the star across a range of choices, then the importance or exclusivity of performance of that factor must be weighed. How long will it be important and exclusive? Are its costs elastic or inelastic? Can the company lock up its source? Is it protectable (and for how long) through proprietary processing or patents? If it is a short-range, unprotectable factor, then will it be a fast-moving, high-margin fad opportunity? Is it quickly communicated—or is prospect education needed? Is it better—or only *apparently* better?

Judgment Grid

Sometimes all of the key judgment factors can be laid out in such a way that each concept in a set can be quite easily screened.

Here's an example. For a food products assignment, a tic-tac-toe grid (Figure 15-5) was erected as a quick way to sort out concepts that have a variety of differences, but no single revolutionary improvement. Usually, the category under study will allow assignment of predetermined weights to certain factors.

Figure 15-5
Concept Sorting

Package	Portion	Components
Occasion	User	Convenience
Value	Substitution	Preparation

In this example, after poor scorers were eliminated, new weights were assigned to the *other* important characteristics, and the survivor concepts were regrouped. This method quickly screened several hundreds of concepts down to 40, then to 20 that went into consumer concept research.

A similar evaluation method is to determine the principal attributes of the interest category. Then rank these attributes according to the performance of the entrenched competition. Then do it for the concepts under question. First, this isolates whether the concept really addresses a need or a gap. Second, it helps answer whether its promise is in an area of significant interest.

As an example, for hair shampoo, the attribute ranking in order of importance might be:

1. Quick, large, and copious suds
2. Quick conditioning effects
3. Easy rinsing
4. Fragrance/lack of fragrance
5. Cleansing ability

As this list shows, a concept for a superior conditioning shampoo that, however, did not suds well might have outstanding efficacy—but still fail. A concept that offered cleaner hair than any other shampoo would provide a marginal benefit and might create a fear of stripping and drying the hair.

Gap Analysis

A frequently used approach in evaluating new product concepts is *gap analysis*. Such factors as brand identity, attributes, differentiation, reward, and payoff are arrayed across a horizontal plane. On the vertical axis are listed the concept categories to be evaluated, such as those five cited in the shampoo example above. For each competing brand, the relevant information is entered in the boxes created by the intersecting horizontal and vertical lines. This matrix tends to isolate the gaps in the competitive market. If the concept under consideration fills the gaps, it may have a competitive edge.

Outsiders Who Are Insiders

Probably every concept in the preliminary set has a sponsor. The initial cut can be made by the coach—based on experience and ultimate responsibility for subsequent performance. Or it can be made by noninvolved insiders unaware of ego-attachments carried by the various concepts. A "ranking" approach, which tends to be impersonal, is asked of each. Sometimes a briefing (in writing) precedes. Clusters of top and bottom ranking emerge. Top ranks and those middle ranks with a few top scores survive. Others are cut, unless a fervent champion makes an extremely strong case for moving ahead with further investigation.

The Champion Screen

Throughout this book we champion the Champion—that individual who is willing to risk ridicule or a career for belief in an idea. To such a strong belief, heed should be paid—there are few enough champions in business, yet they are often the most important factors in the truly new.

Here's an example. A classic example of research versus instinct was well-described by Bob Shanks in his book *The Cool Fire* (Vintage Books division of Random House, ©1976 by Comco Productions).

The Ford Motor Company researched the introduction of a new automobile tirelessly and expensively and came up with the Edsel. A few years later, Lee Iacocca fought for his instinct that Americans wanted a hot car—and came up with the Mustang, Ford's single greatest success.

Incidentally, *after* the failure of the Edsel, I attended a seminar on new product development in Detroit, which featured a presentation by a Ford research director. His case history of a model meticulously managed research program was that done for the Edsel. No matter that the program provided misdirection—it was well planned and executed!

Concept research is used for new products, new services, new advertising themes, new movies, and new television shows. Still, creative judgment cannot be replaced by any standardized evaluation technique. As TV producer Bob Shanks says:

Frequently, networks will themselves make up concepts for shows, test them, and, if certain ones do well, commission shows to be written and produced, based on these concepts. Again, this research is normally used prudently by network executives.

Executives who are trained up through law, research, accounting, or sales generally rely more heavily on this so-called objective evidence; those who have come up through the creative ranks usually rely more on instinct, a sense of actually experiencing what audiences like by having exposed themselves to audiences.

The Experience Screen

Often, the best research is experiential. This comes only from hands-on observation in the field. Not from books. Not from case histories. Not from GIGO[1] computer programs—or any kind, even some that have been validated. After all, while every experience isn't exactly original, each one isn't exactly the same, either. Repeated observations and participatory experiences tend to cluster common themes, which become the basis for trained judgments.

One bad (or good) experience is apt to be misleading. How often have we heard something like this: "That may concept test well—but it will never sell. We tried a product just like that a few years ago and it flopped." Often, upon examination, you find that the referenced concept was not just exactly like that old flop—or that it had a different audience target, times have changed, etc.

Sometimes personal tastes (rather than observations of the behavior of others) unduly affect business judgments. One of the factors contributing to the failure of a frozen main dish line was the absolute blandness of the products, achieved over the protests of the corporate kitchens and food technologists. The CEO just didn't like onions in anything—and that went for lots of other spices and seasonings, too.

What's Left Goes Forward

The mere writing of a clear concept statement can often reveal flaws in the offering—underneath the fancy dress may be a pale figure of an idea. If so, eliminate it from consideration.

As for others in the cut-down process, use experience, personal taste, pragmatic data-based judgments, field observation, etc. Set a target: Only ten

---

[1]"Garbage In, Garbage Out," which means you only get as good as you give, from computers like anything else.

concepts can go into the research screening phase. This will force-fit the selection.

And now you move ahead, to develop rounded stimulus materials and more reliable screening methods. The costs are mounting, but progress is being made. Research among true prospects will help determine the path ahead. It will be the basis for the next important commitment of the company's funds.

16

Screening Research

There is a principle which is a bar against all information, which is proof against all arguments, and which cannot fail to keep a man in everlasting ignorance—that principle is contempt prior to investigation.
—*Herbert Spencer*

The secret is to fail with small dollars, learn from your mistakes and succeed with big dollars. Innovation and risk-taking are the critical skills.
—*H. B. Atwater, Jr.*
Chairman/CEO, General Mills Inc.

General investigation to seek knowledge at minimal cost is the first step in screening research. As the project progresses, the stimulus becomes more refined, the research technique more precise, and both the promise and the investment escalate.

This chapter is devoted to those research steps that help to refine the guidelines for prototype products and communications.

Sometimes, research is an overpromise. Remember, it can yield perspective on yesterday (depending on who writes the history), a snapshot of today (as accurate as the aim and focus, the speed of the film, and the truth of the colors), and the basis for a close-in tomorrow. Predictive research at its best can be no more accurate than its unpredictable subject: the marketplace.

In a paper presented at the 41st annual meeting of the Institute of Food Technologists (June 7–10, 1981, Atlanta, GA), David K. Hardin, then chairman of Market Facts Inc., noted:

Satisfaction with new product screening and product testing results is relatively low. Hardly anyone feels that his or her techniques provide a very good prediction of new product potentials. Two out of five believe that the techniques are not really very good.

Many experts agree. In a review contained in *Harvard Business Review on Management* (Harper & Row), an overview of qualitative methods, time series analysis and projection, and casual methods provided these ratings on seven applicable basic forecasting techniques. In paraphrase, these evaluations are:

A. Qualitative methods (forecasts of long-range and new product sales, forecasts of margins)

    1. Delphi

       Accuracy: Fair to very good.

       Identification of turning points: Fair to good.

    2. Market research (systematic, formal, and conscious procedure for evolving and testing hypotheses about real markets)

       Accuracy: Short-term (0–3 mos.): Excellent.

                  Mid-term (3 mos.–2 yrs.): Good.

                  Long-term (2 yrs. +): Fair to good.

       Identification of turning points: Fair to very good.

       Data required: At least two sets of reports over time, including a considerable collection of market data from questionnaires, surveys, and time series analyses of market variables.

    3. Panel consensus (technique based on assumption that several experts can arrive at a better forecast than one. There is no secrecy—unlike Delphi—and communication is encouraged. The forecasts are sometimes influenced by social factors, and may not reflect a true consensus.)

       Accuracy: Short- and mid-term: Poor to fair.

                  Long-term: Poor.

       Identification of turning points: Poor to fair.

    4. Visionary forecast (prophecy using personal insights, judgment, and, when possible, facts about different scenarios of the future. It is characterized by subjective guesswork and imagination; in general, methods used are nonscientific.)

       Accuracy: Poor.

       Identification of turning points: Poor.

    5. Historical analogy (comparative analysis of introduction and growth of similar new products, which bases the forecast on similarity patterns)

       Accuracy: Short-term: Poor.

                  Mid- and long-term: Good to fair.

       Identification of turning points: Poor to fair.

       Data required: Several years' history of one or more products.

B. Time series analysis and projection

    6. Trend projections (technique fits a trend line to a mathematical equation and then projects it into the future by means of this equation. There are several variations: the slope-characteristic method, polynomials, logarithms, etc.)

       Accuracy: Short-term: Very good.

                  Mid- and long-term: Good.

Identifications of turning points: Poor.

Data required: Varies with technique used. Good rule of thumb is to use a minimum of five years' annual data to start. Thereafter, the complete history.

Typical application: New product forecasts (particularly intermediate and long-term).

 C. Casual methods

  7. Life-cycle analysis (analysis and forecasting of new product growth rates based on S-curves. The phases of product acceptance by the various groups such as innovators, early adapters, early majority, late majority, and laggards are central to the analysis.)

Accuracy: Short-term: Poor.

      Mid- to long-term: Poor to good.

Identification of turning points: Poor to good.

Typical application: Forecasts of new product sales.

Data required: Minimally, annual sales of product being considered or of a similar product. Often necessary to do market surveys.

Learning (as Well as Testing)

One of the reasons for widespread dissatisfaction with new product research is that too much is expected. In reality, as opposed to research that monitors on-going experience, new product research is learning, as much as it is testing.

Unfortunately, all too many researchers in new product areas opt to design research instruments (questionnaires) that are highly structured: lots of multiple choice, agree/disagree, and checklist types of questions that, in most cases, facilitate "testing," but deter "learning." Such testing does build up big numbers at a relatively low cost. Numbers tend to be objective support for facts. And objectivity tends to carry more weight in the decision process.

Closed-end or check-off questions are appealing because:

- They're easy to administer.
- They're easy to tabulate.
- They're easy to compare with norms or pars from other tests.
- They're less expensive to both administer and to tabulate.
- They're easy to understand (require no thought).

Closed-end questions yield "scores," "norms," "pars," "means," and, if the sample is large and random, are readily susceptible to a vast variety of statistical analyses.

In new product work, however, particularly in the early stages, highly structured, closed-end questions serve to gag and to straight-jacket the respondent, rendering him/her the freedom to only nod or shake his/her head when presented with agreeable or disagreeable stimuli. These stimuli, unfortunately, are based on the assumption that we have learned all there is to know about a new product—and that all that is left for research to find out is what numbers of people feel this way or that.

Research Guidelines

Whether it be qualitative research to seek knowledge, projective techniques to make forecasts, or testing to evaluate scenarios, professional disciplines are necessary to assure comparability and validity within the scope of the test.

The Advertising Research Foundation has published guidelines for the public use of research. Although the purpose was to provide an aid to the evaluation of the validity and reliability of research results and of the weight to be given to them in public use, a relatively easy modification of these guidelines is useful when approaching new product screening. Thus, this excellent document has been adopted for the purposes of this chapter.

The approach is both realistic and pragmatic. According to ARF:

Few absolute standards of quality ever apply to market and opinion research. Decisions about what to do and how many cases to study, and what words to use to communicate what meaning are often pragmatic and, on occasion, somewhat arbitrary. The realities of the field make compromise inevitable and perfection impossible. Nonetheless . . . it is essential that [research] be fairly and competently conducted and that it be honestly reported.

The ARF guidelines group the relevant factors into seven areas of evaluation:

- **Origin**—What is behind the research
- **Design**—The concept and the plan
- **Execution**—Collecting and handling the information
- **Stability**—Sample size and reliability
- **Applicability**—Generalizing the findings
- **Meaning**—Interpretations and conclusions
- **Candor**—Open reporting and disclosure

Although much of this is just common sense, it is surprising how often these disciplines are overlooked. Therefore, it is useful to emphasize that those who do the research and those who sponsor and design it should acknowledge responsibility for it and, when the research is reported, should say whether they concur with the findings presented.

Likewise, research should be designed to produce fair measurements and honest information. It should not try to mislead its users. It should not pretend to an objectivity or a significance it does not merit. In planning, the time, money, and skills to be invested in the research should be balanced against the impact of the expected information. Important decisions ought not to be based on poorly conceived and grossly inadequate studies, nor should great efforts be invested to produce trivial data. After all, the integrity and value of research depends on the competence and honesty with which information is collected and processed. Care in performing these functions determines, in large measure, how good the data finally are.

Here, then, are the key questions and quality checkpoints essential to each step in new products screening (as adapted from the ARF work).

Origin—What Is Behind the Research

Key Questions

Is there a statement of the purpose of the research that says clearly what it was meant to accomplish?

Are the suppliers or company departments/individuals identified as responsible for conducting the research?

Quality Checkpoints

Is there a statement by the sponsors acknowledging their acceptance of the research and its reported findings?

Is there a statement from the responsible researchers of their concurrence with the reported findings?

Are the problems to which the research is directed distinguished (in a clear statement) from other related or broader problems that the research was not designed to address?

Is the present use of research the use for which it was designed?

Design—The Concept and the Plan

Key Questions

Is there a full description, in nontechnical language, of the research design, including a definition of what is being measured and how the data are collected?

Is the design consistent with the stated purpose for which the research was conducted?

Is the design even-handed, that is, is it free of leading questions and other bias; does it address questions of fact and opinion without inducing answers that unfairly benefit the study sponsors?

Have precautions been taken to avoid or to equalize patterns of sequence or timing or other factors that might prejudice or distort findings?

Does it address questions that respondents are capable of answering?

Is there a precise statement of the universe or population the research is meant to represent?

Does the sampling source or frame fairly represent the population under study?

Does the report specify the kind of sample used, and clearly describe the method of sample selection?

Does the report describe the plan for analysis of the data?

Are copies of all questionnaire forms, field and sampling instructions, and other study materials available to anyone with a legitimate interest in the research?

Quality Checkpoints

Does the study use a random sample—that is, one that gives every member of the sampling frame an equal or known chance of selection?

Does the research use procedures for the selection of respondents that are not subject to the orientation or convenience of the interviewers?

If the research calls for continuing panels or repeated studies, are there unbiased ways to update or rotate the original sample?

In field use, would the questionnaire hold the interest and attention of the respondents and the interviewer?

Is the information requested limited to what people can supply and can reasonably be expected to give openly and accurately?

Are study or test conditions or responses relevant to the situation to which the findings are supposed to relate?

Where controls or other products are involved, are they the appropriate ones to be included?

Was the plan for analysis set up and agreed to before the data were collected?

Execution—Collecting and Handling the Information

Key Questions

Does the report specify the proportion of the designated sample from which information was collected and processed, or say the proportion cannot be determined?

Is there an objective report on the care with which the data were collected?

Were those who collected data kept free of clues to the study sponsorship or the expected responses, or other leads or information that might condition or bias the information they obtained and recorded?

Quality Checkpoints

Are the coding rules and procedures available for review?

If the data are weighted, is the range of the weights reported?

Is the basis for the weights described and evaluated?

Is the effect of the weights on the reliability of the final estimates reported?

Were there persistent efforts, through carefully scheduled call-backs, to interview designated respondents?

Is the rate of sample completion calculated on the basis of the total designated sample (including all eligible respondents, whether or not a contact was made or attempted)?

Were objective tests made to determine how completing the balance of the sample would have changed the results?

Does the report discuss any substitutions made for any parts of the selected sample, either in the field or when the sample was designed and drawn, or state that there were no substitutions?

Are problems that were encountered in the course of the data collection reported?

Were the interviewers carefully selected, trained, supervised, and paid enough to insure their positive attitude and cooperation?

Were the interviewers compensated on the basis of hours worked rather than on the basis of the amount of work completed?

If the research was part of a continuing design, was the identity of respondents, interviewers, and sampling locations protected to avoid possible manipulation of reported behavior or other contamination of future findings?

Was data gathering limited to what was reported first-hand by respondents or observed directly in the field?

Were there confidential validation checks of the field sampling and the data gathering by unbiased independent researchers with no financial stake in a positive validation?

Does the report give specific information on the result of the field validations?

Does the report give a full explanation of any unplanned or uncommon mathematical manipulation of the collected data?

To the extent that it can be checked, did the data processing preserve the meaning and integrity of the collected information?

Were the research operations opened to objective professional inspection, with full disclosure of the results of each inspection?

Stability—Sample Size and Reliability

Key Questions

Was the sample large enough to provide stable findings?

Are sampling error limits shown if they can be computed?

Are methods of calculating the sampling error described, or if the error cannot be computed, is this stated and explained?

Does the treatment of sampling error limits make clear that they do not cover nonsampling error?

For the major findings, are the reported error tolerances based on direct analysis of the variability of the collected data?

Quality Checkpoints

Is the sample's reliability discussed in language that can be clearly understood without a technical knowledge of statistics?

Is the unweighted sample size reported both for the sample as a whole and for each subgroup for which data are analyzed?

If findings are reported for small numbers of respondents, are appropriate restrictions brought to the attention of the users of the research?

In balancing disproportionate sampling, were reasonable limits placed on the weights assigned to individual cases?

Applicability—Generalizing the Findings

Key Questions

Does the report specify when the data were collected?

Does the report say clearly whether its findings do or do not apply beyond the direct source of the data?

Is it clear who is underrepresented by the research, or not represented at all?

If the research has limited application, is there a statement covering who or what it represents, and the times or conditions under which it applies?

Quality Checkpoints

If the information comes from sources that are easy to contact or specially interested in the subject, is it noted that this information may not be typical of other parts of the population?

Does the report comment on the presence or absence of any exceptional events that might be reflected in the reported data, noting, for example, any audience and circulation drives, brand deals, publicity and promotion, and other transient factors that could affect the results?

Meaning—Interpretations and Conclusions

Key Questions

Are the measurements described in simple and direct language?

Does it make logical sense to use such measurements for the purpose to which they are being put?

Are the actual findings clearly differentiated from the interpretation of the findings?

Has rigorous objectivity and sound judgment been exercised in interpreting research findings as evidence of causation or as predictive of future behavior?

Quality Checkpoints

Is there an effort to make explicit any important assumptions that must be made in drawing conclusions from the research?

Does the report treat realistically people's ability to give valid or unbiased or quantitative responses?

Does the report specifically qualify any data that depend on the respondents' memories over time or their ability to predict future behavior?

Are the effects of the data-gathering instruments and methods made clear?

Candor—Open Reporting and Disclosure

Key Questions

Is there full and forthright disclosure of how research was done?

Have all of the relevant findings been released, including any information potentially unfavorable to the sponsor or embarrassing to the responsible researcher?

Has the research been fairly presented?

Quality Checkpoints

Are all definitions, classification rules, coding procedures, weights, and terminology explained in clear and unambiguous language?

Are the records of the research preserved, and with proper safeguards to the privacy of respondents, and are they available to answer responsible inquiries about the collected data?

Is the presentation free of bias, exaggeration, and graphic or other distortions?

Is there a statement on the limitations of the research and possible misinterpretations of the findings?

Preliminary Screening Steps

With the rules of the game in mind, you can proceed to the execution of the preliminary screening steps. Most often, these involve:

1. Concept exploration
2. Concept testing
3. Positioning testing (which could include name, package graphics, and, possibly, price elasticity testing)
4. Theme testing (to determine the most evocative trigger of buying reaction)

To generate the screening numbers, most product screening tests in the food products field, for example, are done in malls (68 percent), in contrast to in-home interviews (49 percent) or telephone interviews (39 percent). The mail panel and the group interview are not used as often, according to a study conducted in April, 1981, by Market Facts Inc. The shopping mall interview, where shoppers are intercepted for interviewing, represents the major budget area for more than 50 percent of the 142 largest consumer goods companies studied by Market Facts Inc. The growth in this area has been 40 percent in three years. The next most popular approach is the WATS telephone interview, with two out of five companies reporting it as a major spending area. In many areas, face-to-face interviewing is required—because concrete visualization is necessary for evaluation.

Concept Exploration

Qualitative research is most often employed to explore prospect/consumer reaction to concepts, consumer language, and identification of potential target market(s). Frequently, stimulus material takes the shape of concept cards or posters with rough art renderings of alternative product prototypes (developed prior to actual model making, in many cases). Focus groups and one-on-one interviews are usually employed. In certain areas of new product interest, so-called "depth interviews" plumb the implications and psychological triggers behind reactions.

In both types of interactive research, interview guides allow both a free-ranging exploration of respondent interest and a programmed coverage of specific sponsor queries.

As discussed in the preceding chapter on ideaforms, a verbal description may get one score, but its concrete further explication through an illustration may change the perceptions. An actual example is shown in Figure 16-1. This chart shows interest levels for nine of the many concepts studied. Concepts were screened through a series of monadic interviews, then the results were arranged according to the key issues in purchase and repeat use intent. Note how the perceptions changed in various instances after an illustration of the concept product was shown (bottom line)—over-all initial interest went down in one instance (concept P) and up in others. Other evaluations also changed.

Concept Testing

Quantitative testing is used to rank each concept's potential against the others being considered and to provide a rough guideline volume estimate. Several systems generally in use by consumer package goods marketers include:

Mail panel of matched members, who receive concept descriptions and drawings. Each respondent household receives only one concept. Measurement of intent to try the product and intended frequency of buying are the key data of the analysis. The sample size is determined by the dimension of the target market.

Mall or In-Store Intercept, random interviews against predetermined cells. Comprehensive ad-like posters to convey the reality of the concepts are often used to stimulate more dependable reactions from respondents who are in a shopping mode and location. Wide-ranging concepts may be shown to individual respondents. Subtle-difference concepts are used monadically. The resulting intent to buy is scaled numerically.

Figure 16-1
Concept Screening

CONCEPT SCREENING

	HIGH GROUP			MEDIUM GROUP			LOW GROUP		
Composite Rank	1	2	3	11	12	13	20	21	22
1. Concept	Q	A	D	B	T	P	O	U	M
2. Interest and involvement									
a. Overall initial interest	H	H	H	M	M	M	L	L	L
b. Immediacy of perceived purchase	H	H	H	M	M	L	L	L	L
3. Perceived user	F	C/W	C/G	C/G/W	F/G	F	C	C	C
4. Replacement of current product	PRODUCT R	PRODUCT F	PRODUCT Z	PRODUCT B	PRODUCT G	PRODUCT A	PRODUCT L	PRODUCT Y	PRODUCT U
a. Current product replaced									
b. Frequency of use of current	H	H	M	L	M	M	L	H	L
c. Quality of new vs. current	H	H	H	M	L	L	L	L	L
d. Frequency of replacement by new	H	H	H	M	M	L	L	L	L
e. Willingness to pay more than for current	H	M	H	M	L	H	L	L	L
5. Effect of picture	H	H	H	M	M	L	M	L	L

Code: F: Family, G: Gatekeeper (purchaser, but not user), C: Child, W: Woman. (All interviewees were female in this sample.) H: High, M: Medium, L: Low interest levels. Current Product Replaced Summary indicates most frequent product which would be replaced by concept product. (By permission, Pilot Products Incorporated)

Various research suppliers offer proprietary techniques to determine trial and repeat buying intentions from simple descriptions and drawings. Prominent among them are BASES, a pretest market volume estimate technique offered by Burke Marketing Research Inc., employing in-store intercept sampling, with measures on a five-point intent-to-buy scale. Another is E.S.P. (Estimating Sales Potential), offered by NPD Research and designed to project trial, repeat, and volume purchases of new products.

Positioning Testing

This is quantitative testing to help determine which positioning maximizes the impact of the concept. Depending on the nature of the product concept and the primary communications medium of the category, stimulus material may be a mock-up print ad or a live-action presenter or a voice-over still photo presentation on a videotape monitor. With the rapid development of interactive cable television, discrete cable channels, and interactive telephone interviewing, all recognizing the preconditioning of respondents to the medium, more testing is using techniques related to the pervasive electronic medium.

Matched samples of consumers with predetermined purchase patterns are sometimes used on the assumption that the interaction with the new concept-stimulus material represents a universal set; e.g., a 25-year-old middle-income homemaker mother of two children, married to a professional, and a loyal consumer of Twinkies, if geographically dispersed throughout the set, will be representative of similar Twinkie consumers in reaction to each concept position. The incidence of sample stimulus material exposure is equalized against each respondent segment.

Name Testing

Name testing—whether brand name or generic, but most often the former—is approached in different manners, depending on the category. A popular, yet somewhat superficial, method utilizes card sorting. The respondent simply goes through a series of card sorts until a rank order from most to least preferred evolves. An "appropriateness" scale is sometimes also used. Testing of alternative names is best done monadically among a competitive array to allow for measurement of interaction or confusion of the test name vis-a-vis competition.

Competitive Shelf Tests

Competitive shelf tests involve separate panels of respondents evaluating one name or packaging variable within the context of a competitive shelf display. For example, a new name for a Twinkie analog might be monadically tested in the context of a shelf display mock-up containing other current Twinkie analogs, as well as the best known Twinkie competitors. Also employed in shelf testing are eye cameras and similar devices that measure attention and pupil dilation. This purports to document the attention dynamics of the package being tested and its ability to break through the cluttered in-store environment.

Theme Testing

Whereas a "position" is relative to something else (a position has a "location," in the competitive environment, life-style, and/or needs of the prospect), a "theme" is a simple, memorable, attention-getting expression of the new offering's appeal. Occasionally, theme testing is part of new product exploration at this early screening phase. It is most likely to be so in cases where the product differential is little or lacking and the positioning is highly preemptible. In such cases, the "theme" must carry a great burden in the decision to move forward with the new product concept. Techniques employed are similar to the concept sorting techniques, but more likely represent finished advertising language. Whenever possible, it is recommended that theme testing be delayed until a reasonably accurate and differentiating product prototype, with a preemptive position, has been determined.

A Step Forward

Every company works at establishing data norms or, at least, cut-off classifications. Often numbers without meaning in themselves take on credibility through history. By interpolation, X percent of interest in category Y is a better score than the same X percent in category Z, assuming market intelligence about each category is sufficient. According to Market Facts Inc., new product data norms for concept and product success are not universal. About one-fourth of the companies surveyed by Market Facts have established norms, and another one-half have partially established norms. There is obviously a strong need for continuing development in this area.

So far, the risks we have discussed have been within the constraints of a modest investigative budget. A few mistakes won't break the company. What we don't know perhaps won't hurt us—so the concepts that have fallen through the screen are still lying somewhere to be visited another day, possibly by the same company but with new champions or changing market dynamics such as demographics (baby boom) or economics (energy shortage/recession). Meanwhile, some concepts have survived the process—and they must be brought closer to reality.

Section 4
Summary Afterword

Conception is the innoculation of a germ of an idea, giving it sufficient shape to recognize its possible potential. To begin, input is required—something must come from something. With input, ideation is spawned. With ideas, forms become concrete. With concrete ideaforms, the selection process begins.

Matters are specific enough now that a decision can be made to carry forward—or to abandon. In new product generation, the abandonment step is as much a contribution to progress as a blind move forward with all entries. In fact, the act of abandonment liberates time and money to fund the future evaluation of the more promising concepts.

Input can come from many sources. Among them are the following:

- Problems (as input)
- By-products
- Manufacturing process
- Contract packers
- Associated trades
- Inventors and patents
- Licensing
- Men and machines
- Trade schools
- Other trades (parallel ones)
- Other places (beyond business boundaries)
- Getting away from headquarters

- Listening
- Research—R&D and marketing
- Gurus and geniuses

Once you have the input, then it is time to germinate the ideas. We have looked at a number of ways of doing this, including the following:

- Collecting, absorbing, fantasizing
- Lateral thinking
- Rearranging information
- Seeing the obvious
- Seeing the category differently
- Making the product better
- Making the first product of its kind
- Thinking outside-in
- Using peer groups
- Using the Delphi method
- Creating an ideation incentive program
- Learning from consumer mail
- Brainstorming
- Using the Synectics approach
- Role playing
- Roll playing
- Trying the ivory tower approach
- Studying the competitive set
- Using personification
- Learning from self-identification
- Moving from the ridiculous to the sublime
- List making
- Finding an equity
- Determining what and where
- Deciding there will be no holds barred

As ideas become more concrete, we move into more specific ideaforms. Ideaforms have two basic parts: the business term description and prospect communications. Communicating the idea involves several factors. First is writing the ideaform. Then comes concept statement preparation. This must provide product differentiation, some sell (but no ads at this point), and a discussion of the pricing issue. You must know the language territory and be able to provide concept illustrations, if needed.

There are a number of ways to prescreen the idea, before the research stage. They involve identifying the organizing concept, making use of a judgment grid or gap analysis, utilizing outsiders who are insiders (consultants), or depending on the "champion" or experience to do the screening.

Screening research gets more precise. Basic forecasting techniques include qualitative methods (Delphi, market research, panel consensus, visionary forecasting, historical analogy); time series analysis and projection (trend projections); and more casual methods (life-cycle analysis). The process involves learning as much as testing.

Research guidelines include the following:

- Origin
- Design
- Execution
- Stability
- Applicability
- Meaning
- Candor

Under each of these guidelines should be listed the key questions to be considered and quality checkpoints.

Preliminary screening steps include concept exploration, concept testing (through mail panels or mall or in-store intercepts), positioning testing, name testing, shelf testing of the package, and theme testing.

And then one is ready for the next step forward.

Modeling

17

The Product as Communication

Inventing is a combination of brains and materials. The more brains you use, the less materials you need.
—*Charles F. Kettering*

A bad beginning makes a bad ending.
—*Euripedes*

Each product or service is a communication in itself. Although most evolve their personalities over time, some are predestined. Most do not deliver a clear image at the beginning—or ever. Some sharply stand for something from the day of birth—and are carefully nurtured throughout their histories.

The greatest successes know where they are going. Their creators had specific intentions—models—in mind. They worked to assure that the models fit their marketing motivations, that the finished products and their communications enforced those purposeful visions.

Although there are ephemeral categories—the beauty/fashion trades, games and toys, entertainment industry fads come to mind—the most successful of even these have an integral consistency of personality during their brief lifespans.

Model-making is key in the creation of new products. Just as certainly as a blueprint can be laid down for an office building or a libretto, so too can the guidelines for modeling.

Upfront thinking and planning; trial and error; experimentation and screening; user input—all are important to the process.

Family Model

Often a new product has a name before it is born. It is of the IBM or Revlon heritage. If it carries the family name, it must surely appear to be a legitimate progeny. A well-defined corporate or brand image helps set the modeling guidelines. Inappropriate, out-of-focus product dress may mask appropriate function, and lead to failed acceptance.

Most often, a new product is not pioneering a category. It is joining it, with a difference. Therefore, it must encompass the generic descriptor common to the category—but with a distinguishing difference, e.g., not cleansing creme, but deep cleaning lotion; not Arpege dusting powder, but Powdered Arpege for After Bath; not soap with cocoa butter, but bath soap with cocoa butter conditioners. Communicate the class, the difference from others in the class, and, where possible, the benefit.

Preliminary brand name development is a modeling step. Hundreds are generated for screening (including legal screening). Prospects may include in-house brands, as well as newly created brands. They should be appropriate to enforcing the generic descriptor, clearly set apart from competition, and stated in one or a few words, difficult to mispronounce—yet memorable. This distinction and an original graphic appearance will aid in securing the trademark.

Brand Name Bank

Many companies make it a practice to build a brand name bank of their own. Whenever a likely brand name is developed for a category of interest to the company—even if there is no current work underway in the category by the company—steps are taken to register the brand. Labels are printed and affixed to proper product classification lots of lab, pilot plant, or contract maker product. These are sold (in limited quantities) in interstate commerce—sometimes with a minimal direct response advertising support to assure retail transactions but usually simply by providing "guaranteed sale" merchandise at attractive prices to trade channels. Notice is given on the package (TM) that the trademark has been applied for—which is done, leading to a registration®, unless opposed. If opposed, attorneys often work out satisfactory arrangements with the contending party (who was not revealed in the preliminary trademark search). In categories where branding is an important aspect of communication success (package goods), the practice is helpful in protecting the future interests of the company—both offensively (for new products) and defensively (to block competition).

Category Model

Often an entry category sets the tone. Naturalistic product lines that leverage wholesome root values should not veer far from the path of tradition, whereas contemporary cool may be the only design for disc drive.

And, so, form before function—at least conceptually—is often the modeling creed on which a clear marketing communication personality is built.

Trial Parts

Modeling is necessary for function, as well.

Are the knobs big enough and far enough apart for the hands that will twist controls? Don't theorize. Model. Let those hands give them a whirl—*before* expensive working prototypes are built.

Model Instructions

Are the cooking instructions clear and easy-to-follow, and do they have a wide latitude of tolerance? Have the uninitiated try them out before putting the mix into the package and before printing the package. The results may require changes in the recipe formula or the instructions, or both.

Model in Use

Does the toy have play value that will keep youngsters occupied for sustained periods? Will it withstand constant usage punishment? Is it psychologically fitting? Observe a model in use by hidden camera or two-way mirror—and, if needed, with a child psychologist as an expert witness. The results will yield adjustments that may optimize success.

Manual and Model Matching

Does the owner manual match the machine? A model and its manual under use conditions may lead to better illustrations, more (or less) detailed instructions—or even a revision in the machine.

Scale Models

Often, the difference between a functional model and a bench prototype is small—and it is possible for pilot plants to reproduce sufficient quantities for user tests under varying conditions.

But not always.

Full-size models are often uneconomic in the developmental phases. A scale model may simulate the performance characteristics sufficiently well to project to the dimensions of the proposed working prototype. Sometimes, the need is only for cosmetic observation—do the angles balance, do the color breaks clearly relate to use progression or importance, does the overall appearance seem appropriate to the tasks to be performed—or the promise to be delivered? Architectural models are common examples. A mural artist's sketch provides much the same effect. Another example is the wind-tunnel model used in the automotive field—where shape and not material is key, and where velocity of wind drag is computable to the dimension of the model. Figure 17-1 shows some very literal prototype models, and Figure 17-2 shows prototypes of a fruit syrup.

Figure 17-1a & b
Prototype Models

Very literal prototype models used in a sound-and-slide presentation which conveys brand, benefit, position and package in finished format. Target prospect feedback from these exhibits provides direction for fine-tuning of well accepted models.

Figure 17-1c & d
Prototype Models

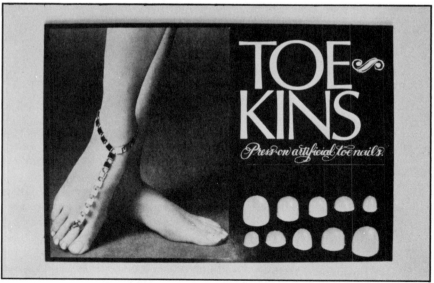

Figure 17-2a & b
Fruit Syrup

Finished prototypes of a true fruit syrup dispensed from a push-button can were used for appeal study prior to home placement of the actual product.

Competitive Environment

> New products live or die by what makes them different. The fact that they are new isn't enough. If it's a me-too version of someone else's innovation, the developer shouldn't concentrate on improving on the competitor's model.

So wrote Robert Cooper, associate dean, faculty of management, McGill University, in *Management Digest*, September 1981.

There are real differences and there are perceptual differences. If the real differences aren't perceived, they are handicapped. If minor, insignificant, or cosmetic differences are perceived as advantageous, they provide a competitive edge.

In either case, it is essential that the differences be perceived. Modeling provides a mode for observation—the means by which the new entity can be seen in its natural end-use environment and (if applicable) in its competitive environment.

In fact, sometimes to be new and different can be more critical than being new and better—if the "better" doesn't show. (In the early years of the foreign car craze, this was the lament of U.S. auto makers.)

Figure 17-2c & d
Fruit Syrup

Modeling is also necessary to understand—and adapt to—the secondary communications, those visual and audio signals that are not product or service themselves: brochures, ads, packages; electronic sounds and visions carried by signage, video, and radio. A well-designed product that does not reproduce well in the pervasive media most common to its marketplace competes under a weighty handicap.

Modeling is necessary to gain a feel for the tactile and a sense of the visual psychology of the product. Certain textures and certain colors send certain signals—not always evident in the planning, blueprint, and elevation sketch phases. The heft and the "hand," the shape and the surround, the color and the contrast—all play a role in product perception—hence the importance of modeling.

Package Model

For many products, the package is the product symbol. It fights for attention on the shelf—in the store, at home in the cupboard, and (sometimes) on public display in the home, such as the perfume bottle, the fire extinguisher, the facial tissue box, the bathroom deodorizer, and the matchbook. Whether it is to make its statement in the store or in use, or both, its model evaluation is a critical early step. Often, the package plays an operational role as well, with a pour spout that readily pops out or a child-proof cap or a push-up applicator stick or a spray-adjustable aerosol. These must be both visually and functionally tested in the modeling phase. Where possible, the modeling test should advance to the phase where final brand and descriptor candidates are in-place on the model in the test—including all of the mandatory legal copy. Often, this affects the final choice. What appeared to be a preferred model in an unadorned state often fails as a final candidate when suitably decorated. Figure 17-3 shows different packaging options for an instant bacon product.

Communications Environment

As surely as the product is a communication, a communication is the product. They are inextricably part and parcel. To study one without the other is to ignore the gestalt of reality.

For this reason, not only must the product fit into the user's mode—it must also fit into the user's information system, the communications that alert and inform.

Whereas a "blind test" of purposely masked competitors may reveal the reality of performance differences, an open-eyed comparison will reveal *different realities*—realities more often true of the marketplace, despite what may be learned in the lab.

Model communication themes are developed and sorted within the context of the model product, with brief benefit descriptions in the context of single major appeals—the differences being a matter of emphasis, nature, and degree of support information. The goal is the development of major selling themes. (See Figure 17-4.)

For this reason, new product developers use communication models. To take the most complicated and expensive example, television, they use analogs of finished commercials to help sort out the most effective communications. (See Figure 17-5.) Sometimes these "commercials" do not include advertising themes, time constraints, or any of the conventions of promotion. The familiar format of television, with its third party authority and cool separateness, is used to exhibit or to demonstrate the model and its promise. Often this is done in an episodic format, so that changeable modules can be inserted to determine changes in viewer-prospect reactions—and to help perfect the model, as well as provide a basis for advertising claims. Then, the models may be used in controlled tests of "model" commercials. The most primitive ones are drawn storyboards on videotape, with sound tracks (animatics). More advanced is still photography with tracks (photomatics). Beyond this are live-action sound on tape or film, but without sophisticated special effects, full orchestration, etc.

Figure 17-3a
New Instant Bacon Prototype

New Instant Bacon could be packaged to reheat in oven or on range, on range only, or in a toaster. Prototype model photographs with descriptive copy helped sort out most appealing options. After successful test market, manufacturing difficulties aborted the project.

Figure 17-3b
New Instant Bacon Prototype

Now pops-up a great new idea—the bacon that you crisp in your toaster. It's easy as toast, and just as fast. Handy toaster packet crisps four lean slices at a time.

In 90 seconds, delicious, hickory-sweet bacon's on your plate—with no mess to clean up, ever. (You throw away the grease with the empty packet.)

The bacon is pre-cooked for you—your toaster does the crisping. (Five packets to a carton).

Figure 17-3c
New Instant Bacon Prototype

Bacon made easy, <u>any</u> way—bakes, broils or fries to crispness in less than three minutes. Here's lean, meaty bacon in a convenient cook-pak—new no mess, no grease, no spatter form. Just zip open new cook-pak and set in oven or broiler —or on top of the burner. In ⅓ the cooking time, crisp, crunchy sweet-smoked bacon's ready to serve. No pan to clean, no soiled oven or broiler. Saves you cooking time, clean-up time. Leaves just the eatin' for you.

(6 slices to a cook-pak, 3 cook-paks to a carton.)

Figure 17-4a & b
Hair Color Appeals

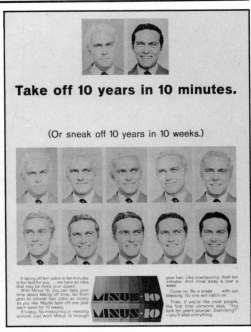

The youth craze spawned a lot of interest in hair coloring for men. These four appeals in finished print advertisement format, as well as those of the competitors, were tested.

Similarly, tipped-in editorial features with model photographs are used as a stimulus. This presents the new product in the appropriate editorial environment. At another stage, when the model is perfected and the appeal tightly identified, comprehensive advertising layouts are tipped in—to help sort out those with the greatest executional appeal.

Model Result

Throughout this process, changes have been made in the models, both of the new product and of its secondary (media) communications. From this is obtained guidance for developing the prototypes that can confidently compete in the reality of the marketplace.

With modeling, the goal has been to develop both the product and the communication prototypes in a compatible system, hopefully synergistically superior within the competitive set in appealing to the target prospect.

Figure 17-4c & d
Hair Color Appeals

Figure 17-5a & b
Preparing a Prototype Commercial

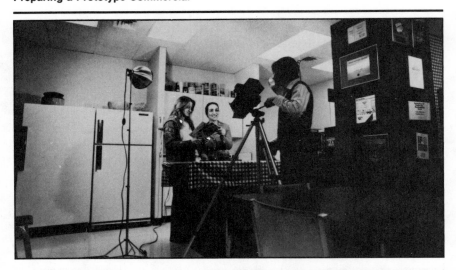

Putting together a new product prototype commercial for use in on-air research. Top: Agency's foodservice kitchen prepares finished product close-up shot. Bottom: Original music track recorded in agency studio. (See opposite page.) Top: Lighting rehearsal on location. Bottom: In-house final edit puts together all scenes, separately recorded tracks, optical effects for test of introductory television commercial. Internal production of all elements of new products research materials helps maintain critical confidentiality prior to in-market use.

Source: Campbell-Mithun, Inc.

Figure 17-5c & d
Preparing a Prototype Commercial

18

Research Guidelines

Numbers keep order.
—*George Katona*

Order is a lovely thing.
—*Anna Branch*

It takes two to speak the truth—one to speak and another to hear.
—*Thoreau*

Report to me and my cause aright.
—*Shakespeare*

It seems so obvious, but it cannot be repeated too often: The research must fit the knowledge goal. Therefore, the stimulus and the method must yield actable results related to the true need. Unfortunately, the new product development success record is frequently marred by inappropriate research yielding misdirection. The life cycle, the usage pattern, the degree of consideration, the seasonal attractiveness—these are but a few of the factors that may influence the success of a product more importantly than those attention and performance measures characteristic of most syndicated and proprietary research dedicated to building supplier or corporate norms.

Each new product—even a simple line extension—presents a new problem for research. If it doesn't differ to that degree, then it is likely not justifiable as a market entrant.

Therefore, start with the question:

"What do we want to find out?"

Not:

"What kind of research do we want to do?"

Nor necessarily with the decision:

"It is Phase I—so put this in our standard Phase I test."

Although there are many excellent syndicated proprietary techniques, it is often necessary to custom design research to yield the specific knowledge you need. Often, critical research is demanded in the model development phase. The most valuable part of this step is defining the knowledge sought. Professional researchers then have little difficulty in recommending an existing program or devising a new design and procedure.

Videotaped Demonstrations

When developing new products where the cost of the prototype is high and building several by hand for research purposes is prohibitive, the greatest boon to the researcher is videotape.

A high-ticket, mechanical new product prototype can be tested virtually anywhere among any target audience merely by videotaping the product demonstration. It's not hands-on—but it's next closest.

The Campbell-Mithun advertising agency has done this for Gates Battery, Toro (articulated-frame riding mower), and the toy division of General Mills (producing videotape demonstrations of 15 different toys ranging from slotless race car sets to board games).

When absolutely necessary, a nonoperative mock-up of the prototype can be made inexpensively to give respondents a more intimate feel for the size, proportions, design, and some of the features. (See Figure 18-1.)

Use-Trial Diary Panel

Where a new product requires some fairly concerted effort on the part of the user or where a slight oversight or mistake can cause user complaints, dissatisfaction, and disaster, there is a simple technique that can be used to avoid in-market failure.

An example: A consulting home economist for a food products company had developed what looked like a very complex bread recipe—one that eliminated the need to dissolve yeast in hot water before adding it to the other dry ingredients.

To confirm at-home success, several groups of novice breadmakers were recruited, given the recipes and $5 for ingredients—then turned loose in their own home kitchens. Each was also asked to complete a "diary" containing 25 questions to be answered at various points during the total baking experience. The diary invited them to jot down opinions, suggestions, points of confusion, and interpretation difficulties, as well as logistical information such as where the dough was placed in the kitchen to rise, total rising time, total kneading time, etc.

The homemakers then reconvened in groups, bringing their diaries *and* sample loaves of the end product. The recipe was discussed and comparisons made of the size, color, texture, and flavor of the baked bread.

From this, an absolutely fail-proof recipe was written, with several of the homemakers' suggestions incorporated.

Figure 18-1a
Product Development

Product development in Industrial Design Department of Honeywell, Inc. includes scale models, which reveal relationships between elements, colors, surface finish, proportion, and accessibility. (From left, Martin Gierke, Staff Designer, Tom Wolfe, Manager of Industrial Design, and Jim Odom, Staff Designer).

Source: Honeywell, Inc.

Figure 18-1b
Product Development

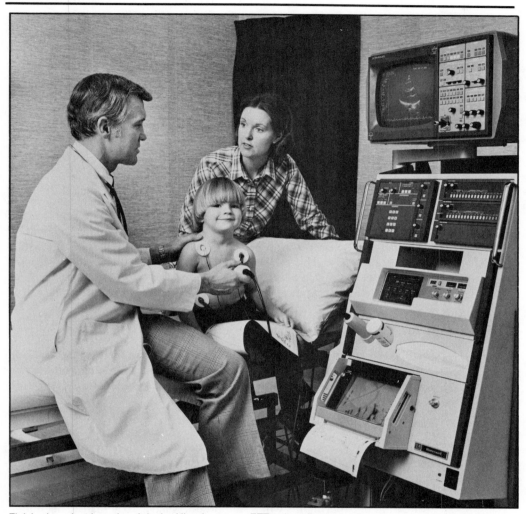

Finished product in action. It is the Ultra Imager, a FFT pulsed Doppler, 2D real time and M-mode all in one integrated system. It reliably and noninvasively obtains clinically significant information on blood flow and turbulence pattern within the heart and great vessels.

The food manufacturer learned, in this case, that the consulting home economist's kitchen is one thing, but that the kitchens of America are something else—that oven temperatures are not always perfectly accurate, that the temperature of "hot tap water" varies from home to home, etc.

This type of "diary research" is relatively inexpensive and can help a new product marketer avoid what otherwise might be a tarnished new product introduction. The technique is applicable to any recipe, assembly instructions, installation directions, complex "mix" products, or in designing electric or petroleum-powered products requiring periodic cleaning and/or maintenance.

Unobserved Observation

Sometimes it is necessary to peek-with-permission.

An understanding of the operational aspects of a competitive game—or of the reactions to a highly private personal care product—can be aided by two-way mirrors or videocamera monitor and/or taping. Respondents are told that expert professionals will observe their use and/or reactions, but will not participate or be present. Shortly after beginning, respondents drop play-acting inhibitions and become involved in the subject at hand. The play value of toys, comprehension of computer-screen instructions, simple use of tools, and creative crafts, all have been evaluated effectively in this mode.

Conventional, Projectable Methods

We looked at guidelines for an approach to conventional, numerical, and judgmental methods in Chapter 15. The Advertising Research Foundation's approach is applicable to model research as well as to ideaforms.

Blind Tests

As previously stated, these are recommended for laboratory (R&D) and engineering (R&E) guidance. However, they are not satisfactory for determining market preference. Even two unknown (invented for the purposes of research) brand names and/or generic descriptors can influence performance evaluation in experiments where the products have, in actuality, been identical. When a well-known brand with appropriate equity to the product being evaluated is put on an identical product to *test against* another with no brand or a less appropriate brand name, the perception of performance characteristics will differ. In certain cases, such a test method may be devised to determine appropriate brand names. Does the peanut butter taste fresher, spread easier, and smell more like real peanuts if it's named A, rather than B? Is the taste sensation better if the generic is "crunchy" or "chunky"? A mere word may make a difference.

As an example, when identical margarines were compared in side-by-side, in-home usage, one bearing a leading margarine brand name and the other with a leading butter brand name, the famous butter branded margarine product won on all counts: color, spreadability, taste, frying, etc.

Usage Tests

The farther the model testing moves from controlled environments to reality, the more likely it is that the results will translate into market predictability, assuming unanticipated variables do not intervene.

In-home or in-office or in-factory usage tests are superior to central location trials. If a sales impulse can move the product into its usage environment, this is even better.

Simulating Sales Response

There are many systems and services that offer methods that simulate sales responses when products are in early developmental phases. Perhaps only a limited quantity of prototypical bench samples and a variety of sales appeal statements are available. Perhaps the product and communications model-making is further advanced. Here are some typical approaches used in the packaged goods field, several of which are theoretically adaptable to other categories.

A prototype selling statement and package (no product)

Concepts are sorted on a relative basis to determine which will stimulate highest trial. Respondents are exposed to renderings of the proposition (a poster and a package, for example), which includes price. Each respondent is given the opportunity to buy the product (possibly, to be received at a later time—or, possibly, to be received as a substitute and a small gift for participating in the study) and to indicate a repeat intention or rate of purchase, based on the sketchy stimulus. Although this method is commonly employed in shopping situations, it is also applicable to interactive cable and mail techniques.

Small quantity of packaged product and print ad

The actual packaged product is sold against the proposition in a comprehensive print ad to help determine the rate of purchase—trial, repeat sales, and, subsequent to use, how the selling theme and/or formulation may be improved to increase product appeal. Occasionally, this approach is executed in shopping areas using videotape communications for stimulus, in a van or bus or mall location. The method is also applicable to cable, where viewers are given a telephone number to use in calling in orders or (on interactive cable) to punch up a home delivery order. Direct response techniques using the mail may also be employed; this is usually used when a broader geographic dispersion of specific psychographic characteristics, using extremely sophisticated sampling cells, is desired.

Pre-test market sales

To answer the question "which presentation of my new product (or which new product) will produce more trial and repeat sales volume?", Frevert & Hall Research Associates Inc., Spring Park, MN, claims to offer the only pretest market service that measures both trial and repeat sales potential by actually selling a new product directly to a nationwide sample of shoppers. The service is called RSVP (*R*elative *S*ales *V*olume *P*otential). RSVP aims to provide direction in evaluating alternative presentations of a new product, i.e., communications or formulations, as well as providing inputs for projecting sales volume.

The procedure involves showing supermarket shoppers the new product's marketing communication, such as a print ad or a commercial. Shoppers are also shown a "New Products Introductions" offer letter with an order blank for the new product. If shoppers decide to buy, they pay the regular retail price for the product at the check-out counter. Triers are thereafter contacted by telephone and repeat orders are accepted throughout the sales period. Buyers also pay the regular retail price for all repeat purchases. (As an option, print advertising may be mailed to triers to further register the sales message throughout the repeat phase).

The study yields regular reports on the percentage of buyers who repeat with each offer, cumulative repeaters, total repeat orders, repeat unit sales—and may also be expanded to determine the reasons underlying the purchase decisions, reactions to product attributes, and product usage information. This information is reported for buyers, repeaters, and nonrepeaters.

Store test

Another possibility is the controlled store test, utilizing only one or several stores. Here the packaged product is put into the appropriate store section, with a realistic share of shelf and display space. Depending on the information needed, various techniques are used. Introductory pricing flags on the package, frequent "store-cast" announcements over the supermarket's speaker system, shelf-talkers, etc., call attention to the product. An in-pack coupon offers a bonus for cooperating purchasers, allowing for callback interviews. For products in categories with high-volume repeat sales, observer/interviewers may intercept purchasers to ask for cooperation and complete the purchase impulse phase of the questioning.

One variation is to intercept recruits in shopping malls. After exposure to the ad, a respondent is led to a controlled store and given several items with incentive money provided, to obtain a purchase effectiveness score.

In other categories, such as home electronic entertainment products, store demonstrators and specially trained factory sales personnel intercept prospective purchasers and ask for relevant comments to obtain a measure of interest and understanding, with special emphasis on how the product is placed in the competitive set regarding features, price, brand, image, etc.

Mathematical Model Research

A number of developing mathematical model research programs have been devised to reduce the risk of new product introductions. Joseph D. Blackburn (Vanderbilt University) and Kevin J. Clancy (Boston University) presented such a concept at the Second ORSA/TIMS Conference on Market Measurement and Analysis (Austin, Texas, March 15, 1980). They stated:

Some firms have turned to a combination of sophisticated test market research integrated with mathematical models of the new product introduction process. The objective is to provide more accurate forecasts of new product market performance and to discern how the product concept or marketing plan should be shaped to maximize the likelihood of success. Several mathematical models, which are designed to use test market data as input, have been developed in recent years. These include NEWS[1], Tracker[2], and Sprinter[3].

Many firms have taken a different approach to this problem, choosing the alternative of relatively inexpensive simulated test markets, such as Yankelovich, Skelly and White Inc.'s Laboratory Test Market (or LTM).[4] Such simulations attempt to compress in time and dollars a test market experience. Some marketing managers use them as a low-risk step prior to a full-scale test market, while others have replaced traditional test markets with their simulated counterparts. Still other firms have adopted systems which combine the simulated test market with a mathematical model. Management Decision System's ASSESSOR[5] is a pioneering example of this approach. LITMUS, a new mathematical model developed in conjunction with Yankelovich's LTM, is another.

LITMUS is an interactive stochastic [educated guess] model designed to forecast, diagnose, and improve the performance of alternative marketing strategies for new package goods either before or after test marketing. Using inputs derived from the new

[1]There have been numerous publications and presentations on the NEWS model, most published by BBDO Inc. and authored by Lewis Pringle, senior vice president of BBDO and director of research services. Among them are "BBDO Technical Report: The Theoretical Basis of NEWS" (1971) and "The News Model: A Technical Description" (No date).

[2]Blattberg, Robert, and John Golanty, "Tracker: An Early Test Market Forecasting and Diagnostic Model for New Product Planning," *Journal of Marketing Research*, May 1978, pp. 192–202.

[3]Urban, Glen L. "Sprinter Mod III: A Model for the Analysis of New Frequently Purchased Consumer Products," *Operations Research*, September–October 1970, pp. 805–853.

[4]This research was funded, in part, by Yankelovich, Skelly and White Inc. who also provided data for the model tests reported later.

[5]Silk, Alvin J., and Glen Urban, "Pretest Market Evaluation of New Packaged Goods: A Model and Measurement Methodology," *Journal of Marketing Research*, May 1978, pp. 171–191.

product's marketing plan, other empirical relationships, and Laboratory Test Market research, LITMUS forecasts brand awareness, trial, current usage, sales, and market share. The model's built-in sensitivity analysis then provides the planner with insights into the likely effects of changes in each strategic and tactical input on key measures of campaign effectiveness, notably sales and market share. In this manner, the reasons underlying the predicted success or failure of the new product launch can be quickly diagnosed and recommendations made which will improve the expected performance of the new product entry.

On the surface, LITMUS appears similar to its predecessors, especially NEWS, Tracker, and ASSESSOR, in terms of its objectives, easy-to-use conversational mode, input parameters, and published evidence of successful forecasting. However, surface similarities can be deceiving, for although LITMUS shares some of the strengths and weaknesses of other models, it has some distinctive features. Two such features are the large number of marketing mix variables and the extensive number of states of nature used to capture the richness and complexity of the new product introduction process.

The heart of LTM is the laboratory test. A cross section of 500 or more potential buyers are invited to a theater (30–35 at a time); the theaters are set up in markets throughout the United States. Following the completion of a brief, self-administered questionnaire (demographic information, as well as marketing), consumers are exposed to a television program in which a commercial for the new brand and competitive products are embedded. Afterwards, consumers are led in small groups to the "store," a store which stocks the brands advertised in the commercial and others which enjoy a significant market share in the testing area. Upon entering the "store" consumers are provided with a fixed amount of money to stimulate purchase. A fraction of the people go on to buy the "test" brand, others do not. This fraction, adjusted by LTM norms, experience, and marketing plan data, leads to an estimate of the probability of brand trial, given awareness.

Some time later (the lag dependent on the product category), consumers are reinterviewed by telephone to gauge their reactions to the product. These data, again adjusted by norms and experience, generate an estimate of first repeat purchase probability. Often, however, a sales wave or extended use test is incorporated in the research design and these data are used to estimate multiple repeat purchase probabilities. All of this information is then used to forecast brand sales and/or market share.

What LTM cannot do easily, however, is to evaluate many plans or assess the individual contribution of many variables in the marketing mix to market share. As the more creative use of media flourishes, for example, there is a growing need by LTM management to forecast the effects of media variables, such GRPs and advertising impact, on new product performance. Hence the interest in coupling the LTM output with a contextual model.

In its current state of development, LITMUS bases its projections on a given marketing plan [variables 1–10 and 19 in Figure 18–2]. However, as an interactive aid to the marketing manager, sensitivity analysis of the relationship between projected sales and specific components of the marketing plan can be carried out to indicate how to improve the plan. The program could be imbedded in an optimization model in which the marketing plan is characterized perhaps by a budget constraint. Then nonlinear search techniques could be employed to determine optimal (or near optimal) levels for each component in the marketing plan by purchase period. Future research will be directed toward this end.

LITMUS is a new product planning model, used in conjunction with LTM, de-

Figure 18-2
Model Inputs

Type	Input	Source
MARKET CHARACTERISTICS	1. Size of potential market (in millions of buyers 2. Number of units per case 3. Size of market (in millions of cases) 4. Estimated number of purchase cycles per year	
MARKETING PLAN CHARACTERISTICS	5. Average cost per 1,000 GRPs 6. Advertising dollars or GRPs per period 7. Average cost per sample dropped 8. Average cost per coupon 9. Percent of market couponed per period 10. Percent of market sampled per period	MARKETING PLAN
	11. Maximum likely brand awareness 12. Attention-getting power of advertising (1.0 = average) 13. Attention-getting power of media (1.0 = average)	COPY AND MEDIA RESEARCH
	14. Probability of remembering brand one period in the absence of additional exposures (1.0 = maximum)	MANAGEMENT JUDGMENT
	15. Probability of brand trial intention given awareness of advertising 16. Probability of brand trial given intention and distribution	LABORATORY TEST MARKET ESTIMATES
	17. Probability of brand trial given coupon 18. Probability of brand trial given sample	EMPIRICAL RELATIONSHIP OR CUSTOM RESEARCH
	19. Distribution per period 20. Trial purchase size (1.0 = average)	MARKETING PLAN
	21. Probability of first repeat purchase in period following trial 22. Probability of second repeat purchase in period following first repeat 23. Repeat purchase size (1.0 = average	LABORATORY TEST MARKET ESTIMATES
	24. Price per standard unit (1.0 = average)	MARKETING PLAN

Source: Yankelovich, Skelly and White Inc., Laboratory Test Market (LTM).

signed to forecast, diagnose, and improve the performance of alternative marketing strategies and tactics for new packaged goods before or after test marketing. Though still in an exploratory stage of development, the model has shown evidence of the kind of construct and predictive validity that might be expected given its "genetic structure" through its "parents" LTM and NEWS.

Testing Communications Models

Now that the product model has been optimized and the selling theme has been identified, advertising and promotion communications models become true prototypes—and methods must be selected to identify the most persuasive sales motivators.

Judgment is not to be cast aside at this critical step. The options for execution are so many and varied that judgment must, of necessity, be exercised. The cost of making test executions and of testing them is so great that further disciplines are needed in the selection of materials. Also, the cost of the media to deliver the messages is so high that a reasonably accurate means is needed to make a final selection. For some entrepreneurial marketers, personal subjective evaluations are sufficient—and successful. But as companies become publicly held, volume becomes larger and the organization more cumbersome; as the founding entrepreneurs give way to the professional managers, and the professional managers move up the organizations, partly based on performance adherence within company disciplines and procedures—the objectivity of research becomes the rule.

Because creativity in commerce is hardly an art—but does possess aspects of art and its artifice, and not necessarily business—it assumes the halfway status of a craft. Whereas objective research could not forecast the market performance of a Mozart or a Van Gogh, it might well be properly used to measure interest in a Rubic's Cube or the Jolly Green Giant. Before determining the directions for creative strategy and selecting those executional roughs to go forward into testable format, it is necessary to determine guidelines for this subjective decision. Some tips follow later in Chapter 21, which stresses singleness of purpose and the shaping of a distinctive personality with sustained appeal.

Television Commercial Models

No two research techniques available to measure any aspect of communications are exactly alike, although many disguise from respondents the specific, commercial focus within a program and/or multiple commercial clutter. This makes it incumbent upon the new product research sponsor to have a clearly identifiable, ranked set of priorities to obtain the desired measurements. Most techniques measure one or more of the following attributes:

- Recall
- Attention (commercial intrusiveness)
- Impact (degree of reaction)
- Commercial holding power (sustained attention throughout message)
- Understanding
- Wear-out
- Persuasion (purchase intent)
- Actual purchase

In the majority of techniques, diagnostic research is additionally available to help understand the scores achieved. Most communicators agree that such direction is necessary to provide a basis for effective improvement or for entirely new communications.

An analysis of 25 selected syndicated television advertising research suppliers and techniques[6] using on-air central location (theater, van, enclosed mall) and direct response (mail and telephone) methods of forced or random viewing illustrates the necessity of understanding all of the most popular offerings before selecting those most appropriate to your new product introductory advertising task—or, alternatively, devising a proprietary technique to meet special needs. Most of the available services have developed norms in the most advertising intensive categories.

If the new product commercial models fit these categories, then select a supplier whose service measures the most critical element of the message during its introductory phase (brand recall being most often paramount), and has the most reliable norms (recency and size of base are considerations).

Other considerations involve the phase of product development, and whether preliminary checks are needed of many very rough materials (e.g., chalk storyboards with small cast tracks) or of fewer, more comprehensive materials that are preliminary to finished production for on-air use. Although cost should not be the determining factor, it also enters into consideration. The trade-off for a low-cost test of more options that will yield limited, grossly directional information as opposed to a more reliable, sharply defined test at greater cost is judged in relationship to the phase of development, the willingness to make management decisions from broadly directional information, and the financial risks involved. If the next developmental phase is to be a controlled mini-market (a learning experience), the answer may be different than if the next step is a conventional test market, regional expansion, or major introduction.

Many central-location test methods necessarily reflect the demographic and life-style biases peculiar to the area. This is also true of mall intercepts (unless the sample is widely dispersed to represent the population), CATV viewer recruits, on-air tests of limited market scope, and other forced interview techniques. If a new product is targeted to a particular city size, region, program-content viewing habit, livelihood, discrete competitive set, etc., then it may be necessary to tailor the syndicated technique (several suppliers will do this at an extra charge) to the need—or to customize the technique exactly to the purpose, which likely obviates normative data. However, as

---

[6]On-Air: ASI-Recall Plus Test, Burke-Marketing Research Inc., Gallup-Robinson Syndicated Subscription Service (TPT—Total Prime Time), Gallup-Robinson Custom Pretesting (In View), Gallup-Robinson (Custom Post Testing), Mapes and Ross, Sherman Buy[c] Test-Option Three, Westgate; Theater: ARS, ASI (Audience Studies Inc.), McCollum Spielman (AC-T Format); Forced Exposure: Harry Heller Corporation B/EST (Benefit Estimated Share Technique), Palshaw, Rabin Research (Search), Recap, Schrader Research & Rating Service, Schrader Copy Lab, Schrader Research & Rating Service Recall, Sherman Buy[c] Test—Option Two (clutter exposure), Telcom, Tele-Research, Video Storyboard Tests, Inc., VOPAN.

earlier noted, the learning and direction correctness of the answers are often more important than the "score."

Radio Commercial Models

Radio commercial testing is done in similar fashion to television testing, except that on-air testing is rarely used, and telephone research is frequently used, inasmuch as the audio communication is what is to be evaluated. Because radio is less literal than two-dimensional television communication, the range of emotional responses is likely to be wide for dramatic and musical stimuli. Because radio production is much less expensive than television, it is less costly to do modular variations in a manner that helps to optimize final production.

One service, ERIS (Emotional Response Index System), performs a content analysis of the audio (including voiceover characteristics), sound effects, music, etc.) based on word and symbol response scores of a previously analyzed test group of 7,232 respondents. This system indentifies and measures the elements in a commercial that will capture attention and create involvement with the message. The primary output of the system is the diagnostic information that specifies what makes a given commercial effective, or lessens the impact or memorability. The ERIS diagnostics further explain reasons for these findings, which enables improvement before final production and airing. In a review of ten popular syndicated radio commercial measurement techniques,[7] costs appeared to be similar to television studies, except that media costs are usually not involved and the production elements studied are apt to be far less costly.

Print Advertising Models

Natural in-home viewing and forced exposure are the prevalent environments for print advertising research.

In-home readers receive targeted publications with tipped-in model ads, usually with as near to fully comprehensive reproduction as possible. Telephone and in-person callbacks are common. Most services offer standard audience magazine norms, but will customize studies with special-interest books for an extra charge. In most instances, respondents know they are participating in a test; often, callback timing is unnatural for routine readership habits.

Forced-exposure readers are recruited at central locations (shopping malls or mobile units, most likely) or visited at homes or offices. Coupon-redemption techniques are available to help determine trial purchase. Spe-

[7]ASI, Burke, ERISCO Inc., McCollum/Spielman & Company, Inc., Radio Recall Research Inc., Schrader Research, Sherman Buy^c Test, Spencer Bruno Research Associates Inc., Telcom, Tele-Research Inc.

cial-analysis techniques (voice-analysis of respondent comments, eye-movement photography of view-scanning of an ad projected on a screen) can provide helpful additional insights about design and copy effects.

Most of the 14 syndicated services studied[8] reveal one very important characteristic of print research: editorial environment. This is rarely a factor in the broadcast advertising model studies. In broadcast cases, the editorial (program) environment is often used as a comparable common thread, with the advertising elements being the only differences. In most print research, the environment fits the target audience—hence is more directly segmented than other media surroundings. Additionally, it is therefore more adaptable to special interest areas—merely by selection of the most appropriate publications and audiences. Except in the high-circulation general and women's service categories, there is likely to be a higher charge for this service and little or no current normative data. (Exceptions to these observations are those out-of-home techniques that use a standard "bogus" proprietary magazine to assure little or no editorial target bias, those that use print ads as individual posters, and those that project slides of print ads onto large screens.)

Ancillary Aspects

The critical elements of any communication are the impressions made by the visual and audio elements that represent the offerings. Although the gestalt—the total effect—must be integrated, involving, persuasive, and memorable, certain elements are more critical than others.

For new products, these include:

The brand—often unknown.
The generic descriptor—is it clear, appropriate?
The package—often unique; just as often, disguised by family resemblances, if a line extension or a flanker.
The product—does it quickly register?
The promise—does it fill a (possibly only latent) need?
The personality—is it distinctive, appropriate, attractive?

Additional probes and questions may often be added to the formats of syndicated research, to help in isolating these elements sufficiently for precise study. In the case of the brand, descriptor, and package elements, the commercial model studies may be the first instance of their being studied within the complex of a total selling message—even though they may have been "shelf-tested" and "use-tested" prior to their incorporation into model

[8]In home-viewing: ASI, Burke, Gallup-Robinson, Mapes and Ross, Sherman BUY[c] Test, Spencer-Bruno Research; Forced exposure: AHF Marketing Research (Competitive Environment Test), Palshaw, Perception Research, Print Animatic Tests Inc., Sherman BUY[c] Test, Telcom, Tele-Research, Vopan.

advertising. The interactions among these committed elements and between them and the newly added presentation elements must be optimized for maximum selling effectiveness.

For those new products that will spring forth on the world with a patron—whether it be a contrived character ("Mother Nature" or a dove flying through the window) or a real one (Bill Cosby, John Houseman, Orson Welles, The Osmonds, etc.) or an actor-authority (Mrs. Olson, Madge the Manicurist, Juan Valdez, etc.)—the patron must lend authority to the new product, but not be so powerful as to overwhelm the message or its meaning. Often, it is necessary to study such a persuasion element separately—prior to studying the complete communication—in order to understand as well as to screen likely candidates. Once done, the patron-in-place in the advertising may be tested by those techniques reviewed above.

Positioning-Advertising-Copy-Testing (PACT)

Overview guidelines on copy testing—no matter what the medium—were published in January 1982, in a consensus credo representing the views of leading members of the American Association of Advertising Agencies[9], along with several committee participants who had formerly been advertisers and the then incumbent chairman of the Advertising Research Foundation. A brief review of their credo is useful in both planning and assessing model development for advertising research on new product communications. The following review refers *only* to those aspects that are particularly salient to introductory advertising. Here are the nine principles laid down in the PACT credo:

1. **A good copy testing system provides measurements that are relevant to the objectives of the advertising.**

   For new products, this means:

   Reinforcing current perceptions, if they relate to a parent company or brand that has purchase influence and, possibly, providing greater saliency for a brand or company name.

   Encouraging trial of a product or service.

   Encouraging new uses of a product or service, especially where these new uses provide a point-of-difference for the new product.

   Changing perceptions and imagery and announcing new features

[9]Sponsors of PACT are N W Ayer, Inc.; Ted Bates Worldwide Inc.; Batten, Barton, Durstine & Osborn Inc.; Benton & Bowles Inc.; Campbell-Mithun Inc.; Cunningham & Walsh Inc.; Dancer Fitzgerald Sample Inc.; D'Arcy-MacManus & Masius Inc.; Doyle Dane Bernbach Inc.; Grey Advertising Inc.; Kenyon & Eckhardt Inc.; KM&G International Inc.; Marschalk Campbell-Ewald Worldwide; Marsteller Inc.; McCaffrey and McCall Inc.; McCann-Erickson Inc.; Needham, Harper & Steers Inc.; Ogilvy & Mather Inc.; SSC&B Lintas Worldwide; J. Walter Thompson Company; Young & Rubicam.

and benefits if the mode of the new product is to make the parent brand more competitively contemporary.

2. **A good copy testing system is one that requires agreement about how the results will be used *in advance* of each specific test.**

    Action standards should be set *before* testing, so that the evaluation of the results will be against such goals as:
    *   Improve (or achieve positive new perception) of brand perception, as measured by _____
    *   Achieve an attention level of _____ percent or better, as measured by _____
    *   Perform at least as well (or _____ percent better) as (specify execution, which may be an ad norm, as previously tested model, etc.)
    *   Produce no more than _____ percent negative responses, as measured by _____

3. **A good copy testing system provides *multiple* measurements—because single measurements are generally inadequate to assess the performance of an advertisement.**

    As there is no universally accepted single measurement that can serve as a surrogate for sales, determination should be made in advance of testing as to which method will be used to determine the measurement of how much the studied advertising will contribute to sales. Obviously, each measure will not be given equal weight—and, therefore, prior agreement is needed about the decision-influence of each finding.

4. **A good copy testing system is based on a model of human response to communications—the *reception* of a stimulus, the *comprehension* of the stimulus and the *response* to the stimulus.**

    To succeed, advertising must have an effect on several levels: It must be received, it must be understood, and it must make an impression. Questions to consider:
    *   Did the advertising get through?
    *   Was it understood?
    *   Was the proposition accepted?
    *   Did the advertising affect attitudes toward the product/service/ brand?
    *   Did it alter perceptions of competing brands?
    *   Did it cause response to direct action appeals?

5. **A good copy testing system allows for consideration of whether the advertising stimulus should be exposed more than once.**

    In the light of experimental work, PACT agencies share the view that the issue of single versus multiple exposures should be carefully considered in each situation. There are situations in which a single exposure would be sufficient—given the objectives of the advertising and the nature of the test methodology. There are other situations where a single exposure could be inadequate—particularly for high risk situations or for subtle or complex communications or for resolving questions about executional diagnostics.

6. **A good copy testing system recognizes that the more finished a piece of copy is, the more soundly it can be evaluated and requires, as a minimum, that alternative executions be tested in the same degree of finish.**

   The judgment of the creators of the advertising should be given great weight regarding the degree of finish required to present the finished advertisement for test purposes. If there is reason to believe that alternative executions would be unequally penalized in pre-production form, then it is generally advisable to test them in a more finished form. (If alternatives are tested in different stages of finish within the same test, then it is not possible to insure that the results are not biased.)

7. **A good copy testing system provides controls to avoid the biasing effects of the exposure context.**

   Examples: Television commercials tested off-air versus on-air; in a clutter reel versus a program context; in a specific program context versus another specific program context. Each of these variables affect the perception of and response to the stimulus and must be carefully controlled to prevent comparative biases.

8. **A good copy testing system is one that takes into account basic considerations of sample definition.**

   Testing should be conducted among a representative sample of the target audience. (Limited testing among the general population without provision for separate analysis of the target audience can be misleading.) Geographic differences, where critical, and sufficient sample size should allow for a confident decision based on the data obtained.

9. **A good copy testing system is one that can demonstrate reliability and validity.**

   To be reliable, the system should yield the same results each time the same ad is tested. External variables always must be held constant.

   To be valid, the system should yield results relevant to marketplace performance. This is a major and costly goal and requires industrywide participation. While some evidence of predictive validity is available, many systems are in use for which no evidence of validity is provided.

Now that the communications have been developed and the product prototypes sorted, the investment increases. However, the risks have been reduced by the thoroughness of the early phases, so the new product next moves confidently forward into scaled-up development toward commercialization.

Section 5
Summary Afterword

Because the new product is in itself a communication and because the carrying of that message off the catalog sheet, shelf, or television set is inextricably bound to the total selling personality—modeling of *both* the product and its marketing media must proceed down parallel courses. Each affects the other. In many instances, it is difficult, if not impossible, to determine which is more important. It is known, however, that an alteration of either element can affect the future success of the product. This explains the time and money premium placed on modeling.

Model-making provides the blueprint for the further development of new products, offering the opportunity to experiment and screen ideas. The model may grow out of a family name and its heritage, or an entirely new brand can be developed. Many companies build a brand name bank, on which they can draw as new products evolve. Also influencing the model are the generic descriptor and the product category itself.

There are many different kinds of models. They include models for functional parts, instruction/direction models, and scale models. It is also useful to experiment with the model in use, and to evaluate it against its competitive environment. Questions to consider include: Is the model different, as well as being better? How does it feel, heft, and generally fit the surroundings? The package model acts as a symbol of the product, but it can also be functional, as with a pour spout.

Does the model fit the user information system? Communications modes, as well as the product, should also be modeled. One way of evaluating this is through blind testing. Or television (VTR) can simulate models in test modes. Television provides a third party objectivity in evaluating communications models.

Every new product presents a new problem—hence, a new research or judgmental decision. The type of research undertaken must fit the knowledge goal. Videotaped demonstrations can simulate working models, as well as providing a method by which to perfect instructions.

Conventional, projectable research methods include blind tests, use tests, and the simulation of sales response. This last can be accomplished in several ways: with a prototype selling statement and package (without product); with a small quantity of the product plus a print ad/poster; through pretest market sales; or through store tests. Mathematical models include the use of a laboratory test market or an interactive aid to assess variables, such as LITMUS. The communications models can be tested in all forms of media, including television, radio, print, and ancillary aspects.

A system known as PACT (Positioning-Advertising-Copy-Testing) also can provide relevant measurements. There should be advance agreement on the use of results. PACT provides multiple measurements, including measures of reception, comprehension, and response to stimulus. It allows multiple-exposure testing, and testing of different messages in the same degree of comprehensive finish. It targets the sample and is generally regarded as reliable and valid. Controls are in order, however, to avoid bias in the exposure context.

Marketing

19

Plan, Simulation, Selection

Dispatch is the soul of business; and nothing contributes more to dispatch than method. Lay down a method for everything, and stick to it inviolably, as far as unexpected incidents may allow.
—*Lord Chesterfield*
(Letter to his son, February 5, 1750)

The marketing plan begins with a "Fact Book" assembly of all of the relevant known data about the product category, as well as the new product introduction company. Never is there enough data. Where there are gaps in information, it is determined that:

1. The missing information is *not necessary* to the planning process, or
2. It *is necessary*—however, a consensus assumption is satisfactory to the process, or
3. It *is necessary*—and the data needs to be gathered and/or updated from syndicated sources that may be purchased, or generated from consultants in the field (or contract packers, trade groups, parts, materials, and ingredient suppliers), or requires an original research project which is justified on a cost-benefit basis.

Fact Book Planning Guide

A typical outline of a fact book may be as follows:

A. Executive summary
B. The industry
    1. Total sales volume of industry (units and/or dollars)
    2. Sales trends over 4–5 years
    3. Consumer penetration of product/service by total industry

    4. Major competitors—with unit and dollar shares

    5. Estimated margins

    6. Recent distribution trends in industry (overview only; details requested later)

    7. Future industry outlook

    8. Outside influences facing industry (government controls, shortages, etc.)

    9. Recent activities

    10. Financial analysis of parent corporation of leading competitors

    11. Reconstruction of corporate charter and style, based on performance history

C. The subject company(ies)

    1. Brief history

    2. Total sales/profit trends (all products) over 4–5 years

    3. Sales/profit trends of *this* product/service over 4–5 years

    4. Organization

D. The company's new product/service

    1. Description (brand name, function, recent improvements)

    2. Main user benefit(s)

    3. Consumer profile
- Target prospect
- Target trade[1] factors
- Income category
- Ethnic factors
- Geographical influences
- Seasonal influences
- Psychological influences/factors
- Any differences from major competitors

    4. Main selling points (packaging, pricing design, production, state-of-art advancement, prestige of manufacturing, etc.)

    5. Secondary selling points

    6. Exclusive selling points

    7. Primary selling appeal(s)

    8. Product/service prospect appeal barriers
- Price
- Lack of recognition
- Packaging
- Etc., etc.

    9. Foremost barrier

---

[1]In many categories, the consumer—the end-user—is a trade factor. In other situations, the characteristic of the trade may be peculiar to the consumption pattern, e.g., although grocery outlets are thought of as the trade factor in pizza consumption, it may be a characteristic of the consumer profile that they buy pizzas not in restaurants and not at grocery stores, but at taverns, which are the "consumer" of conventional frozen pizzas also available in groceries.

        10. Frequency of purchase

        11. Frequency of use

        12. Type of guarantee or warranty; compared with competition

        13. Quality control performance, reputation

        14. Consumer awareness level

        15. Resumé of other market research findings (indicate who conducted research)

E. Distribution/Pricing

    1. Chain of distribution (distributors, jobbers, brokers, direct, etc.)

    2. Markups/commissions/other incentives

    3. Weak links in distribution setup (e.g., inexperience, lack of training, apathy, low level of product knowledge, etc.)

    4. Exceptional distribution and sales operation strengths

    5. Distribution system compared with major competitors

- Structure
- Quality
- Number of dealers, outlets, etc.

    6. Elements in subject company's distribution that handle competitive brands, if any

    7. Available selling tool(s)

F. The current advertising/promotion program
(for subject company and major competitor)

    1. Media history, past 2–3 years, on intended new product/service area

- Total media investment
- Percent of total by media
- Media inhibitions peculiar to subject company or industry

    2. Current selling appeals of leading competitors

    3. Advertising effectiveness measures

    4. Typical customer sales promotion material characteristic of category—including merchandising of advertising

    5. Field acceptance/use of these materials

    6. Use/value of trade shows, conventions, etc.

    7. Use/value of sales development aids

- Couponing
- Sampling
- Loaders
- Tie-ins
- Etc.

    8. Use/importance of publicity/public relations

    9. Use/importance of direct mail

- Trade
  Size of list _____   Type of mailing _____
- Consumer
  Size of list _____   Type of mailing _____

- Assessment of value _____
_____
_____

G. Objectives for new product
    1. Share of market
        - Year 1 ____ percent
        - Year 2 ____ percent
        - 5-year goal ____ percent
    2. Volume

	Units	Dollars
- Year 1		
- Year 2		
- 5-year goal (if known)		

    3. Other objectives
H. Introductory communications and marketing strategy
I. Long-term brand personality goal
J. Vital missing information

Preparing the Executive Summary

One of the most useful steps in analyzing the "Fact Book" is the preparation of an executive summary. This forces separation of the critically salient information from the less important. It allows for a spotlighting of the atypical differences from the field demonstrated by the leaders, the growers, and the faltering factors in the category.

Finding Gaps

In nearly every marketing category there are uncovered opportunity areas. Analyze all of the market facts including the strength and weaknesses of the product/service offerings, distribution system, geographic and trade class coverage, media selection, target audience, historic developments, recent management structure and personnel changes, annual report analysis, stock performance, legal actions, union arrangements, location and modernity of manufacturing sources, shipping and warehousing, purchasing policies, etc. Array these factors against the new product entrant's strengths and weaknesses. This will show the gaps in the principal competition that can be attacked in the new product introductory plan—as well as illuminating the sponsoring company's own areas for improvement or, if the company's already especially strong in key attack areas, for major leveraging against the field and/or any strong competitor in the new product's target segment of the category.

A gap grid can be built for each area of analysis, with an assigned power number for each competitor and for the new product entry from the market planner company. This will provide a solid directional basis for the planning.

Information Sources

In those areas where the assessment of potential competitive activity is particularly critical, there are a number of perfectly legal secondary research approaches. For example, let's look at how IBM does it. As reported in the *Los Angeles Times*, March 21, 1982:

International Business Machines Corp., by any measure a competitive powerhouse, has assembled an elaborate intelligence-gathering apparatus that relies on published sources and detailed reports from its salesmen all over the world.

Trade meetings, scientific seminars, and professional junkets can present invaluable opportunities for quick-witted technical people and executives to pick the brains of colleagues.

Intelligence Consulting
The article continues:

For executives who want more than casual information, Washington Researchers, a consulting firm based in the nation's capital, offers a "company information seminar."

A brochure advertising one seminar says the consultants will show participants how to use public sources to find out, among other things, the nature of a competitor's marketing strategy or whether the competition is opening a new plant.

Reverse Engineering
And there's more, according to the article:

Such major manufacturers as automobile makers routinely examine their competitors' products as they appear on the market. Breaking down a rival's marketed products in this fashion is known as "reverse engineering," a technique so common in industry that most courts find it acceptable as a competitive practice. Reverse engineering is a particularly valued skill in such high-technology industries as electronics, where it is often an important step toward duplicating or improving on a competing product.

Freedom of Information Act
Even the government helps. As the *LA Times* article points out:

But perhaps the most important "legitimate" source of inside information about competitors is the federal government, which for regulatory and contracting purposes requires public corporations and even private companies to make extensive disclosures about their products, finances, and operations.

Over the years, businessmen have become adept at using the federal Freedom of Information Act to extract some of this data. Although the 1966 law was tailored to help the press and public obtain information about the workings of government, in practice it has been more useful to businesses looking for information about their rivals . . .

According to a 1980 study by a University of Oregon professor, 37 percent of the freedom-of-information queries submitted to 29 federal agencies in 1978 (not including the FBI and CIA) were to the Food and Drug Administration. That agency is the repository of millions or even billions of dollars in proprietary formulas from cosmetics and pharmaceutical makers, among other companies.

Other studies suggest that the vast majority of information requests to certain regulatory agencies comes from corporate probers rather than from the general public or press. The Food and Drug Administration reported last year that of the 33,000 requests it answered in 1980, about 85 percent were from companies in the industries it regulates.

IBM's Model System

IBM perhaps has the most sophisticated business intelligence-gathering system.

Many businesses regularly glean information about their competitors from newspapers and magazine articles, press releases, and other publically available documents. But few have assembled intelligence-gathering systems as sophisticated as the one put together by IBM. In fact, it has served as a model for other companies.

So reports the *Los Angeles Times*. According to the *Times*, two major divisions of IBM have been responsible for scouting the competition. The commercial analysis department of IBM's data processing division has produced quarterly reports rating each of IBM's major products as "superior," "equal," or "deficient" to the competition.

The assessments were based on reports filed by IBM's far-flung network of salespeople, as well as on internal analyses prepared by various IBM divisions . . . a modified version of [this system] is still in use today.

A single example of how this works is sufficient. Here's how IBM profiles its competition, according to the *LA Times*:

A largely upbeat 127-page study of the Burroughs Corp. in 1967 included data on the company's costs for research and development, production, sales, and administration, and a profile of . . . the energetic Burroughs chairman . . . The Burroughs study listed 36 published sources, including annual reports and newspaper articles. It credited 30 IBM agencies and departments for contributions to the report.

The Planning Process

All parties involved in the execution of the plan must play a part in the planning process. This means every player in the company in every affected division. Perhaps it seems unbelievable, but companies have had costly new enterprise failures in taken-for-granted areas for such reasons as unanticipated waste disposal regulations (the new product produced waste dissimilar to that with which the company had previous experience), misinterpretation of industry guidelines (for product and/or communications), lack of alternate sources (or source planning) for critical ingredients, incomplete cost-of-goods sold build-up, off-target (inefficient) media planning, inappropriate product-sizing assortment to address regional differences (lines were limited to the industry's best selling variations only, based on national averages—failing to take into consideration that the best sellers differed from region to region—so that the *average* leaders represented necessary coverage in only a few markets), etc.

Use of Specialist Experts

Failure to use specialists when entering a new field has also led to more expensive failures than the cost of employing these experts in the planning phase. Too often companies believe that because they can make the product competitively, can handle sales and distribution competitively, and will communicate competitively, there is no reason to employ the specialist in the new field. After all, these experts may be expected to provide the industry cliches of the competition—while the very opportunity for the new entry is a new approach to the market. Nonetheless, informed experts can save time and money, provide valuable input, and tell a company what competitive reactions are likely to be when the new entrant takes its original noncliche approach to the marketplace. The new product manager can decide whether to rely on the expert's advice and, if so, how to use it, if at all.

There are expert generalists, and there are expert specialists in every major industrial category. Both can be helpful to procurement and manufacturing, sales and distribution, legal and finance, staff recruitment, etc.

Elements of the Plan

All of the up-front work has been completed.

Now you must obtain management approval.

In seeking management approval for a full-scale go-ahead, it is necessary to review the highlights of the entire development program in an executive overview. Marketing, finance, legal, production (including manufacturing, supply, shipping), technical (including R&D, engineering, medical, etc.) all participate in the combined recommendation of the new products team.

The elements of the recommended plan may include:

1. **Situation analysis** (including market potential and competitive analysis, e.g., product, sales, pricing, etc.)
2. **Business objectives** (volume for Year 1 and after in units and dollars, cost of goods sold, gross and net margins, etc.)
3. **Product strategy**
4. **Development review** (whether internal, acquisition, joint-venture, or outside supplier made, assembled, and/or packed.)
   - Includes findings of concept and prototype screening.
   - Includes all physical (or operational service) elements, e.g., product, package structure, but not graphics; shipping cartons; on-site final assembly and/or service, etc.
5. **Detailed financial analysis of market's present entries**

6. **Price perception study results** (field entries plus new product)
7. **Benefits and claims study results** (present competitors and recommended new product entry)
8. **Marketing strategy**
9. **Communications strategy** (includes advertising, customer and trade promotion, sales incentives, media plan, etc.)
10. **Legal review** (includes product, price, communications, patents, etc.)
11. **National theoretical plan, all elements** (for stimulation)
12. **Financial review** (includes timing and capital risks)
13. **Test market simulation** (or otherwise) plan or (alternatively) major launch with other test methods

Upon receiving executive clearance, the normal course of events finds the new product team coordinating their efforts along these lines: (Code: M = Marketing, T = Technical, P = Production, F = Finance, L = Legal)

- Finalize creative (M)
- Finalize package structure (T/P) and graphics (M)
- Obtain patent, labeling, and other package copy, and distribution policy clearances (L)
- Conduct dealer impressions study (M)
- Conduct final advertising creative execution tests and produce advertising elements (M)
- Conduct factory-production user trial tests prior to release of selling samples (M, T, P)
- Conduct final manufacturing feasibility measures (T, P)
- Scale up for production and shipping (P)
- Begin manufacturing (P)
- Conduct benchmark awareness study in test markets (M)
- Sell-in to trade (M)
- Set shelf detailing and displays (M)
- Start advertising (M)
- Follow-up test market awareness study (M)
- Conduct distribution and price audit (M)
- Develop buyer profile study (M)
- Develop repeat awareness, audit, and sales measures (M)
- Project test market performance against plan (M)
- Make management recommendation to expand, abort, or revise plan (M, with new product team consensus)

Being First

The most wonderful new product and the best possible marketing plan avail little against a competitor who beats the innovator to the market with a similar new product. The "new" has been taken away. The trade that has taken on the first entrant isn't going to enthusiastically add another "me too" item until it is demonstrated that the new product will build or enlarge a category sufficiently to leave room for variations.

Predictive field surveillance of the category, and of the likely competitors, must be intensively continued throughout the marketing planning phase. Where certain categories have pronounced regional skews, these areas should be surveyed with care. If the competitors have foreign marketing operations, they should be monitored also. If there are major foreign competitors, then their activities in their home countries should be monitored. Frequently, the products are tried at home before being exported.

Beyond this, in those categories where test marketing is common, all of the syndicated test market cities plus those cities most commonly used for conventional test markets should be surveyed to see if new product tests are underway. If so, tests should be audited because the marketing planning needs to take into consideration the test activity. For example, it may be decided to "read" the competitor's test while readying the new enterprise company's product for a regional or national launch—foregoing the originally planned test market to beat the competitor to the broadscale marketplace.

Even so, doing it right is more important than doing it first—if doing it first means short-changing the optimization of the product or key elements of its launch. The risks should be carefully weighed. Where the test market is part of the plan because of prudence and fine-tuning, rather than a real need for important learning, then, if the down-side trade-off for a preemptive strike prior to competitive moves is not great, skipping the test market may be justified. Other alternatives present themselves also.

Test While Launching

Go ahead with the test exactly as planned, but make the major launch at the same time. This will enable the test market laboratories, with all of their in-built controls, to provide detailed information not available from the operation of the free-market, large-area introduction. With test-market information at hand, adjustments of the broader roll-out area can be based on a quicker, more detailed (hence, less risky) reading of the situation than available from the broad, uncontrolled market situation.

Another alternative is available for certain merchandise categories. For low-ticket, frequently purchased, package goods, it is possible to put together a sales test among a limited number of high volume, geographically-dispersed, controlled-test stores to measure shelf movement, assuming that a reasonable simulation of advertising communication is available. The best use of this technique is where differences are being measured in terms of price, packaging, brand, or sales theme emphasis, and store panels are well matched.

Contingency Planning

What we covered above are some of the downside issues. There are upside issues also. On occasion, new products are far more successful than anticipated. This means rapid step-up of manufacturing or a slower roll-out than planned or product allocation or fewer trade-category channels than planned or a cut-back in promotion—or a combination of all of these. Lost sales are sales never made. Since initial trial is so important—especially if they are to be gained during the heaviest introductory advertising/promotional period— an ideal marketing plan considers contingency activity under all circumstances, including:

1. Everything goes according to plan. How to optimize.
2. Outside events intervene, affecting success. How to meet and control events, or take advantage of them.
3. Product acceptance is less than anticipated. How to take remedial action—or to cut losses.
4. Product is more successful than anticipated. How to leverage this opportunity and/or how to deal with the problems (supply, out-of-stocks, media commitments, etc.).

In other words, war game strategies and tactics are employed. The games can be played in the marketing planning phase, in order to anticipate all possible contingency planning needs, make financial allowances, and predetermine actions that will be triggered by various circumstances. In this way, little time is lost and funding provisions are both predictable and manageable.

Simulation

Presuming that the marketing plan calls for a test simulation, then the guidelines for the simulation need be laid out prior to selection of the test areas.

To do this, the universe must be defined.

In very few instances is the test universe defined as contiguous-state U.S.A. Even for those new products that are expected to be on sale nationally after a successful test, this is true. And, where it will truly be a nationally distributed brand, state and regional differences—often legal (local regulations), more often developmental or psychographic—need to be considered. Average markets and average marketing approaches exist only in statistics and, unfortunately, in far too many marketing plans. How do you avoid this?

Because any simulation in several or more geographic market areas will represent the true picture throughout the intended major marketing area in only the most gross sense, this should be recognized early—in both the market selection and in the guidelines for performance analysis.

It is probably true that in nearly every new product category, success *must* be obtained in certain markets or market-types because performance in other areas will not make up for poor performance in these key areas. If this is true, then you will want to stimulate those distinctive characteristics that have major influence in these critical key markets, with weighted allowances used to project results to the entire universe of eventual sales.

County size, population concentration, industrial vs. rural, all play roles in marketing reception. Sometimes, for presumed cost savings, relatively small, lightly industrialized test markets are selected to simulate marketing performance for a new product that must have its leading successes in large, heavily populated urban areas with an industrial and/or business service base. If this is the case, the cost savings are illusionary, because the misdirection thus supplied may result in faulty projections.

After all of the (updated) demographics and psychographics have been analyzed—but before you make any further commitment to the choices—the projected test markets should be visited in person by those responsible for market selection. Oftentimes, what is on-the-scene is different than what is on paper. Circumstances change rapidly and affect prospect behavior—whereby statistics and Chamber of Commerce descriptions tend to have mostly historical significance. Unless you carefully check local conditions and incorporate them in the plan, the phasing of the test pattern may not take into account consumption biases and such influences as an influx of migratory workers, illegal aliens, or across-state-line shoppers (where there are influential tax variances or legal marketing restrictions, such as controlled liquor stores, price advertising of professional products and services, etc.).

If possible, arrange to have some of the early consumer research panels set up in intended test market candidates—and ask questions about more than the product area. Find out who are the most credible spokespeople on the media, which are the "innovator" bell-cow store outlets (if they are not the big chains, their importance won't show up except in an apparently unimportant statistic), reputations of *local* competitive companies, and brand franchises, etc. Weigh all of this. Is it relatively representative? Will it affect your simulation marketing plan, media balance, etc.?

Although the simulation will represent the marketing plan quantitatively, how are *local qualitative decisions* made? If, for example, the national plan calls for use of network personalities, shouldn't the local plan do more than merely represent the gross rating points? Shouldn't it also use any available appropriately credible local personalities? Does a weighting adjustment need to be made for network ratings as simulated by local spots—or national print space as simulated by local print or regional editions? More pertinent to the plan to be simulated, should all major media be bought on a national scale?

If the new product will have (at least initially) biases by area size or location, perhaps the national plan should be highly regionalized in design. In this way, each area should be given the expected weight in sales potential and respective marketing spending. The simulation translation will be merely an execution of the plan for that particular area. In this way, the sales projection will be against its predetermined importance to the total marketing plan—a big difference compared with its unweighted arithmetical proportion of the national goal.

Not only does the plan require simulation of the proposed national product, package, pricing share-of-shelf, and share-of-mind—it should also simulate the minimum trade acceptance and distribution level. If this is not achieved, then the test should be delayed or aborted in the market before media are unavoidably committed and heavy shipments are made—or continue. The "start-up" must be simulated properly. If it is not, then this most critical aspect of the plan cannot be projected.

Too often, it is assumed that what is being tested is the prospect's acceptance of the new product. While this is usually true, many times what is being tested is the quality of the sales force, the reputation of the service organization, and the relations with the specific trade factors represented in the test markets.

Be certain to identify these issues before simulation plan guidance is given to the selection of test markets. It is possible that the new product requires a different type of sales organization or a different style of buyer persuasion than that which has been successful for the company in other areas. It's best to learn this in test market. If such factors contribute to unacceptable new product performance, but customer satisfaction is high among those few who did purchase, then this indicates that there are elements that can be corrected either in an expanded effort or in a retest (perhaps, and probably, in another "nonpolluted" area).

Test Market Selection

Under ideal circumstances, test markets are definable, projectable entities, which differ from the goal universe only in scale. Naturally, this objective is not achievable.

Because no one market or set of markets can replicate an entire population, the key decision in market selection is to set priorities regarding the information needed. This done, markets are selected that best represent opportunities to yield the most accurate measures, at least concerning cost.

Selection Considerations

Essential considerations in selecting a test market include:

1. Availability of in-place syndicated market measurement resources
   This often provides historic performance information within the category of interest. Because it is in place, it is less costly than the building of a proprietary service.

2. Establishment of a proprietary resource

   Some companies have continual performance audit markets that measure sales trends in all categories of corporate entry and contingent interests. Others establish fresh test markets to meet measurement goals in new categories of interest, if neither existing syndicated nor proprietary resources are available or appropriate.

3. Prospect demographic/psychographic mix

   Except for mass appeal, broad consumption products, most products are targeted at markets more refined than a national cross section. In such cases, care should be taken to identify over- or under-representation of the target audience in test markets. This means using care in selection and care in projection. During unsettled economic periods, the unemployment index (by type) is also apt to be a key factor in selection.

4. Trade penetration mix

   Equal care is devoted to the trade mix, often a reflection of economics, ethnicity, age of the control city, maturity of local brands, recovery of competitive introductions, dominance or lack of it by individual trade factors, local price wars, coupon misredemption aberrations, etc.

5. Media mix

   Consideration should be given to the number of competitive TV and radio stations; local aberrations in viewing or listening; the strength of dailies, weeklies, and suburban shopper newspapers; the strength and character of city magazines, etc. All types of media planned for the national introduction should be represented in the test markets.

6. Pricing of media

   There is a pricing penalty in simulating the national plan on a local scale. All else being equal, select the lower cost-per-thousand media market. Media spill-in/spill-out should be at minimum levels. Further, the cost of media within each market is of primary consideration. Also, network TV affiliations and the possibility of regional local magazine translations should be investigated.

7. Location

   When several test markets are selected, they should be in different regions, representing parts of a projectable whole—not looked at individually. Where shipping costs will be critical to profit margins after expansion (large, bulky items from a central plant), nearby key markets of sufficient size for profitability are needed. Performance *must* make it where there is no added shipping burden. Minimize transshipments to other geographic areas so as not to blur the assessment of sales performance readings.

8. Seasonal effects

   Nearly every seasonally related new product should be tested in areas where seasonal influences represent the average peak timing and length of the planned roll-out marketing area.

9. Competitive set
   Consider the competitive industry mix—where competitive shares by *type* of product (e.g., sports cars vs. sedans) are either representative of the whole, representative of the target, or are measured for an otherwise identifiable reason. Look at the competitive brand share mix. Competition should be typical of the planned expansion market area.

10. Recent, accurate information
    This should be obtained by on-the-scene investigation by local and regional services, not limited to published economic and societal data, but including the business, editorial, and news press, trade management, in-place company sales representatives, applicable professional groups, etc.

11. Retail pricing
    This should be typical of the rest of the planned expansion area.

12. Sales force
    The proficiency of the company's sales force in the test area should be typical of its performance throughout the rest of its entire trading area.

13. Projectability
    The test market(s) must be statistically projectable. Most experts feel 3 percent of U.S. households is the minimum test market size for consumer package goods. Often, marketers go as small as 1 percent of the U.S., however, with care to see that the per capita consumption index does not vary more than 10 percent. Use of more than one market is recommended, to hedge market readings against unpredictable influences, such as layoffs, strikes, atypical weather conditions, etc.

The importance of selection, measurement, and performance interpretation in test marketing cannot be overstressed. According to International Multifoods, in their study of package goods test marketing, the research of a test market costs three times as much as the production of the product itself. (See Figure 19-1.)

The Actual Markets

Now that all those factors that match the national plan have been laid down for the simulation guide, the actual test markets must be selected.

There are likely many more candidates than are called for by the needs of the test—perhaps two to four, unless matched sets are being used to test price, media weight, or communications strategy differences.

Figure 19-1
The Test Market Dollar

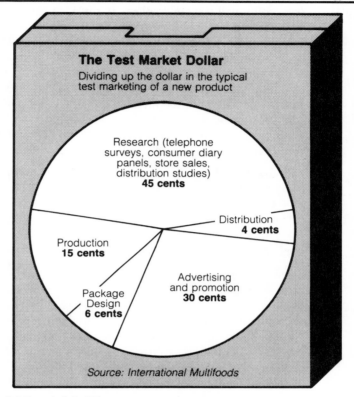

The Test Market Dollar

Dividing up the dollar in the typical test marketing of a new product

Research (telephone surveys, consumer diary panels, store sales, distribution studies) **45 cents**

Distribution **4 cents**

Production **15 cents**

Advertising and promotion **30 cents**

Package Design **6 cents**

Source: International Multifoods

Source: New York Times, April 11, 1982.

Choosing the Candidate(s)

These are further cut down on the basis of geographic dispersion and, possibly, by such logistical considerations as factory location, best air connections for headquarters staff, freight tariffs, special competitive biases, etc. Also to be considered is test wear-out. Some more or less representative areas have been used so many times that they are product cluttered. Others may currently be the scene of above average detailing or special promotional efforts by the company's own sales force—or competition.

Competition may be testing products in a similar competitive arena. In this case, it may be decided to monitor one or several without a face-off, to get a "pure" early reading—while, perhaps, facing competitors directly in others, to determine their reactions. In most instances of the latter scenario, if the second entry goes in with a reasonably projectable plan, a sophisticated competitor will stick to its plan—to see what happens in what could become reality in larger areas. Unfortunately, sometimes a war ensues—and marketing spending becomes out-of-line with anything that could be feasibly spent on a broad scale. In this instance, the only winner is the customer. The warring new products haven't been submitted to a true test.

Where sales are being projected from sales audits, it is sometimes found that the promising initial success occurred because of sales made to competitors picking up sample products for analysis. At least one wise national package goods supplier always sends a case of its new products to its competitors as it ships to the trade, with a letter that says:

Our new X product is on its way to you for analysis. We'd be interested in your comments. Meanwhile, you'll be spared the trouble and the expense of picking up the product and, hence, your reading of our sales performance will be more accurate.

If you'd like another case of X product, just let us know. Catalog sheet enclosed.

Simulating Simulations

There are, of course, methods whereby conventional test markets may be themselves simulated. Where "control"—rather than unfettered reality—is needed, isolated mini-markets with managed controls are often used. These are especially useful in measuring variables between matched pairs, e.g., store or shelf position, price, promotions, sales activities, marketing spending, etc. On occasion, controlled markets are used in pairs against conventional markets. Where, for example, distribution and shelf facings are controlled in the managed markets and subject to haphazard circumstances in the others, it is possible to get a relative measure of sales force effectiveness, attractiveness of trade promotions, as an element in sales success, etc.

Show and Tell

Now that the marketing plan has been approved, the simulation guidelines laid down, and the test markets selected—now is the time to put the communications together that will tell the world about the new product about to be born.

This communications development process has been moving along parallel with product development. The learning process has contributed modifications that now will come together in the marketplace.

New-Product Communications

You're only young once, so make the most of it.

Like a new baby, a new product is born only once—without a name (although its birth certificate may identify parentage), neither given (brand) nor surname (generic descriptor).

This is the most opportune time to get this youngster started off right—to help assure its successful future.

There are so many decisions to make. How will it be dressed? With whom will it associate? How often will it be seen in public—and where? And, most important in its productive life, what will its personality be?

Many factors enter, most importantly:

- The product
- Its performance
- Its name
- Its package
- Its price
- Its display
- Its advertising

Unless the new baby is a product of genetically matched parents, even its complexion, structure, and style are subject to many design variations for the marketplace. Even if it's a clone, a line extension, or a cousin, a flanker—there are opportunities to send the powerful signal of newness.

247

After all, "new" is one of the most arresting and trial-persuasive words in the marketing lexicon. "New" cannot be said for long (in many cases, it is legally limited to six months in your advertising and promotion.) So, during this brief period of letting the world find your new baby, say "new" powerfully, frequently, and with great audience reach.

That is why it is so critical to understand those elements which send the signal of communications "newness."

The Product Itself

You want a product that is equal to or better than the competition. In a true commodity category, you must move the merchandise at almost any cost, because it is too costly to store, is perishable, or is subject to frequent vagaries of Mother Nature or market speculation. In such a classification, you must move the tonnage and (often unfortunately true) hang the profit margin.

But most marketers are not moving commodities. They are making products to provide a range of new benefits. Often these benefits relate to new life styles and changing demographics.

Within the constraints of technology and legality, and of perception and actual fact, there are geometric combinations of new product performance possibilities. Most of these are based on known technologies, readily available skills, and quickly communicated benefits.

The architecture, engineering design, texture, color, and assembly of the product must set it apart from the competition, while at the same time associating it with the field sufficiently to make a quick communication. It should not appear, feel, or behave so differently that it is misperceived or overlooked as not belonging to its category.

As discussed earlier, your new product selection has the greatest opportunity for success when it fits a strength of your company. New products are not an end in themselves, they are a means of leveraging your company's strengths to increase volume and profit.

Make no mistake, the product selected is a communication in itself. Everything about it is a communication, including the outwardly manifest enthusiasm of the corporate new products group, from science to manufacturing to marketing. This initial commitment often sets the pace for later marketplace achievement.

Product Performance

A new product must be both different and better to be an outstanding hit in the marketplace.

Experience tells us that it should be only a little bit different. Users tend to understand, accept, and adopt that which is close to the familiar. The signals are clearer. The differences are easier to accept—and, hence, more apt to be believed.

There are countless examples of major improvements that sit in the laboratories, in patent application files, or in the heads of their inventors—but will not reach the marketplace for years. All of the know-how necessary to make these products exists today—but their concepts are too advanced to find ready acceptance. This is true in every culture. It is also true that what may succeed in another culture, although possibly superior to what we offer in this one, may fail here because of sociological, regulatory, or other reasons unrelated to the performance superiorities of the new product.

And, so, great breakthroughs are usually *not* the order of the day. Those few exceptions have mostly been entrepreneurial commitments that have built businesses, not products per se.

Most new product managers will work for established companies. Few will be founders or have the benefit (and constitution) to be a working part in the conceptional explosion of the genius of an Edison, a Disney, or a Land. Perhaps typical of a truly inventive attitude is that of Polaroid founder Dr. Edwin H. Land: "Any market already existing is inherently boring and dull." (Quoted in *Business Week*, March 2, 1981). He stresses *invention*, rather than innovation or improvement.

Contrary to this view, the action for most industry is in responding to the marketplace: the user habits, evolving technologies, competitive actions, available capacities, and distribution opportunities.

That is reality for most new product managers. And that is the way of the free marketplace.

As for being *better* . . .

Experience tells us "a lot better" is desirable if we are not "a lot different" at the same time. However, in the laboratory, being a lot better often goes with being a lot different. That's the rub. History shows that tiny performance advances usually appear to have the greatest opportunities in the market *precisely because they are easy to communicate and do not require habit change.*

Because small performance differences are most easily achievable, opportunity plays into the hands of communicators. New product performance just a slight bit ahead of competition is easily communicated through comparison with past user experience or by direct comparison with attributes of competitive offerings.

That slight difference is the trouble, also.

If it is only slightly better and only slightly different, then it will ordinarily take only a slight amount of effort and a slight amount of time for competition to catch up. For these reasons, the product's performance must constantly improve over its life cycle—to allow its producer to constantly renew its benefit claims. At the same time, the product's positioning in the user's mind should remain distinctive and relevant, and its personality must be so strong as to be nonpreemptible.

The Name

This is one of the most critical decisions a marketer must make. Prospective user research is essential. Often, in the case of line extensions (another size, another color, another flavor, another horsepower, etc.), circumstances dictate a strong family resemblance, with just enough difference to indicate another selection.

Sometimes what appears to be an appropriate name for a flanker or for a new item sends the wrong signals. For example, a famous brand name of women's hair coloring was used for its parent company's pioneering brand of men's hair coloring. The logic went: this is the leading brand of hair coloring. Therefore, it will say to the prospect that he can trust the product, because it is made by the leader. However, what the brand actually said was: This must be a feminine product, because that brand name is associated with beauty parlors and cosmetics. Since I am hesitant about trying a hair color, I certainly don't want to use something that will diminish my self-image of masculinity.

A famous package goods company, the maker of leading toiletries, went into test market with a line of frozen foods. Because the company's most famous brand was its toothpaste, it branded the food products with that name—and failed. Consumers probably couldn't separate the prestigious brand name from its peppermint flavor, its cleansing (and spit out) usage.

Every well-established brand has a meaning, a boundary. Often this establishes a capacious level of preliminary reception, as well as readily defined limits of extension for any new member carrying the family name. Johnson & Johnson found that its brand name meant "gentleness." Well-known and a leader in many fields, it learned that J&J's "gentle" meaning is nonetheless *not* appropriate to introduce a powerful germ fighter or its leading analgesic, Tylenol.

Betty Crocker is one of the best known brands in the food business, yet General Mills has been careful to see that it is applied only to an appropriate range of new products. Studies have shown both the new areas that fit its image as well as those that are inappropriate.

Such studies are a requirement for every company with one or more strong brand names, or a corporate identity with a specific meaning. Usually, it will be found that the strong names carry great close-in opportunities and equally potent problems when entering new areas of consumer perception.

Often almost as important as the brand name itself is the generic description. Is the product "cosmetic beauty bar" or "Step 2—Nightly Skin Care System" or "solid beauty bath" or "toilet soap"? All of the above are essentially the same product, but with different generic descriptors. As you can see, this can make an important difference in the product's perceived personality, price point—and possibly even its distribution channels and advertising media selection.

The Package—Construction and Graphics

For some products, the function of the package may be almost as important as the materials it contains. For example: Years ago, an attempt was made to improve the troublesome method of dispensing toothpaste through a tube with aerosol delivery systems. Today, two marketers are selling toothpaste in a new type of pump dispenser, developed in Europe. This unique new package is being offered by Colgate MFP Toothpaste as well as by an entirely new brand, CheckUp™ Adult Tooth Paste with Flouride and Microsil™, distributed by the Oral Hygiene division of Minnetonka Inc., and made in West Germany. Other toothpaste brands are already following this lead.

Most packages, however, are designed chiefly for display purposes, secondarily providing protection, a pedestal to rest upon, and space to readily identify the contents, provide printed directions, etc. Other packages are integral parts of the complete product appearance: the television set cabinet (the set will work perfectly well without it) and, at the other extreme, the cleansing tissue box. Both serve an appearance function as long as the product is in use—but play no critically necessary function in product performance. And both the packages—the cabinet and the cardboard box—send a message about the contents. Although the contents in each case may provide similar performance to other dissimilarly packaged products, the package appearance will affect how we perceive the product's newness, quality, and value.

Recognizing this, Crown Zellerbach Corporation, a large West Coast marketer of consumer paper products, successfully brought the first line of designer tissues to market, in prominently signed dispenser box designs by Vera. (See Figure 20-1.)

This cosmetic dress sends a message with its materials and their arrangement, as well as its decorations. These graphics superimposed on these constructions begin to shape the product's personality. Together, particularly for mass distributed products that are displayed on shelves, they often send more messages, more often, and with more continuity than all of the advertising exposure. This is why it is important to pay equally great attention to the package, as well as to the product. Packages are advertisements for their products. Packages are the heroes of much advertising. They must send a clear message, easily reproduced in visual media. Their brand language must be phonetically easily pronounced in word-of-mouth as well as on audio media.

Figure 20-1
Facial Tissue Packages

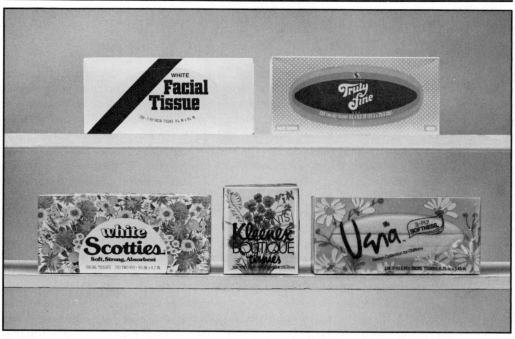

Package graphics and construction send a message. Facial tissues are continuously on display, from store shelf to bathroom counter. They must command attention among competition, and they must fit the home or office environment and the purchaser's taste. Here is an array of examples, from upper left to lower right: A generic brand, a store brand, a popular brand, a boutique shape popular brand and a popular west coast brand with graphics by a name designer.

Its Price

Price, of course, must reflect value. But it must also speak of the position and the personality of the product. Something that is priced at $1.99 is not the same as something priced at $2.00—what a difference that penny makes!

Years ago, a miniaturized reel-to-reel tape recorder was introduced by Webcor. At the time, such items sold in the $79.95 to $129.95 range. Ads ran in hi-fi store retail newspaper space. Webcor's excellent performance, high-tech styled machine was introduced as the Microcorder in *The Wall Street Journal* at $175. The price, the product name, the style of the package (the case), and the environment of the media all combined to set the product above its field, in the minds of the consumers, the trade, and throughout the company itself—with sellout results.

Price communicates a message about how your company values its product and about how much a consumer might expect from its performance. Price tells a consumer how to value the product.

It is always possible to lower a price (in promotional periods or permanently). Except when the entire industry takes a price rise, it is often difficult to unilaterally price-up in a dynamic category.

Set a price that is appropriate to your personality, even if this does not reflect the price structure of the category or the minimum acceptable profit margin goal. If you cannot do this, then alter the factors: your product's cost, its committed marketing dollars, its profit goals, or its position in the competitive set. All elements of your communication should be integrated—consistent with your total personality. If that appears impossible, rethink the personality to fit the price. Be realistic. Rely on user research to help you establish a ceiling (as well as a basement) for a reasonable price range.

The Display

Most products and services are displayed somewhere—at a trade show, on a selling sheet or an ad, on a counter or a shelf, on a showroom floor, in a shopping cart or a shipping case, in an office, factory, or home.

And most are displayed more than one way at different times.

Establish the "look" of your new product from the very beginning. Send quick visual signals; symbols; clean, quick logotypes; proprietary color schemes and design elements; a style carried forward in typography, setting, and illustration—a fitting background for your products or services. Be pervasive with this in everything you do from the very beginning.

Do not leave any of this to chance. Do not assign it to uninvolved specialists. And do not look at display out of context.

Just as you look at and study your packages in their usage environments— look at your displays in their selling environments. Look at displays full of products and in the context of their trade use, such as next to other dissimilar and possibly similar displays.

See that your displays are functional. Do they do what you want? Are they single-minded? Do they lead the viewer to the focus or action you desire— without distraction or unnecessary additional elements? Are they compatible with various types of lighting and other display conditions? Are they easy to assemble quickly? Will they stay fresh-looking for their reasonable intended life—or are they easily refreshable?

And do they fit the personality that is being developed for the new product—not only fit it, but reinforce it? This is a must—to make the most of exhibiting the new offering under conditions the marketer controls.

The Advertising

Marketing communications must be based on an advertising strategy. This is used to develop creative direction for the communications executions in advertising, promotion, and all other media-carried support.

The creative execution is a tactical result directly flowing from the direction provided by written guidelines. In most cases, these guidelines are jointly developed by the advertiser (who will market the product) and the advertising agency (which will prepare the advertising). It is the advertiser's obligation to help develop and to approve guidelines that will be specific enough to form a basis for evaluation and for assessment of research results.

On the other hand, the direction should be general enough to allow for freedom in the creation of a variety of effective executions. Such executions should be consistent with the long-term strategy for the product throughout its marketing life. The executions should build one upon another over time, so that the introductory marketing investment will be leveraged after the brand has been well established and the mission of the advertising shifts from an informational to a reminder mode.

Although the execution is expected to persuade triers, buyers, and referrals, it must first attract attention before it can create desire. For this reason, awareness and recall measures are particularly critical in measuring introductory product advertising.

Advertising may be expected to help generate trial, and it may be expected to help remind initial triers to try *again*. However, it cannot be expected to generate retrial if the product does not deliver on the promised benefits. For this reason, it is mandatory that the advertising does not overpromise nor the product underdeliver. Overpromise can generate fast acceptance—and early rejection. Not infrequently, advertising has *underpromised*. The result is a slow buildup of consumer acceptance—rather than the fast take-off that may result from an accurate portrayal of product delivery. For this reason alone, it is essential that advertising execution communications be studied in conjunction with product appeal testing.

Advertising agencies and advertisers use different formats to provide creative direction. However, they generally include the following elements:

1. Business communications objective to be achieved by the advertising
2. Description of the target consumer in the category and, if different, for the new product entry (Include attitudes toward category and product offering)
3. Single most important product benefit, stated as its strongest supportable (and demonstrable) claim. This tells what is different and better than competition about the new product.
4. Image, equity, character, or personality to be established for the offering (and to be established and reflected by the advertising, as well as all other communications)

To this add various caveats (restrictions and mandatory requirements) affecting the range of possible media selections, trade style, brand registration, patent, trademark, and copyright notice, point of origin credit, code authority guidelines, etc. Backing this up, add a Fact Book that includes all of the essential information in summary form regarding the marketplace conditions, product composition, competitive activities (including their advertising executions), and relevant consumer research concept, product, and communications testing results.

The Organizing Communications Concept

Personality, as we have seen, must be the organizing communications concept. All other elements are apt to become fugitive because of events beyond the maker's control, such as preemptive competitive activity.

As the pervasiveness and impact of communications increase, it takes more and more to stand out, to be recognized—and to be remembered.

In the old days of advertising, a simple claim, forcefully and repetitively presented, often sufficed: "Fights headaches 3 ways" . . . "Contains Irium" . . . "Contains chlorophyll" . . . "Contains fluorides" . . . "Biggest, best, tallest, cheapest, longest-lasting, cleans whiter, less tar, more vitamins," etc., etc.

Always necessary is the exclusive "reason for being"—the selling justification for selection of one product or service over another. A tangible, objective consumer benefit is needed for the newly introduced product. It is essential to find these benefits—whether naturally built-in or purposely engineered.

Today, however, this is simply not enough.

Why? Because most heavily advertised products are near-commodities, and they are subject to parity, or better, counterclaims. It takes more than an exclusive, differentiating consumer benefit claim to sustain the forward momentum and continuity of an introductory advertising campaign without changing the character of the product personality (often to be built over the years with millions of media dollars).

It is easy to understand the success of The Marlboro Man, The Green Giant, The Hamm's Bear, A Piece of the Rock, The Pepsi Generation, The Real Thing, etc. They all rely on the personality of the product offering— one that will be sustained no matter what the specific concrete consumer benefit offering may be. The personality is a benefit also. A favorite research technique is to ask: "What kind of person am I if I (buy, drink, use, etc.) Product X?" This reflects the personality signals of the communications—not the hard claims. It is often the most important factor in a successful product's life cycle.

As an example of the sustaining power of a product personality, there's "Madge, the manicurist," and her soaking bowl. She's still going strong, after successfully launching Palmolive Dishwashing Liquid in August 1966 (following market testing).

Colgate-Palmolive Co., through its advertising agency Ted Bates Advertising/New York, uses the professional endorsement authority of Madge to sell their light-duty liquid detergent. Over the years, Madge has maintained the brand's strong presence against many major competitive introductions.

How has Madge done it?

When Palmolive entered the fray, the generic attribute of all light-duty liquids was efficacy, i.e., gets dishes clean. Beyond that, consumers looked for, and all brands promised, a secondary benefit. When Palmolive Liquid was launched, all brands were making secondary mildness claims.

Palmolive made that secondary claim their reason for being, an end-benefit perceived as superior to those of its competition. It was highly specific, simple, relevant, supportable and durable: "Palmolive softens hands while you do dishes." It cut to the heart of the mildness (good for hands) benefit sought by consumers. This statement was delivered by a relevant, hand-care expert: a manicurist (who would know more about hand care?) who illustrated how mild the product was by using it to soften a customer's cuticles prior to a

---

Figure 20-2
Madge—Yesterday and Today

Palmolive Dishwashing Liquid's famous Madge the Manicurist, as portrayed by actress Jan Miner, has been an appropriate, durable, sustaining product personality since 1966 for this leading brand of light duty liquid detergent. Madge and her soaking bowl made mildness a preemptive Palmolive claim in a field where others placed selling emphasis on cleaning efficacy. Here's how Madge looked in the early days (left) and today.

Source: Ted Bates/Colgate

manicure. Research shows that "Madge" and the soaking bowl afford Palmolive Liquid instant consumer identification. They are virtually synonymous with the brand. (See Figure 20-2.)

It is likely that the continuous use of this well-positioned authority for a prime benefit is a prime factor in the low A/S spending ratio. The positive familiarity with Madge makes each message instantly recognizable, understandable, acceptable, and efficient.

In summary, a new product should start out its communications life with an enduring personality that will sustain and build over time.

To sell an idea, product or service, the most important communications equity is its personality.

It must be distinctive, integrated, consistent, positive and memorable.

Nothing else is so important as a vivid personality.

Competition may copy claims and product.

It will not copy personality.

Personality is non-preemptible.

It is a marketing obligation to discover and to build personality into new products communications.

Personality builds sales over time.

21

Media/Promotion/Payout

It's still the same old story,
A fight for love and glory,
A case of do or die.
The fundamental things apply,
As time goes by.
—"As Time Goes By"
   by H. Hupfeld (Harms, Inc., NYC)
   from Casablanca, Warner Bros., 1942

Now that the product people have produced this wonderful new product, somehow it has to be sold.

To be sold, the consumer has to know it exists.

For the consumer to know it exists, you—the marketer—have to communicate it. Better yet, you have to promote it.

To promote it effectively (and effectively means at a profit!), there is one clear challenge: Execute a program that satisfies everyone's selfish interests. That's the true test of a good sales program.

Everyone knows that a new product should satisfy a need—real, perceived, latent, *or basically* essential.

Not everyone knows that a successful new product introduction has to satisfy not only user needs—but seller needs. In other words, there has to be something in it for everyone.

Use the media to tell consumers about the product and about the trial purchase incentives—coupons, samples, trial sizes, etc. There's never enough to do everything, but with creativity and by phasing various elements so that the financial impact doesn't hit all at once, a lot may be accomplished. With a new product introduction, however, many of those costs do hit at once. That's why the introductory year (or two) is often an investment against future profit potential.

Serving Selfish Interests

Let's review those selfish interests that must be served in the introduction of a typical new package good.

Company Sales Force

The sales force is being asked to add an item. Maybe they're being asked to do this while maintaining the volume of all the other items out there. Maybe they are being asked to do it at the expense of one particular weak sister in a competitor's line—or in the company's own line.

The manufacturer is choosing—not the trade. Never mind the computer read-outs, the sales force must sell the substitution headquarters recommends. They're being asked to put that item in a certain spot in the store, in a certain department, on a certain shelf, next to a certain other product. Maybe sales people will get a little detailing muscle for assistance—but the sales force has to sell the program.

Or, maybe not. Maybe a broker organization will replace the sales force for this item. So? So they're losing an opportunity to add a new item to their line. Sure, the work is skipped—but the opportunity for gain is lost also.

No matter what the situation, there has to be something in it for the sales force—or else the new product isn't going to get all of the attention it rightfully deserves. Build in some incentive bonuses for performance: money, prizes, recognition—maybe all three. Do this first step thoroughly. If you miss on this one, much else that follows will have little effect.

Don't forget: on the average, 37 percent of all sales growth and 31 percent of profits for most marketers will come from new products in the next five years, according to a 1982 study by Booz, Allen & Hamilton.

So, doing this basic first step right is the foundation for all of the communications and promotions that overlay the field selling plan designed to get the introduction started off just right. Not only should there be the selfish-interest incentives, there should also be the tools of the trade to help serve that selfish interest. A full array of fact sheets, sales brochures, advertising media plans, and examples of the creative communications must be in the selling kit.

The Headquarters Distributor

Also in the selling kit must be something to appeal to the selfish interests of the chain headquarters and/or wholesaler.

The sales force is going to ask some very big businesses to change their assortment of merchandise. This means something has to move over to make room. The salesman has a suggestion, of course. Kick out that slow-moving competitor. However, he must have the facts to support this suggestion. Also, because the newly inventoried item means record-keeping changes for the merchandiser, sales must pay for this one-time cost. As an added incentive, the sales force will offer an introductory allowance to encourage a sufficiently large opening inventory to help the stores meet the predicted demand with plenty of merchandise at a "hot" feature price during the introductory advertising/promotion program. This allowance may also include add-on sweeteners to underwrite store advertising, support in-store and/or retailer ad couponing, pay for displays, and perhaps underwrite in-store sampling.

The Retail Level

But, it's not that simple. Every store manager is his own boss. No matter what headquarters recommends, in most instances the store manager has the authority to elect whether or not to take on the item, in what assortment, and in what quantities. So—his selfish interest must be served also.

The new product may be a big deal at headquarters, but out at 2nd and Central, it's another matter. "My market isn't your average market. My customers are different. I am very careful about what I throw out, after all I picked that stuff in the first place—and my customers rely on us to carry it." And so a way must be found to squeeze in the new product—even if on a trial basis.

Right now, at introductory time, there may be a way for the local manager to benefit by a big consumer sweepstakes. If policy isn't against it, if the consumer winners are his customers, he can win the big award that goes to the retailer who cooperates by putting up the big sweepstakes display (which requires a lot of merchandise as well as those tear-off pads). Then, there's the "mystery shopper" program—if the mystery shopper sees someone buy the new item, the purchaser gets a prize, and so does the store!

That's the idea. A little cut of the pie for everyone. If the store is a big one and there are department managers, there should be something in it for them, too. After all, it's a big event—giving birth to a new product.

Marketing Interrelationships

The Quaker Oats Company, an active new products marketer, has collected much information on the related effects of various new products marketing forces. The following section, passed along to the author by Quaker's past president, Kenneth Mason, contains much information specifically interesting to the package goods industry—but also principles that cut across many new product marketing needs.

Figure 21-1 illustrates first-year retail sales for four ready-to-eat cereals from three leading manufacturers, each introduced in different years, but, considered together, representative of a typical cereal introduction pattern. The Quaker Oats report, "The New Item Problem," says:

Figure 21-1
4 RTE Cereals—Retail Sales

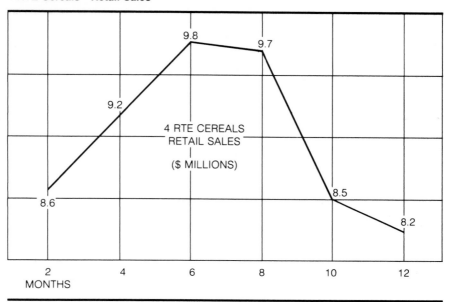

Source: A. C. Nielsen.

For the first A. C. Nielsen reporting period, the combined retail sales of the four cereals would have been $8,600,000 for the first two months; $9,200,000 for the second two months—with a general trend of from about $8,000,000 to $10,000,000, then back to about $8,000,000 where the trend levels off. This is the pattern of the industry.

Why this particular pattern? Why do the sales of new products start at a certain level, rise to a peak, and then level off? Does the answer lie in advertising? As a new product is launched, advertising builds to a peak and sales follow. When advertising levels off, sales level off, creating this pattern. This sounds logical, but it isn't so.

As Figure 21-2 shows, advertising does not always start at a low level and then build up. In this example, media spending started at a very high level and then descended to a lower level: Advertising level and sales level are exactly contradictory!

If it isn't advertising, then it must be consumer demand that causes our sales pattern. Demand builds up as the advertising becomes effective.

But Figure 21-3 shows that consumer demand starts at a peak and then levels off.

Our illustration uses Nielsen figures showing sales per point of distribution. Our illustration shows that where these products were available, they moved almost twice

Figure 21-2
4 RTE Cereals—Advertising Expenditures

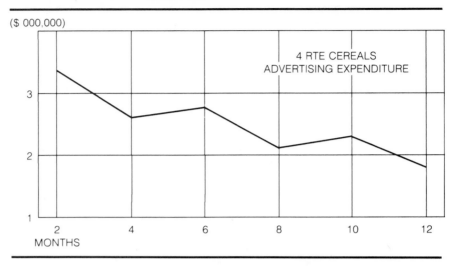

Source: A. C. Nielsen

as fast in the first period. Indexed at 100 percent, they show 189 percent the first two months. The products were moving off retail shelves at a rate almost twice as fast in the first two months as they did in the 12th. In other words, products were turning over faster *where they were stocked*.

Consumer demand starts at a peak, advertising starts at a peak, then why do sales start low, rise and then level off?

The only thing that correlates to the sales trend is effective distribution, as Figure 21-4 shows—"the gradual build-up of effective distribution from about 60 percent in the first two-month period to 88 percent at the end of the year."

Figure 21-5 suggests that:

We have produced a marketing model. As an industry, we are peaking advertising at the point where availability is lowest. We then let advertising—and demand—level off while availability rises. *In terms of profits, this model is very inefficient and really does not make sense.* [Author's italics]

What is needed is an improved model [see Figure 21-6], where availability is at its peak from the start. We don't mean 100 percent distribution—we are talking only about the distribution actually attained—in this specific case, 88 percent distribution at the end of the first year.

[Figure 21-7] shows the improved results. If we could alter the marketing model so that distribution/availability is at its peak from the beginning, a completely different sales picture emerges.

Figure 21-3
4 RTE Cereals—Consumer Demand

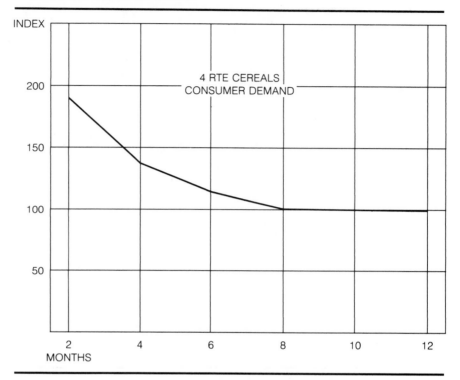

Source: A. C. Nielsen

The bottom line is the same line we showed in the first chart [Figure 21-1], the actual retail sales of the four ready-to-eat cereals. The top line shows what could have happened to those retail sales if distribution/availability was at its peak from the start. Actual sales were $54 million. Potential sales were $66 million . . . a difference of $12 million, or more than 20 percent. Filling this gap in sales required neither additional expenditure nor additional cost. The manufacturer has the same investment, the same sales costs, and the same advertising costs. The retailer has no increased distribution, except that stores that will ultimately carry the product have it when advertising breaks.

To test the hypothesis, Quaker Oats Company ran a similar tracking of six newly introduced semi-moist dog foods from three major marketers, with the same general results.

The conclusion:

Figure 21-4
4 RTE Cereals—Effective Distribution

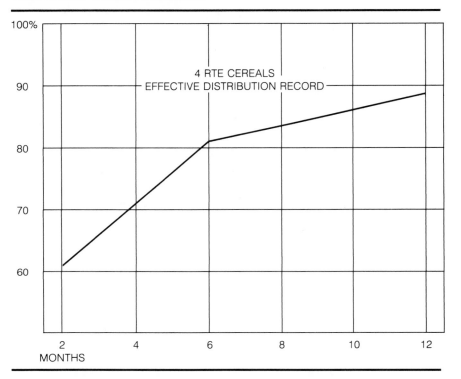

Source: A. C. Nielsen

These figures relate to consumer purchases and not manufacturers' shipments. The profits here relate more to the retailer than to the manufacturer because, in the new product explosion, a single manufacturer does not participate in the entire explosion. He participates only when he himself introduces a product and, for most manufacturers, this is really quite seldom. A retailer, however, participates in all the new product introductions . . . in any given year, more than ten percent of the business done in a retail store may be in new products.

Presumably, then, if the 20 percent loss of new product introduction effectiveness is overcome, the 10 percent of business can produce a 2 percent increase in the total sales of the retailer.

The Quaker Oats Company concludes that by getting new products on the shelf at the height of introductory promotional efforts, both the manufacturer and the distributor can make more profits with the same investment.

To achieve this, the following is necessary, says Quaker:

Figure 21-5
4 RTE Cereals—Marketing Model

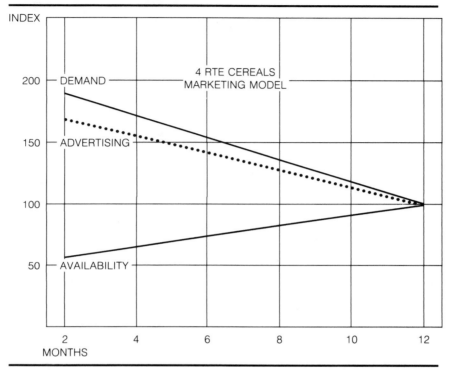

Source: A. C. Nielsen

1. A better job on the manufacturer's part in communicating with the retailer.
2. Coordinating new product introductions better and timing them so that the big advertising and promotional emphasis come when the retailer is ready with the product on his shelf—and . . .
3. A healthy respect on the part of the retailer for the tremendous extra profit potential that exists for him by working together and coordinating these new product introductions—to tie-in distribution with the manufacturer's efforts.

The Consumer

Even if all of this has been done right, nothing much will happen unless the ultimate consumer is served. The customer is always right—and serving that selfish interest is paramount.

To serve that consumer, of course, the right assortment of merchandise has to be in the right place at the right time.

Figure 21-6
4 RTE Cereals—Revised Marketing Model

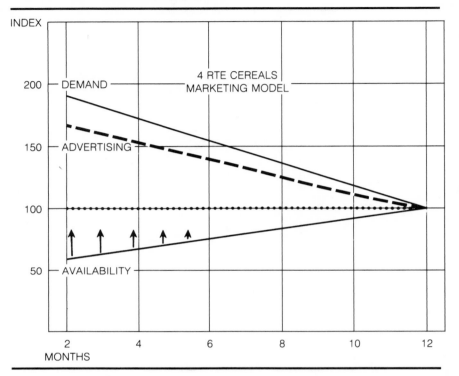

Source: A. C. Nielsen

The advertising will direct the consumer's attention to the selfish interest the new product serves, whether it be reflected glory and status or a way to do a tough dirty job quicker, easier, and cleaner—or any of the many gradations between.

It will also tell the consumer about the special incentives being offered to encourage trial purchase. The deep price discounts, the high value coupons and bouncebacks, the free samples, the premium offers, and the contests will all be advertised and promoted.

The sales force, the trade headquarters, the retail store were all logistically easy to reach. They were fixed entities in known geographic locations with known sales potential. But the consumer—ah, that's different.

Here's where skillful media and promotion planning can make or break the introduction. If the research backdrop for the launch has been done in terms that can be translated to the audience characteristics available in the census

Figure 21-7
4 RTE Cereals—Retail Sales Projection

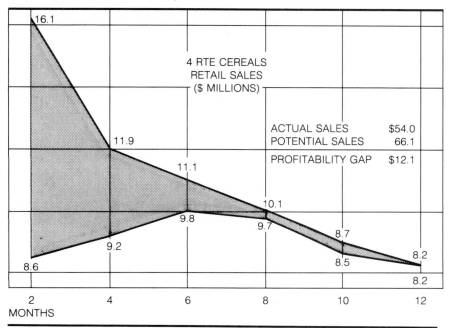

4 RTE CEREALS
RETAIL SALES
($ MILLIONS)

ACTUAL SALES	$54.0
POTENTIAL SALES	66.1
PROFITABILITY GAP	$12.1

16.1

11.9

11.1

10.1

9.8

9.7

9.2

8.7

8.6

8.5

8.2

8.2

2   4   6   8   10   12

MONTHS

Source: A. C. Nielsen

and zip codes, in media audits and guides, in the computer programs of the major advertising agencies—then efficient media planning can begin.

Media Planning Guidelines

Media planning involves targeting the audience, determining weight levels in terms of reach (coverage) and frequency, and timing. All of this translates into media efficiency: How well and at what cost is what percentage of the target reached at goal frequency within a specified period?

The Numbers

All of that is programmable. If the target is numerically defined and located, media measures can be cranked in and the best use of any media daypart or combinations of dayparts can be computed and, given some fairly reliable assumptions, combinations of major media.

There are important qualitative considerations, also, which are often overlooked.

Qualitative Considerations

During the birth of a new product—before it is known for itself alone—its close associates affect its perception. Therefore, editorial climate is important. This means that subjectivity enters into the selection of the specific publications and programs that will carry the advertising. In the case of spot broadcast advertising, program adjacencies are taken into consideration. Or, in the case of r.o.p. (run of press), newspaper section and editorial adjacencies are considered. In certain product categories, even the day of ad appearance becomes important (e.g., "best food day" for grocery products, aimed at the highest traffic periods, and weekends for major-ticket items where more than one member of the family may participate in the purchase decision).

The numbers are not the most important factor, although they are a reflection of the spending pattern.

Timing is critical. Heavy introductory weight designed to stimulate new product trial must not fall on deaf ears (wrong season, wrong day or day-part, wrong program or publication) or empty shelves (empty of the new product, because it either hasn't appeared yet or was understocked and is already sold out before the advertising begins).

There are space and time elements in media. How big should the ad be? How many colors? Should it have a pop-up coupon? Can we tell the story in 30 seconds? Does it need a full minute? Or is the budget so big and the product so sensational (yet easy to communicate) that 10 second announcements are needed also, to get into crowded time periods and to extend the frequency? What about cable and direct broadcast? Will they reach the target with greater efficiency?

Is continuity of media needed? Perhaps the new product has a relatively flat seasonality and is frequently consumed. This may mean year-long advertising is necessary. After the big introductory blast, how much is left to carry that continuity? Can it be on an every day, every week, every month, every season basis? Are low levels spread across the calendar preferable to a flighted plan of clusters of advertising—or a blinking pattern of a week in and a week out? Will one time slot (or one type of publication) carry the target, or does the new product need several dayparts? Will a scatter plan across the board be most effective— or should roadblocks be used, to be certain that no matter what channel is turned on for the 6 o'clock news, the new product word will get across?

Targeting Directions

Media experts will know how to put the plan together. The new product marketing team, however, is responsible for precise targeting directions.

It is possible that one planning pattern is indicated for the introductory period—a media program that will reach all of the interested target segments—while a sustaining plan must of necessity concentrate only on those prime prospects in the center of the target. The introductory plan, in other words, reaches "Definitely" and "Probably" and "Might Buy." After the product is well established (perhaps a year or two later), the lower spending level sustaining pattern is best aimed at "Definitely," with media selections that will peripherally pick up bits of the wider target.

Sometimes a product has a dual audience: The user and the purchasing agent. Toys are an example. Toys for toddlers are advertised to mothers. Toys for older youngsters are advertised to user (purchase influencer), even though the purchaser may be a parent. Soft drinks, fast foods, and confections may be advertised across-the-board, with different creative approaches in different media and at different time periods aimed at different segments. A mammoth advertiser such as McDonald's, for example, has advertising creative and media tailored to kids, tweens, teens, and on up the segmentation of ages and life-styles. Sometimes there are shared experiences. All-family ready-to-eat cereals may be advertised to adults in one style and the same theme carried forward in another style in another time period to the high-volume kid consumer.

Bartered Media

There are many ways to buy media beyond the negotiated deal. Barter buying is common. Barter means simply paying for media with merchandise instead of cash. Merchandise is valued at a demand value, determined by the method of distribution by the barter firm and the guidelines laid down by the manufacturer, which may wish its goods released outside its trading channel areas. Product overruns, obsolete models, etc., are commonly used in barter deals.

Syndication Trading

Syndication trading is also done in broadcast. A station receives a program it wants (with, possibly, some additional cash) in exchange for an advertising schedule. Because the program rights are syndicated across a number of stations, the per-station cost to the media buyer is minimal, while the value to the station is significant. For this reason, it may be possible to buy more media for less cash—especially if these arrangements can be made well in advance. (A leading program trader is Cash Plus Inc., Minneapolis, MN 55402.)

Another type of syndication is where the program is provided gratis, but includes one or several program-sponsored commercials in place and mandatory to run—with several open commercial interruptions to provide the stations with sales opportunities.

In both barter and syndication deals, be certain of firm schedules running according to plan. Scatter-shot is not for new products where controlled reach and frequencies are essential.

The bottom line is that the new product marketing group should lay down the target audience guidelines. If economy is more important than flexibility, then upfront money committed well in advance may pay large dividends in efficient buying or bonus advertising units.

Effective Introductory Promotions

There are literally hundreds of promotion devices employed in the marketing life of any product. Generally, they are divisible into two areas—trade promotions and consumer promotions.

Trade Promotions

Trade promotions are designed to enlist trade cooperation in efforts to stimulate trial use of the new product. For consumer package goods products, off-invoice allowances and trade programs (displays, premiums, contests) are frequently employed.

The trade is often offered a per case payment for promotional support (e.g., display store ads, storecasts, hot feature pricing, etc.) for new orders placed during a specified period. These are used to sell-in the product, gain shelf facings, build inventory—to build trade support for an introductory consumer promotion.

- **Display allowances** pay for specific display performance only during the specified introductory period, generally while the new brand is being otherwise heavily promoted and advertised.
- **Buying allowances** grant a reduction in the list price of a product during the introductory period (within specified limitations). They are designed to obtain initial distribution, build trade inventories, and (if desired) reduce the inventory shelf price, increase trade support behind consumer promotion, and (occasionally) meet unexpected competitive threats.

Consumer Promotions

Immediate value promotions attract attention by lowering the price, adding value, or both. Examples of the former are "off-label packs" (with the cents-off offer flagged on the package); examples of the latter are in- or on-pack premiums (free FM tuner module with full-price cassette player). Established brands often use delayed value incentives that encourage the consumer to do something before being rewarded for purchasing the product. These are less effective (but less expensive) for an introduction seeking immediate trial impact.

A review of the most frequently used consumer promotion techniques indicates the following are most effective for new product introductions:

- **Off-label packs**
- **In- or on-pack premiums**
- **Coupon packs**

  Inexpensive distribution can be combined with an off-label pack to provide both trial and repeat incentive. There is little or no cost involved on either incentive until actual purchase.

- **Cross-ruffs**

  The established brand carries a sample and/or coupons for the new product; the new brand can reciprocate. Where targets are compatible and products noncompetitive, this can work well within a company's product array or with another company or industry association. For the established brand, it provides an additional incentive for retrial and early repeat; for the new product, it provides an accepted, established-value premium to loyal users of the established brand. It is workable both ways—or either way—to stimulate new product acceptance.

- **Mailed coupons**

  These packages can be zip-code targeted to the most susceptible prospects—thus cutting down waste distribution. The consumer makes the purchase decision at the mail receiving point (home/office) away from competitive influences. It is efficient in stimulating trial of new and low-share products. Costs are often spread among a number of non-competitive participants in a single mailing. One drawback is that misredeemers and nonredeemers dilute the total effectiveness.

- **Product sampling**

  This technique is extremely expensive, difficult to police, and hard to control. It is best used for unique products, those with high repeat usage, or those in low unit cost categories (example: street corner sampling of mini-packs of new cigarette brands).

- **Media coupons**

Payout

There has been a tremendous expenditure to bring the new product this far. Now, it must pay off. How long will it be before it will pay out?

This differs in every case. It also differs by product category. In many consumer package goods categories, there are tried-and-nearly-always-true formulas. One is this: Year 1 New Product Introduction: Spend at *double* the Share Goal. In other words, if the year-end share goal or average Year 1 share is 20 percent of market, then media advertising spending should be 40 percent of the total media advertising in the category.

Here's how it works:

Market size:	$100,000,000	(factory dollars, not retail)
20% share goal:	20,000,000	
Total category Advertising Spending:	20,000,000	
Spend at 40% of total advertising:	8,000,000	
Assume Year I Sales:	$ 15,000,000	(reflecting retail movement)
	5,000,000	(year-end field inventory)
Total	$ 20,000,000	
Less:	8,000,000	for advertising
	4,000,000	for trade promotion
	6,000,000	for cost of goods
	1,000,000	for freight
	1,000,000	for advertising & promotion production, inventory events, miscellaneous
	$ 20,000,000	

This mythical Year 1 break-even, using the "double the category share-of-voice goal," is merely for illustration. Even for a product with 30 percent cost-of-goods, it is unlikely.

However, as can be seen in Figure 21-8, it is worth it—for a successful new product. The life cycle concept, espoused by the management consultant firm of Booz, Allen, & Hamilton for 30 years, illustrates that new products are essential to the life of any marketer. It illustrates that like Man, products go through cycles—some with more revivals than others. Sales volume grows faster than profit margins, with absolute profits lagging behind the margins—but with an important dollar profit return growth during the maturity/saturation periods. This chart is based on the average of studies of 700 companies and 13,311 new product introductions. It recognizes the investment spending necessary to get a new product going, as well as the importance of doing that.

There is no absolute in approaching what must be invested, how fast it must pay out or what incremental volume it must add. It depends on many factors. Figure 21-8, it should be stated, represents new products of several definitions: Only 10 percent are new to the world, while 19 percent were new only to the organization. The remaining 71 percent were all changes within current product lines—much less costly to develop, introduce, and manage over time. These were additions to existing product lines, revisions or improvements, cost reductions, and repositionings. Their lesser cost helped pull down the total new products investment percentage per company. In other words, not only the mature products but the close-in line extensions, flankers,

Figure 21-8
Basic Life Cycle of Products

Basic Life Cycle of Products

Sales Volume

New Product Profit

Profit Margins

Introduction | Growth | Maturity | Saturation | Decline

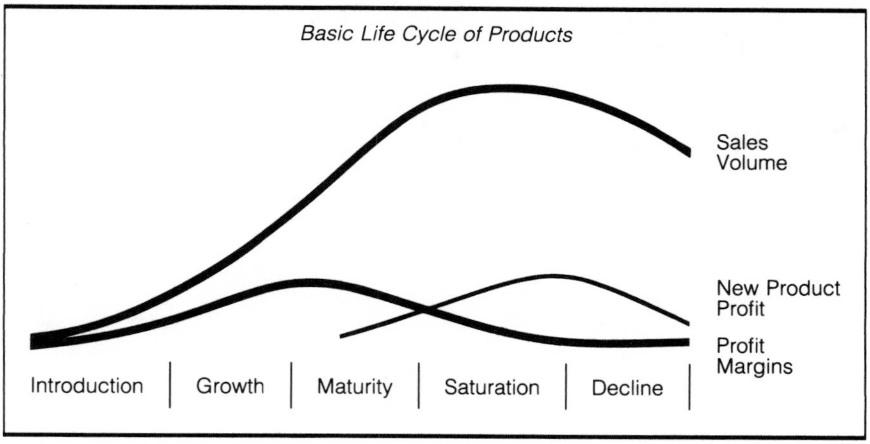

By permission, (c) Booz, Allen & Hamilton, Inc.

and repositionings helped carry the company while it funded the investment in the dynamics of establishing truly new products.

This underlines the fact that every vital organization needs a program of new products, ranging from the easy-to-execute and none-too-risky line development items all across the board to innovations and inventions. It is this balance that will keep the new product flow going, at the same time making it all affordable by keeping the company profit dynamics in tune. Watch the individual payout, of course—but the payoff is at the corporate level, which benefits by the total effect of a skillfully managed new product development and marketing program.

Section 6
Summary Afterword

Once the product is ready, we enter upon the marketing phase. This involves planning, simulation, and selection of the test markets; determining the new product communications; and measuring the promotion payout.

Building a "Fact Book" is essential in planning. After determining the meaning of all the assembled facts, an executive summary should be prepared to provide needed perspective. This indicates where the opportunity gaps are to be found and what information sources might be used—intelligence consulting, reverse engineering, making use of the Freedom of Information Act.

Then comes the actual planning process. Here is where to consider the importance of being first, the possibility of testing while launching on a wide scale, and the importance of contingency planning.

In moving on to the actual selection of test markets, various candidates may be considered and rejected before lighting on those most suitable for the new product. There is also the possibility of simulating simulations by going into isolated and controlled micro-markets (extremely small test markets).

The product then is ready to move into test market. Now we must communicate its presence. Any number of factors enter into product communications, not the least of which is the product itself. Its personality should be established at birth, assuring newness and that the product is both better and different.

Then come all the other factors of communication: product performance; its names, both brand and generic; its package—the construction and graphics;

the price—what it communicates about the product image; product display, both on the shelf and at home; and the advertising.

The advertising, of course, is perhaps the most elaborate part of product communications. It is derived out of the business communication goal; the category target (and if different, the new product target); the communication of the product's most important benefit—both different and better; and the establishment of an image, equity, character, or personality that will be sustained over time in all communications.

Now you are ready to tell the world about your new baby. Keep in mind that this involves due regard to all the selfish interests involved—the company sales force, the headquarters distributor, the retailer, and the consumer.

Media planning guidelines should go beyond the numbers and include qualitative considerations. While the media experts can draw up the media specifics, it is up to the product manager to determine the targeting directions. Not to be overlooked are the possibilities of using bartered media and syndication trading.

Effective introductory promotions encompass both the trade and the consumer. Trade promotions include rewards for retail purchase performance, display allowances, and buying allowances. Major consumer promotion techniques include off-label packs, in- and on-pack premiums, coupon packs, cross ruffs, mailed coupons, product sampling, and media coupons.

If all is handled right, the payout—and payoff—will extend over the product life cycle. The key is the development of a balanced new products program, taking into account the full range of risks.

Market Testing

22

Start and Monitor

We must ask where we are and whither are we tending.
—*Abraham Lincoln*

Hope is generally a wrong guide, though it is very good company by the way.
—*Lord Halifax*

Good merchandise finds a ready buyer.
—*Plautus*

The marketing plan has been approved.

The product is feasible. Scale-up tests confirm the costs. On-stream plant production yields the same product quality as laboratory or engineering prototypes and the pilot plant runs. Quality control guidelines are confirmed.

The test markets have been selected to simulate conditions of a successful later major launch.

The new product is about to be born . . .

Born into the real world—not an incubator.

That controlled environment with extra-special attention is hard to resist. Everyone wants to do everything possible to see that the newborn is a success. The president flies into the markets and makes a few suggestions on how to improve matters. The general sales manager drops in at the district sales office to give an extra pep talk. Product managers swarm over the market, measuring, counting, photographing, computing. The advertising agency massages the local media—maybe even the program and editorial folks.

That's not how to give birth to a new product. If there's to be a silver spoon in its mouth, don't force feed it in—let the prospect discover it.

Getting Off the Ground

Certainly, the sales force should receive just as enthusiastic an introduction as will be made if the product successfully expands its marketing area.

If there is a national sales meeting planned prior to launch, then this should be simulated also—at headquarters if possible.

The more the sales force knows about the careful targeting, product benefits, and superiorities vs. competition, about forecasted sales success based on controlled test or simulated model projections, about share-of-voice vs. market share goals—the more the sales force knows, the better. It will help them communicate that enthusiasm to their customers.

But, make it easy for them. Provide visual aids: catalog sheets, videotapes or continuous-loop films of commercials, ad proofs, advertising and promotion schedules, demonstration guides, selling samples, and whatever else is necessary to tell the story quickly and effectively. Be sure the salespeople know all about the total market, its progress, competitive moves and positions—literally everything a sharp prospect may know or question.

If there is a national press conference planned for the eventual expansion, then a mini-local press conference should be held in each test market. Invite the press, the trade, the sales force, and have a (quotable) headquarters executive make a few remarks and respond to questions.

Programmed Introductory Goals

Every plan should have market penetration goals. For mass marketed retail distributed products, this goal is usually a percent of distribution per size, per item—often with a shelf position and share of shelf target. There is trade acceptance, which is one positive level. There is actual appearance at retail, which is the more critical level. Products don't sell to consumers out of wholesale warehouses. They must be accessible.

Coping with the Slow Start

Where possible, advertising and promotion start dates should be keyed to the achievement of a certain percentage of availability to the consumer. If there is likely to be genuine difficulty in meeting the minimum distribution goal in time for the introduction, then the introduction should either be delayed or a plan to "feather" in a lead schedule of advertising/promotion before major weight is added should be prearranged with the trade and the media. Go for all of the flexibility possible on a national program. (Here the term "national" is used to represent the maximum expansion area, presumed to be significantly larger than the test market area.)

Coping with the Fast Start

Be certain there is adequate stock in the market—and in back of the initial shipments. It is very difficult to "read" the dimensions of a success if it is characterized by out-of-stock empty shelves. The business goes elsewhere.

Important opportunities have been lost, at a time when the "newness" is most attractive.

It is even possible that if the new product appears to be a really hot item, the trade may jump the planned start date. One trade factor may hit the market long before your planned advertising introduction, possibly putting the product in the retailers' own ads at a "hot" feature price. This tips the competitive trade factors, who may follow suit.

This is the reason to have plenty of merchandise on hand to ship—or, better yet, in nearby warehouses. This is also the reason to have a flexible advertising plan, one that will allow for an earlier-than-planned introductory launch, with a shift of media scheduling at a moment's notice. The sales force should be alerted to these possibilities. Although an effort should be made to start everything off on the planned date, flexible programs to deal with early starts as well as slow starts should be in hand—and communicated to the sales force.

In those instances where a trade factor jumps the gun out of enthusiasm for the product, the trade deal, etc.—and many other trade factors are still hanging back—there is an opportunity for the sales force to use the renegade gate jumper as leverage to bring in the other slowly reacting factors fast. If they do, the sales department can promise earlier, stepped-up efforts— flexible devices such as an overlay of an early coupon drop on top of the introductory trade deal, a stepped-up cooperative payment for exceptional store advertising and mass displays.

Paired Market Sets

Often, test markets are paired—the combination being judged to provide a demographic mix more representative than either individually. Sometimes there are several pairs. One pairing of two-market sets may be designed to measure price differential, another pairing may be designed to measure spending level differentials, another to measure different creative strategies.

When part of a set behaves differently than the other part—such as one jumping the gun and another being laggard in gaining distribution—the difficulties in interpretation fall into the arena of subjective judgment, with a range of possible projections.

One such experience occurred with the test marketing of a famous beauty soap. The low-level spending market outperformed the high-level spending market. Distribution was gained much faster in the low-level market, although spending against thinning distribution was out-shouting its competition at a greater clip.

Because test markets are learning experiences, however, the manufacturer reasoned that if the product could sell so well at the lower level, it should perform even better at the higher level if factors were equalized. The product was left in both markets, the advertising adjusted up in one market and leveled-off in the original high-level market. Pragmatic reasoning ruled.

Projections were relative only to in-market performance. However, a pool of triers and repeaters was developed and studied thoroughly.

From these studies, the package design was revised, the color of the bar changed, the advertising execution refined (while maintaining the successful strategy). Then, the product rolled out to a successful national introduction. It was more of a risk than if the paired test had been one that behaved according to plan—but less of a risk than if the product was retested while competition gained the additional time. The many important areas of refinement made possible by the dislocated test market pairing had enhanced the new product's successful launch.

Premature Success

First, there is the excitement of commercialization and the test market launch. Then there is the "it's too early to read" period. Then, the numbers start coming in. If they are right on target—or better—chances are conversation begins to suggest plans to abort the test early while the expansion commitments are advanced in time.

Another popular suggestion is an expansion from the test areas—to roll-out into divisions and regions from districts.

There's nothing wrong with enthusiasm.

But, if the planning stage was handled correctly, these exigencies were anticipated. There is a plan in place that triggers action under the best and worst circumstances. Under most circumstances, it is advisable to move up the capital clearances in preparation for a rapid expansion—while remaining cautiously watchful until sufficient multiple repeat purchase has been measured—and competition comes out of the woods.

Early Failure

So, the numbers are not so good. The crepe begins to hang.

Now's the time to use a test market for all it is worth. Unless the failure can clearly be traced to bad product—the food turns rancid because of a poor package seal, the machine falters because of a poor component or an assembly goof—or unless the apparent failure is clearly caused by some other readily identifiable circumstances—find out why the flop.

This can require a great deal more searching study than originally planned. The start-up went according to plan—but the take-off never occurred. No need to be terribly concerned about giving the market a little extra attention now. Question every channel of the trade. Question more users in more depth more often and in both qualitative and quantifiable modes.

Often, it is a little thing—overlooked, perhaps. Sometimes the little thing is a last minute "improvement." Sometimes the little thing is an adjustment made necessary when scaling-up from prototypes, an adjustment not thought significant at the time: a different closure on the package, a change in type-face to fit a slightly different dimension, a confusing promotion added to the package back, a change from a simple declarative description of the product to more esoteric or industrially sophisticated language. Tear down the differences between what is going on in the market and what was originally designed and planned. Do "reverse engineering" on the faltering new product entrant.

The inexplicable failure is very rare.

In the face of failure, there are many experts willing to point fingers. Listen. Test every reasonable hypothesis. When the fault or combination of faults is found, determine if it is worth fixing. If so, fix—and move ahead, to a new set of markets if the fixing or the faults indicate this. Then, erect fail-safe procedures to prevent recurrence of such events.

So-So Introduction

Well, it's not a barn burner—but it is still smoldering. It's not bad enough to abort—and it's not good enough to move ahead.

This is a much tougher decision point than the out-and-out flop or the run-away success.

Still, it is "only" the *introduction* of the new product that is a disappointment—not the test.

Patience—and some tinkering, perhaps—is required.

Go after it like the flop—but try to find the flickering spark that is giving it early life as well as the smothering factors that keep it from bursting into flame.

Sometimes the product is just fine. It is only that the proud parents were overly ambitious. A scaled-back program may still sustain the new product with sufficient velocity to justify its existence—and to sustain a profit within a reasonable payout period. Too much has gone into the development of the new product to give up too early.

And, remember, this is only the beginning.

As the new product continues to live in various degrees of success, plans change. They're remade as a result of the test market introduction knowledge, now providing new insights to the monitoring of sales progress and expansion plans.

23

Assess and Expand

You can see a lot just by looking.
—Yogi Berra

Don't go down to the ocean with a notion of what you will find.
—Mason Williams

It is a bad plan that admits of no modification.
—Syrus

The higher you peak, the higher you level. That's been almost axiomatic in assessment of test market experience. That's why heavy promotional efforts, front-loaded media plans, and intensive sales training and motivation go into those early efforts. The communications assault means more when it is "new news" rather than the same old story.

Understand the Plan

Another old axiom is "plan your work, work your plan." Although there is often a temptation to improve on the plan, be careful. Sometimes the goal is achieved, and the input appears to indicate that the horizons might be even broader—so the expansion is modified based on a subjective interpretation of the implications of the findings (rather than the findings themselves).

Because a test market is a learning experience, modifications nearly always *should* be made in the expansion plan. However, care should be exercised to control those brilliant insights based on wishful thinking—rather than on tested performance.

As an example, some years ago, a major personal products company developed an extremely refreshing antiseptic toothpaste, with a flavor so powerful that it almost stung the tongue—and lingered on many minutes after rinsing. The hypothesis was that such a dentrifice would not only be hygienic—but the user would be able to "feel" the cleanliness. A realistic

284

share of market goal was set for the aggressively flavored paste, which had proven to have an intense liking score among a hard core of triers prior to the market test.

The test was a success. The market share goal was achieved. Although the average repeat scores were relatively low, they were extremely high among a significant but small segment. The product quickly built up a very strong brand loyalty among users who could sustain the share goal on an on-going basis.

Then, middle management changed.

The new marketing director read the findings differently than the planners and operators of the test. Whereas the premise had been to build a significant business on the special properties of the intense-tasting toothpaste, the newly assigned executive looked at the huge percentage of triers who had rejected the product because of the extremely aggressive flavor. "Yes, we have a success," he reasoned, "but look at how much more business we could have if we just reduced the flavor intensity to make it more broadly acceptable."

This was done. Advertising strategy was switched to "a pleasantly refreshing dentifrice"—away from the former "shockingly clean feeling" approach. An expanded regional market roll was begun, with higher share goals.

Of course, the result was a new product failure. Although more triers found the product acceptable, they did not find it sufficiently different from their regular brand to make a firmly committed repeat switch. The product was insufficiently differentiated and became just another new brand with generally parity properties.

"Don't fix it, if it ain't broke," is the lesson to be learned here.

Assessment Steps

Too often marketers read the numbers—but do not talk to the customers.

Of course, pre- and postawareness checks should be made. Sufficiently large samples of telephone checks of either the target market or the general population, depending on the nature of the new product, should be executed. The premeasure gives a level of competitive product awareness (which can be related to their share-of-voice media spending and longevity in the market) and, surprisingly, sometimes finds a level of awareness for the as-yet-to-be-introduced brand—which relates to historic reasons (other similar names used in past) or other circumstances. At any rate, these levels of unaided and aided awareness of brand and generic classification become the basis for periodic postintroduction measures that will be tracked in relationship to marketing spending, competitive activity, and time.

Too often, the communications value of a sales presence is overlooked. In markets that are paired in all respects except retail shelf visibility, it is not surprising to find that awareness is higher in the market with strongest distribution and display. Marketers sometimes forget that there is the potential for huge numbers of impressions on the shelf—because it is the reach (coverage) and frequency of media and promotional devices that are usually related to sales performance.

Measuring Awareness

Experienced marketers have awareness goals to achieve at various stages in the development of the test market. As these are reached, exceeded, or underachieved, analysis of the causes may create the need for fine-tuning some aspect of the program. Such changes should always be projectable to the national plan's pay-out plan.

Meeting Competitive Moves

In some rare instances, of course, where special local competitive efforts are mounted, a marketer may decide to sacrifice the projectability of the test market in order to make abnormal counter-moves to blunt the competitors' further interest and their ability to read their effect on the test.

The trade-off for this type of tactic is rarely advantageous in the long run. Better to find out how well the planned program can stand up to out-of-scale competitive moves, meanwhile measuring and projecting the competitive activity to determine if it is in fact a program that could be mounted against the new product on a major geographic scale.

Meaning of Awareness

Behind awareness are perceptions. A broadscale telephone survey can ask how the brand is evaluated, based on awareness—and relate this to whether the awareness is unaided or aided, and whether the respondent is a trier, trier-rejector, trier-repeater, or considering trial. In each case, the rationale for the mode is reported. The ability to play back advertising is often key. Is the playback related to the advertising's creative strategy, its central theme—or to something peripheral such as executional elements that may assume greater importance than the promise of the new product itself? This measure may be related to buyer attitude and trial.

Point-of-Sale Audits

While sales from the order sheets and withdrawals from the shipping department and warehouses are measured, actual shelf momentum (in retail goods terms) is the best indicator of whether stock backups or out-of-stocks are problems ahead. These shelf audits may be conducted on an actual count basis, using special detail services, syndicated research, service of some retail chains employing universal product code measures, etc. In fast moving categories, even cursory but periodic visual checks of a sampling of key retailers can often spot the trends. The technique, in other words, should fit the circumstances. In any event, it is important to audit the activity at the point of final sale—not just at the point of factory sales.

Talking to the Customer

Until now, consumer reaction to the product has either been achieved in a controlled or laboratory situation during the early phases of product development—or has been the result of structured telephone (or, possibly, mail) interviews. In some instances, interactive cable television may have been employed.

During communications development, it is likely that group interviews and/or one-on-one intercept point-of-purchase interviews and/or carefully designed and guided individual interviews in depth had taken place and provided guidance.

Now, buying is taking place under real circumstances—off the shelf, in response to an offer made in person by a salesman, a commercial, an ad, or a mailer. Now is the time to again talk to a buyer, a user and—in many product categories—a potential repeat prospect.

As early as planned awareness has reached a substantial level, respondents should be sought for person-to-person discussion of the product reception and rejection, use-experience where applicable, elements of the paid (as applicable) editorial, and word-of-mouth characterizations. Depending on the product category, these may be conducted in the office, in the factory, in the home, through mall intercepts, or in central location groups.

Just as the point-of-purchase audit is an important indicator, so too is the prospect/consumer audit. Often, the predictability of the test progress is signalled at this juncture.

Talking to the Sales Channels

If the product moves through one or several channels before reaching the ultimate user—which is always the case except in certain direct response situations—then interviews should be conducted at each level in the process: sales force, wholesaler, distributor, broker, shelf detailer, chain buyer, merchandise manager, store manager, store department head, purchasing agent, etc., as applicable. Don't miss an element in the marketing chain!

Periodic Repeat Research

The factory-to-user research we have just described should be repeated at various points in the test market's development. Early wear-out of the message—or of the product's reception—can be spotted before either may be reflected in sales figures. Opportunity for modification of both, with clear direction, may result from the program of repeated research.

Occasionally, opportunities for product accessories, feature deletions or additions, line extensions, flankers, and peripheral product opportunities are suggested as the new product gains market acceptance and user familiarity. This test market study process then may become a staging area for expansion of the opportunity as originally conceived.

This type of study has also led to revisions in pricing strategies, restructuring of trade deals, reengineering of package structure, resizing (size-ups, size-downs, multi-packs, etc.), retiming of marketing spending, rebalancing of the media mix, etc.

The history of new product test markets is such that rarely is there a repeat opportunity to gather this information prior to major capital expenditure and market investment if the product achieves the test goals and is subsequently launched in a major way. Therefore, make the most of this one-time opportunity!

Market Checking

Make sure the travel department knows of every test market. When booking trips, the department can furnish a supply of appropriate store check questionnaires with a simple letter of instruction to each traveler. The request is simple:

If you can find the time on your trip to (city names), please stop at as many (class of trade) stores as possible, and note the information needed in spaces provided. Route completed Store Check forms to the travel department for distribution. Thank you— you are helping us keep track of (name of category and key brands) progress.

The Fast Way

Ingenuity can sometimes save time, save money, and make a better record.

One time, the author had to cover three widely separated test markets in the same day. By commercial airline, it would have taken several overnight stays and hotel charges.

Solution: Charter a plane. Arrange in advance for each airport to have a rental car handy, complete with map and route list. Take along a VTR or a small 8mm camera. Start early in the morning, ring each city to hit suburban shopping centers, with one drive through the city center on the way back to airport.

At each stop, photograph identifying locator—name of shopping mall on sign or, if not appropriate, street sign at crossing. Photograph signage over store entrance, photograph line-up of checkout counters (by counting the cash registers, you can estimate store volume), photograph appropriate store sections and displays. Zoom camera in on price marking, special promotions, etc.

If the city is unfamiliar to business associates, take the opportunity to add highlight shots that provide a characteristic feeling of the neighborhoods surrounding the stores checked. When entering each store, be sure to tell the manager or assistant the purpose of your visit, so he will not become alarmed by the on-scene photography. Secure his authorization.

Managing the Expansion

Early success indications have triggered activities back at the home office. Clearance has been obtained for scale-up to expansion, with various dates keyed for additional funding should indicated objectives be achieved according to program.

Although the expansion area has been predetermined prior to market testing, it should be reevaluated in light of the knowledge input from the test area. Whereas it was originally planned to expand into the area with the highest consumption of the product category, the test area results may indicate the opposite—that the best initial opportunity will be in areas where the category is not as well developed and where the new product offers a distinctiveness and advantages particularly appealing to category sub-par prospect groups. It may be learned that the major competitive thorn in the test area is a product line with unanticipated advantages in the planned roll-out area. Regional economic factors may have changed since the major introductory plan was approved months or years earlier. Perhaps, even the original assessment that the new product might "cannibalize" (steal sales) from similar products in the company's own line turns out to be just the opposite—if anything, it enhances the appeal of all elements of the line. This also can indicate a change in territorial expansion.

Outside Effects Affect the Plan

During the course of the test market, a major competitive new product may have been introduced nationally or into a major geographic area. This can alter plans, triggering a national launch rather than the roll-out plan, a complementary regional pattern launch (filling in those areas of presumed roll-out by the competitor), or a head-to-head launch in the competitive region.

The company's test market does not operate in a vacuum. The expansion plan should have been made with anticipatory directions understood given those happenstances that are possible to predict. Production planning and parts/material sourcing must be alerted as soon as any such changes become a possibility—even if the indicators come very late in the test program. The new product development team works closely together monitoring the environment—reassessing implications to the approved plan, securing altera-tions to the plan on an as-needed basis, but always with clear bottom line performance objectives. Avoid the swashbuckling attitude: "We'll meet the situations as they come along, then adjust our payout after we ride out the rough waters." Success doesn't mean just to win, success means to win with a profit.

Merchandising the Expansion

The test market success should be packaged in a dramatic way, to turn on the enthusiasm of the sales force and the trade. Now, there are hard facts—share of market, trial and repeat, profit performance for all distribution and sales channels, competitive steal, category expansion, realignment of the trade assortment, and space allocations. Quotas can be set for sales, with bonuses tied to achievement of goals clearly linked to realistic sales levels.

Trade advertising should feature the success as its major appeal—to en-courage broad and deep product stocking while the deals are rich and while the introductory opportunity is most timely. Proven profit results, based on test performance, and the heavy consumer impressions plan, underscores the fact that the trade's opportunity is *now*.

Be liberal with trade samples, professional detailing, or demonstration trials (as applicable). For consumable products, consider sales seminars or introductory trade sessions and sample mailings or personal deliveries to the homes or offices of selling agents, whether they be retailers, service dealers, or any agent between company's sales force and the ultimate consumer. (First, be certain this is not in violation of any corporate, dealer body, or trade policy or custom.)

Here's an intriguing example. A major grocery chain has a policy forbidding its buyers to attend any vendor event where competitive chain buyers are present. One new product marketer complied by inviting the *wives* of every chain buyer—along with a guest of her choice in each instance—to a spectacu-lar fashion showing and luncheon with a famous designer to help introduce its new personal care product. The invitation to the buyer's wife went to her home with a liberal assortment of samples of the product line, along with an autographed design from the famous guest she would meet at the chic hotel grand ballroom showings, which were conducted on a region-by-region basis. Being able to bring a friend along encouraged maximum attendance by the buyers' wives—100 percent of the trade factor wives were represented. Each received another gift favor at the upbeat, sophisticated luncheon, met the famous designer, and was introduced to the dramatic new product line—and shown how to use it for best results. Evidently, each went home to her buyer husband with a great deal of enthusiasm. There was 100 percent distribution acceptance.

Hard to Read Results

Successes and failures are usually easy to recognize.

It is the in-betweens that baffle and chew up corporate innards: fiscally and physically.

Here is where marketing research makes its greatest contribution. It isolates the reason for the so-so reception. Only, usually, it is reasons.

Therefore, don't skimp on marketing research during any phase of development. Monitor everything. Talk to buyers, nonbuyers, repeaters, non-repeaters, multiple-repeaters, single repeaters, heavy users, light users—and likewise to consumers of competitive products. Be aware that competitive products may not be in the industry category, same store section, or even the same store . . . or any store. If another product fills the same void, it is a competitor—even if you initially perceive it as not a part of your market. It competes against you for time, energy, and money—and it fulfills the same craving.

Don't skip the trade. Check the extent and time of distribution development. Check merchandisers, store managers, and, maybe most importantly, the stock clerks. Do store checks independently—not with the company salesman (clear this with the sales department). Have everyone use the same store check forms, dictating devices, or camera techniques. Do not alert store detailers in advance of your calls.

Don't skip the product. Buy a little here and there on each trip. Examine it. Try it. Record the code.

Be aware of special local situations—economic, social, weather, etc.

Sort all of this out. The answer is usually to be found, and often correctable. Sometimes it is so easily rectified that the company can expand the product from an apparent failure. Oftentimes, it is back to the drawing board for revisions and retesting. There must have been good reason to get this far, so there is often good reason to try to keep the project alive. If there is clearly no hope, the sooner the project is terminated, the better for all concerned.

Where Do You Go from Here?

The test market has measured the new product's vitality under actual market conditions, conducted to maximize economy while limiting risk and gaining knowledge. Usually several high quality, geographically dispersed, all-media markets are used. The market performance is a measure of trade and customer acceptance.

Now, the test has been analyzed and projected to success, perhaps with significant improvement modifications. Every aspect of the test has been examined, analyzed, and pumped into the process of perfecting the expansion plan.

Finally, the new product is launched in its major marketing area. Big dollars, careers, and corporate fortunes are on the line.

Hopefully, you've quickly rolled out with a success, filed a failure, or diagnosed an in-between. Summarize the knowledge gained for the record, and then move on to another project—so much the wiser.

Section 7
Summary Afterword

The marketing plan has been approved. The product is feasible. Scale-up confirms production costs. Plant production replicates the prototype quality. Quality control guidelines have been confirmed.

Market entry has been approved.

Caution: Don't overmanage.

While it is tempting to give the new entry every help possible, it is important that the market test mirror as much as possible the broad-scale rollout. While all potential selling tools—including sales meetings and press conferences—should be utilized, the national marketing plan should be translated as closely as possible to the test market.

The plan should incorporate contingency arrangements to deal with coping with a slow start, coping with a fast start, coping with competitive actions designed to confuse test results, what to do when paired market sets don't stay controlled pairs, premature success reaction, and early failures. Moreover, it should also make allowance for what to do in the case of a so-so introduction—when the product is neither an obvious success nor a failure.

The introductory period then leads to. . .

Assessment and expansion. Most important here is to know the plan and stick to it. This is where research comes into play, to distinguish facts from insights. Assessment steps include pre- and post-awareness checks, meeting competitive moves, point-of-sale audits, talking to the customer, and talking to the sales channels. And don't stop there. Periodic repeat research should be conducted throughout the life of the product to keep it fresh and on target.

The product is ready to go into full-scale expansion. Outside effects should be monitored to assess how they affect the plan. Then, the expansion should be merchandised for all it is worth. Make the improvement modifications that are necessary—then go into the full-scale launch!

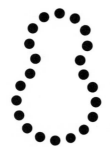

Major Introduction

24

And Now What?

Some of the most significant new ideas in science involve the recognition of new problems.
—*Linus Pauling*

In business, also, problems are among the best sources of opportunities.

So—now what?

Every new product encounters a stream of problems—and imparts a stream of knowledge, which is capable of yielding both solutions and opportunities.

Comprehensive Marketing Plan

After the test marketing has been successfully completed and the major launch has been effectively executed, where do you go from here?

A comprehensive new product marketing plan looks beyond the introductory period.

1. **Revised P&L**

    The marketing plan should provide the expansion plan with a projectable P&L, realistically adjusted from the test simulation forecast to the pragmatic realities of change in operation at the actual time of broadscale launch.

2. **Long Range Communications Program**

    The plan nails down the communications platform on which to build the brand personality over time.

3. **Product and Resource Proliferation**

    The plan recommends close-in product proliferation opportunities. As part of this, it should also suggest extensions of any new (to the company) technologies employed, both as applied to the new product and as a basis for other product improvements or new entries. The same goes for new distribution channels, sales force operations, warehouse locations, etc., added by the nature of the new product. Any one may become an important new avenue for a host of new sales opportunities.

There needs to be a continual program to feed a succession of adjacent new products into the system, be they resizing, repackaging, line extensions, flankers, new segmentation (upscale, downscale), new brands, etc.

Beyond this, there are other, perhaps less obvious, essentials to sound new products direction.

4.   The Refreshment Program

A complete program includes a plan to keep the product offering forever new, a planned program of refreshment that (at the very least) will keep the product "newsy" or "newsworthy."

The aim is to avoid the typical bell curve of rising fortunes, maturity, and gradual demise. While countless new products do not live to ripe old age, others evade the fortunes of the average and greet each new generation of prospective customers with a new face, a trusted, familiar, well-established name, and an integrated personality. Regular, programmed "face lifts" help keep the offering fresh and appealing.

5.   Timely Changes

On the other hand, it is likely that those most familiar with the product will tire of it first. That's what happens to many a manufacturer. All it takes to stir this up are a few soft sales periods.

Chances are, the consumer is just beginning to become acquainted—or, having become acquainted, is just beginning to place the recently introduced new product in his or her repertoire of acceptable products.

How do you guard against premature refreshment—or, worse yet, destruction of a carefully crafted marketing communication concept?

In a large expansion region, a company cannot read the nuances of marketing dynamics as intensely as in test markets. Knowing this, resist the temptation (often, the standard operating procedure) to abort the test market measurements when the regional roll-out is committed. Keep those test markets going. Already, they are months or years more mature than the introductory area. They have a history of product performance. They offer benchmarks.

While the new product is in Year 1 nationally, it is entering Year 2 in the test areas. Manage the test area to simulate Year 2, as closely as possible. Modify the national marketing weight going into those areas as well as can be done, with network cut-ins and plate changes in publications—substitute other company products, promotions, etc.

If this is not practical or practicable, then make statistical adjustments. The worst that will happen is that the marketing effort will be overstated in test areas, if national Year 2 is planned as a step-down.

In that instance, test markets represent an exaggerated exposure to communications—and should flag early wearout or (conversely) signal the important brand-building longevity of the creative executions that helped propel the successful test in the first place. Using test markets as a lead laboratory for the future of expansion areas will often save a marketer from hasty, less well-researched changes that may bring the offering to an early demise—rather than position it for vital refreshment as it moves along a long life of achievement.

6. **Overall New Product Posture**

    While particular new business entities are being nurtured, the company's overall program of development must be frequently assessed. This reevaluation looks at the long-range planning cycle and modes, at the definition of the corporate charter, and at all the other elements attendant to the business, regulatory, social, and scientific environmental changes.

7. **Process Surveillance**

    Constant surveillance of the new product process, as appropriate to the company, staff, and organization, is also necessary—with appreciation of a possible need to change one or all of these components of the pattern.

Maintaining the Entrepreneurial Spirit

Commenting on the need for reexamination, John G. Main, managing director of Main, Jackson & Garfield Inc., a management consulting firm, wrote in the Spring 1982 issue of *Point of View*, published by Spencer Stuart & Associates:

Innovation is a process in which flexibility, imagination, curiosity, intuition, and a large dash of freedom are essential. Managing that process calls for a creative interaction with those elements. And the highly structured, systems-oriented environments in many of today's large corporations are typically neither receptive to nor geared up for that kind of commitment.

Fortunately, there are exceptions—a growing number of companies that are pursuing organizational options aimed at generating a flow of new ideas and new technologies.

Many experts hold that once a company has passed beyond its own entrepreneurial phase of development, it's next to impossible to encourage or to pursue innovation. Main writes:

As a corporation grows larger, it tends to become more set in its ways, conservative in its fiscal thinking, and increasingly dependent on rigid systems and controls. All of this runs counter to the free-wheeling, entrepreneurial setting in which breakthroughs flourish.

Those companies that most effectively maintain the entrepreneurial spirit while leveraging the resources of the corporation employ one or more of the techniques covered in this book, including: *Specially assigned new product managers*, who take over at an early stage; *internal entrepreneurial project teams; corporate venture groups; spin-offs*, which take products from one usage area into another; *cooperative agreements*, which combine the strengths of two companies, one perhaps technologically-intensive while another is marketing-intensive; *acquisition*, buying a new product opportunity; *contract entrepreneurs*, to manage the start-up phase so as to move the operation ahead without encountering the frustrations of the corporate organizational boundaries. Main adds another angle: "*Venture Capital Lending*—making selected portfolio investments in the ventures of other groups."

A change in the established way of doing business, of course, has its risks. However, the trade-offs may be necessary to effectuate a reasonably dynamic new products operation. Here is what Main has to say:

Corporate management can take specific steps to provide an interface and environment that will facilitate implementation and promote full realization of the program's potential . . .

The new activity should be managed continuously by one person or project team throughout its entire evolution—from inception, through research and planning, into an established operation with a structured organization.

The CEO should prepare corporate management to accept and interact with the instinctive and intuitive forces at work in entrepreneurial management. Established views and practices may not be the appropriate response to a venture situation and, in some instances, may well prove counter-productive.

At the same time, the CEO should be alert to individual sensitivities and fears that the new operation and top management's commitment to it may threaten existing positions within the corporate hierarchy . . .

Ultimately, the successful management of innovation in a large corporate environment will hinge on whether the leadership is willing to risk new challenges and explore new management cultures.

New product generation stimulates the entrepreneurial juices that nurture the future prosperity of the corporation—and, more likely than not, identifies the successor leaders.

That is the pattern.

But—there is another element, also.

New product programs do not always go so smoothly.

And now what?

Now—the program must be put back on track or aborted. It's time to discover just what has changed over which the marketer may have control—and to do something about it. Or—to discover the outside influences affecting the program and to determine whether something can affordably be done quickly enough to make the move the best long-term use of expensive capital and corporate energies.

A false start may not presage a poor finish, but a stumble once out of the gate is extremely difficult to overcome. Tenacity within reason, yea; stubborness within blinders, nay.

New Product Lessons

New product managers learn lessons readily applicable to established businesses. They learn to break out of the mold of routine practice, to reap the attention and rewards accorded a new face on the block (even if it *is* an old face with new cosmetics, or a very close kin with something new to show or to proclaim). They know how to make a reintroduction of an old offering more exciting than a bigger trade allowance and a snappy new label. New product managers, the best ones, learn to be iconoclasts, to challenge the norms of today and yesterday so firmly entrenched in all but the most infant industries.

And they are not afraid to borrow from the successful tactics of (presumably) wholly unrelated industries. Nor to seek out consultation from across a wide range of disciplines, peer groups, and target prospects.

New product managers are selective sponges, soaking up everything—and retaining the important differences that leverage the meaning of "new."

New product managers are curious. They're anxious to discover, to turn over every rock, to challenge every clichè, to swim against the tide, and, thus, to create new channels and new tides.

Yet—new product managers know that the degree of change affects the degree of acceptance, most often in an inverse ratio. They know that too much gap jumping may represent true progress, but probably will be beyond the comprehension of the broad marketplace. They learn how much is enough—and how much is too much.

Since the '50s, when the author first saw the formal shaping of the new product process proven in practice, the lessons of this text have been validated. In those early years, the various steps were clearly identified—which my new products development company published in a slim proprietary volume widely shared within the field. Then, as now, that field embraced makers and marketers, advertising agencies, academia, and consultants, and the then newly emerging specialty field of new products development services.

Early co-workers in those vineyards soon spread out across many industries and applied the procedures.

The original go/no-go gates have changed little.

The process works. And it works everywhere—across oceans, across cultures, across real and imagined boundaries.

It is my hope that this book, built on the bedrock of experience in the trenches and biased by the lessons of reality, will be a lasting contribution to the art, science, craft, and gut instinct so important to the field.

This disciplined approach works because it is flexible to the demands of unanticipated events (problems and opportunities). The three outstanding case histories that follow are dazzling evidence of this.

Appendix

Case Histories

Introduction

Success is a journey, not a destination.
—*Ben Sweetland*

The race is not always to the swift, nor the battle to the strong—but that's the way to bet.
—*Damon Runyon*

No text on new product marketing development would be complete without a few case histories that illustrate the principles and disciplines advocated therein.

These "real world" examples put it all together. Each is from a leading company in its field. Each was prepared expressly for this book in full cooperation with the companies' managements. The author is indebted to them for this. So, too, will the reader gain from a careful study of these case histories.

They illustrate:

- Knowledge of market characteristics
- Use of strategy as a management focus
- Management with stringent criteria
- Heavy upfront investment in the early development phases
- Extension of or refinement of the basic corporate charter as a new product directional focus
- Development of new products as either a basis for future proliferation of the line or as an actual extension of an existing brand franchise, or both
- Different organizational structures and different performance incentives employed by the case history subject companies

Each of the companies is continually learning, rethinking, and redeploying its approach to new products. They are seeking ways in which to manage innovation, but also in which to encourage risk-taking entrepreneurship.

Each has a balanced program of new product development that focuses on various investment and longevity goals, so that there is a continuous flow of activity aimed at short-term opportunities, mid-term new business enterprises, and longer term innovations and inventions that require considerable investment in staff and capital equipment and a lengthy time frame. Both opportunistic and programmed acquisitions and joint ventures may play a role in the mid- and long-term programs, while licensing opportunities may be important to the short-term programs.

All are seeking a new product management approach that balances the orderly disciplines of an institutionalized publically held business with the dynamic spirit of vital entrepreneurship. They appear to be succeeding.

The case histories are of the successful development of Land O Lakes Margarine (recently introduced to 85 percent of the U.S.), Fisher-Price children's phonograph, and the Toro Power Shovel (snowthrower), a highly seasonal item.

There are a number of common new product issues to be emphasized:

Name
- Land O'Lakes was concerned that naming a margarine after a butter brand would needlessly cannibalize its leading spread.
- Toro needed a generic "handle" for a lightweight snowthrower that would clearly differentiate it from the conventional machines at a different prospect target.

Price
- Fisher-Price's children's phonograph entry would be at a pronounced price premium. This could be a barrier.
- Land O'Lakes' brand reputation is appropriate to a premium-priced margarine. Although this is a smaller segment of the total market than the popular-priced segment, this could be the appropriate price point.

Seasonality
- Fisher-Price products respond to the gift-giving holiday swings.
- Toro snowthrower sales respond to early significant snowfalls.
- Land O Lakes margarine's introductory effort should avoid the peak holiday butter consumption period.

The consequences of the decisions made on each of these issues—and the behavior of Mother Nature in Toro's case—had major effects on the respective successes of each of the new product introductions.

A

Land O Lakes Margarine

Land O'Lakes has redefined its business. Today, we are in the *spread* business, not the butter business alone. With our well-established leading brand of butter, our recent broad geographic expansion of our new margarine products and more spread products to follow, we expect to be Number One in spreads. There are few brands that carry the quality, wholesome broad acceptance of Land O'Lakes. We intend to make the most of that fact.

—*Ralph Hofstad*
President
Land O'Lakes Inc.

The Company

Land O'Lakes 1983 sales were $2.283 billion. The company was organized as the Minnesota Cooperative Creameries Association Inc., in 1921, under the cooperative law of Minnesota, for the purpose of promoting, posturing, and securing improvement in:

1. Standardization and improvement of quality, through cream grading and proper methods of manufacture
2. Shipping and transportation of butter and dairy products through car-lot shipping
3. Service in the sale of products of Minnesota creameries through closer cooperation with present distributing agencies and wholesale market receivers
4. Cooperative purchase of supplies
5. Advertising of dairy products.

Two years later, Land O'Lakes brand was selected as an appropriate name for the company's sweet cream butter. Through a commitment to producing a consistent, high quality product and building a consumer franchise through advertising, Land O'Lakes became America's largest selling butter, although it did not achieve national distribution until the third quarter of 1983, when it added markets west of the Rocky Mountains. In 1933, its present advertising agency (Campbell-Mithun Inc.) was selected.

In a 1950 presentation, the agency pointed out that 30 companies (mostly meat packers) were making a large profit selling animal-fat based oleomargarine, while thousands of butter processors were operating on a very narrow margin. The packers had no qualms about selling both margarine and butter. The agency expressed the concern that the combined advertising weight of all those margarine producers would put margarine into all American homes and would eventually convince consumers that butter was uneconomical.

For the next 20 years, Land O'Lakes remained involved in food processing and marketing, as well as providing a limited supply of farm products and technical advice to its members.

In 1970, a farm supply and crop processing cooperative named FELCO was merged into Land O'Lakes, adding soybeans and soy oil to its list of products. With this merger came the pressure from FELCO soybean farmers eager to become part of the growing margarine industry, which uses soybean oil in its production process.

Land O'Lakes butter had enjoyed a phenomenal growth in the previous 20 years. However, margarine had overtaken and more than doubled the sale of all butter in the same period. Land O'Lakes took another look at margarine.

Situation Analysis

Margarine in 1970

Industry sales of margarine in 1970 were 1.8 billion pounds—87 percent of households used margarine in an average month; 35 percent of households used butter.

Per capita consumption of table spreads held steady at 16 to 17 pounds between 1950 and 1970. However, per capita consumption of margarine grew from 6 to 10.8 pounds, while butter slipped from 11 to 5.3 pounds. Lower retail price and perceived health benefits of vegetable fat over animal fat were the primary reasons for the shift. Research showed that *price* was by far the most important variable. (When oleomargarines, made from rendered animal fat, gave way to vegetable fat based spreads, the shift had accelerated.)

Many homemakers used both margarine and butter. Land O'Lakes research showed margarine was used mainly for cooking and baking, while butter's chief use was as a table spread, topping for vegetables, and for special occasion recipes such as Christmas cookies. Land O'Lakes butter users had a much higher brand loyalty than typical users and were less likely to accept substitutes.

Demographics

The heavy margarine user was female, 35 to 49 years of age, had children under 18 at home, had five or more in her household, had graduated from high school, and had a household income of $5,000 to $10,000.*

*In April, 1982, this translated to: $15,000 to $30,000.

Margarine came in multiple forms marketed under many brands. In 1970, there were 14 national or important regional brands, plus private labels. The regular stick form accounted for 59 percent of business. Leading brands were Blue Bonnet (Standard Brands), Imperial (Lever Bros.), and Parkay (Dart & Kraft Inc.). Combined, they represented over one-fourth of the market and 45 percent of the regular stick business. The category was (and is) categorized by very little brand loyalty, with the typical consumer buying within an orbit of two to three acceptable brands, and the decision primarily made on a price basis. There were also strong regional differences in terms of butter/margarine share, price points, and preferred forms. (See Figure A-1.)

Figure A-1
Margarine Shares and Prices—1970

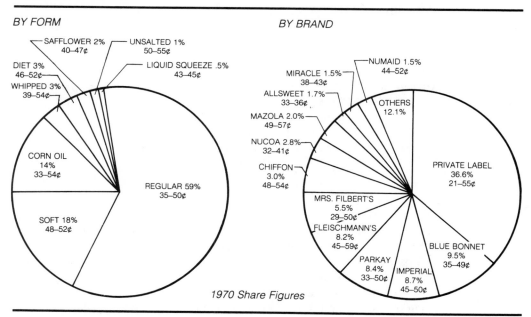

Source: A. C. Nielsen

Competitive Advertising

Advertising Claims/Positioning
At this time competitive advertising claims tended to concentrate in three areas:

Comparison with Butter
1. Blue Bonnet—"Everything's better with Blue Bonnet on it." (A comparison of similar dishes prepared with butter and with Blue Bonnet

demonstrated that internationally known chefs could tell "no difference.")

2. Mrs. Filberts—"Mrs. Filbert's fresh, sweet buttery flavor." (Not a heavily advertised brand.)
3. Chiffon—"Good enough to fool Mother Nature." "If you think it's butter but it's not, it's new Chiffon."
4. Mazola—"No matter how close you feel your margarine comes to butter flavor, Mazola margarine comes even closer."

Taste/flavor

1. Imperial—"Tastes so good, it makes me feel like a king."
2. Parkay—"Country fresh flavor."
3. Allsweet—"Compare the sweet taste of Allsweet with any other margarine at any price."

Health

1. Fleischmann's—"It makes sensible eating delicious." (Emphasized "low cholesterol.")

Spending

Advertising spending was substantial, with the eight leaders spending approximately $500,000 per share point of media advertising. Adding non-advertising promotion, spending approached $1,000,000 per share point or more than $50,000,000 total. The leaders each spend about $4,000,000 to $5,000,000 in media, primarily television. (See Table A-1.)

Trade

Margarine was a better profit maker for the trade than butter (on a percentage basis). In the dairy case, it accounted for 9.9 percent of sales and 7.8 percent of profit, and returned a retail gross margin of 15.6 percent. Butter's comparable figures were 6.1 percent, 2.8 percent, and 9.1 percent. Margarine ranked third (behind milk and eggs) in the dairy case and butter ranked ninth in departmental gross margin dollars.

On the other hand, butter generated more than twice the sales dollars per shelf foot, returned slightly more gross margin per shelf foot, and had a somewhat faster inventory turnover.

Margarine Potential for Land O'Lakes

Further processing the soybean oil of its new members into margarine would bring more consumer dollars to Land O'Lakes and to its members. But entering a large maturing market would not be easy, especially when the market was dominated by several well-managed companies who were aggres-

Table A-1
Competitive Ad Spending
1970 Advertising Expenditures

Brand	Parent Company	Nielsen Share ($)	(lbs)	Advertising Expenditures*
Imperial	Lever Bros.	11.5%	8.7%	$ 5,393,796
Fleischmann's	Standard Brands	11.4	8.2	5,211,690
Blue Bonnet	Standard Brands	10.4	9.5	4,630,709
Parkay	Kraft	10.3	8.4	5,504,621
Mrs. Filbert's		6.6	5.5	105,700
Chiffon	Anderson Clayton	4.2	3.0	2,560,189
Mazola	CPC International	2.7	2.0	2,577,963
Allsweet	Swift	1.6	1.7	135,851
Miracle	Kraft	1.6	1.5	792,129
Private Label		33.0	36.6	

*Source: LNA/Media Records.

sively marketing their margarine brands. Also, the success of a Land O Lakes branded margarine might jeopardize their successful Land O Lakes butter franchise.

Research Projects

A number of related concerns were addressed by research projects with these objectives:

1. Estimate the impact Land O Lakes margarine would have on Land O Lakes butter sales.
2. Evaluate the total potential of a Land O Lakes branded margarine in terms of displacement of butter volume, total butter margarine volume, and return to Land O'Lakes members.
3. Determine likely acceptance of a margarine product under the Land O Lakes brand name, with product technology in line with that of the leading brands.
4. Determine consumer price/value expectations for a Land O Lakes branded margarine.

5. Provide a preliminary planning estimate of the potential for Land O Lakes margarine in a strong Land O Lakes franchise market (e.g., Boston) vs. and average Land O Lakes franchise market (e.g., Indianapolis).

A study was conducted in mid-1971 among a random sample of housewives in representative markets. Respondents saw simulated advertising of one of four brand positionings. (See Figure A-2.) Highly predisposed respondents received a sample product in labeled cartons carrying descriptive copy. Three to ten days later, 921 product evaluations were received from qualifying respondents. (Half the sample had received a leading national brand re-labeled as Land O'Lakes; the other half received a similarly relabeled version of another leading national brand.)

Interpretation of Findings

Results of this test provided encouragement that Land O'Lakes could success-fully position a new margarine product without jeopardizing its butter.

By developing a universe of all spread users, margarine-only users, butter-only users, users of both, with each cell broken out by brand, type, price point, demographics, and spread usage—it was possible to predict probable high and low ranges of acceptance and cannibalization. Against this backdrop, the concept of Land O Lakes branded margarine was tested in Boston and Indianapolis. The study made possible a very preliminary estimate of poten-tial share performance, with both markets performing above goal—Boston projected to more than three times Indianapolis. This was attributed to Boston's historic high performance on Land O Lakes butter.

The study also allowed an estimate for the upper range of potential butter cut-in. This was derived by estimating the current volume of Land O Lakes butter among homemakers who would buy the new margarine. If *all* their butter purchases were converted to margarine, butter sales would decline 23 percent. But since most homemakers saw different uses for butter and mar-garine, the actual expected cut-in should be substantially less than 23 percent.

Respondents who received the sample product rated it highly (although, in fact, each panel was split between repackaged major national brands). The four copy approaches all were acceptable, with no particular positive or negative standout.

Brand Name

Despite the positive findings, concern persisted about use of the best known butter name on a margarine: Would it disproportionately affect butter sales?

Competitive margarine was repackaged as a Land O Lakes brand to test consumer reaction. Margarine users were monadically tested equally, using either a leading national product repackaged as Land O Lakes or a leading

Figure A-2a

Position Posters for LOL Margarine

NOW!
A NUMBER ONE MARGARINE
FROM THE NUMBER ONE BUTTER MAKER

New Land O Lakes margarine gives you the closest thing to butter there is. Natural tasting flavor—rich creamy texture. Land O'Lakes—best in butter—now best in margarine.

Source: Campbell Mithun, Inc.

Figure A-2b

Position Posters for LOL Margarine

NOW!
A MARGARINE FOR ALL-AROUND USE

Now Land O Lakes margarine is a total spread for cooking, baking, frying and table use. If hubby is finicky about your serving margarine, try him on this one—even he will like its rich creamy texture and natural flavor.

Source: Campbell Mithun, Inc.

Figure A-2c

Position Posters for LOL Margarine

NOW!
A MARGARINE PERFECT FOR BAKING

This new margarine from Land O Lakes is perfect for baking. Cookies don't run or burn. Cakes and pastries are moist and rich with no oily taste. The same high quality you expect from Land O'Lakes.

Source: Campbell Mithun, Inc.

Figure A-2d

Position Posters for LOL Margarine

NOW!
A MARGARINE WITHOUT THE OILY TASTE

New Land O Lakes margarine has a rich creamy texture with no oily taste. Less greasy when frying and permits the natural taste of food to come through without the oily or artificial taste.

Source: Campbell Mithun, Inc.

national with its correct brand name. Both the positive disposition and depth of interest scores for the Land O Lakes branded product exceeded the goal criteria. Consumers' predisposition was stronger for the Land O Lakes branded margarine and the product was rated superior to any margarine any of the testers had previously tried.

This convinced Land O'Lakes that the flagship brand name was a major asset for margarine and clearly the brand name to use.

Establishing Measurable Objectives

Key issues were the development of measurable marketing objectives including share, butter cut-in, consumer brand and advertising awareness, trial and repeat, and pricing strategies. This could only be done through testing that would include the actual Land O Lakes margarine product.

Product Development

R&D was directed to develop a top quality product, which could be duplicated in both soy and corn oil margarines. Six different forms had to be created: Soy regular stick, soft, and whipped, and corn oil base regular stick, unsalted stick, and soft.

Taste Tests

Dozens of central location consumer taste tests were conducted in the summer of 1972. The objective was for Land O'Lakes products to be preferred by as many (or more) margarine users as the leading Parkay and Imperial brands.

To qualify for the regular stick soy samples, respondents had to be current users of either stick or soft Blue Bonnet, Chiffon, Imperial, Miracle, or Parkay. To qualify for either of the corn oil test samples (stick or soft), respondents had to be current users of either stick or soft Fleischmann's, Mazola, Imperial Corn Oil, or Parkay Corn Oil.

Quotas were met for each comparison. Respondents tested an unidentified Land O'Lakes product vs. an unidentified competitor. Comparisons were on two pieces of bread and were alternated.

Research Findings

Regular Stick vs. Parkay. An equal number of women preferred each. More men preferred Land O Lakes.

Regular Stick vs. Imperial. A large majority of women preferred Land O Lakes. (No male panel.)

Corn Oil Stick vs. Parkay. The largest majority (all women) preferred Land O Lakes.

> **Corn Oil Soft vs. Parkay**. A large majority of female panels preferred Land O Lakes.

Thus, all three taste-tested Land O Lakes margarine products met the objectives of equal or better performance than competition.

Product Quality

What contributed to this consumer blind test response?

Most margarines are similar in composition. One occasional difference is the level of skim milk content, if any. Some have none. Others use non-fat dry milk solids. Land O'Lakes uses only fresh skim milk. Taste tests indicated that the dairy flavor was positively discernible at the 10 to 17 percent level, the Land O'Lakes formulation range. This may have contributed to its recognition as the top-rated regular margarine by the Consumer's Union as reported in *Consumer Reports* magazine in February 1979.

We established criteria for excellence for a product that resembles butter but isn't butter. Our sensory consultants independently evaluated each brand of margarine against the criteria. The experts tasted at least four samples of each brand. Their combined judgments formed the basis of our ratings.

The top rated product, regular Land O Lakes margarine had no sensory defects. It had the appropriate pale yellow color and an even, solid texture. Its sweet dairy flavor and aroma had a slight vegetable-oil character. It was just a bit salty. And it melted rapidly and evenly. We rated Land O Lakes very good.

Product Manufacturing

Land O'Lakes used contract packer Miami Margarine of Cincinnati, Ohio, to make the product for controlled mini-markets and later test and expansion markets. (In 1976, Land O'Lakes completed its first margarine production facility in Hudson, Iowa. A second was to be added at Kent, Ohio, in 1983.)

Creative Exploration

Development of creative strategy for the product was conducted within this context:

1. Margarine is a low interest category. Consumers are not waiting for new information about it.
2. At the time, there was a strong similarity among competitive claims. Almost every brand "tasted like butter." (Exception: corn oil margarines utilized health claims.)
3. Television was the principal medium.
4. Most competitors made frequent use of exaggerated visual devices: crown for Imperial, magically appearing countryside for Parkay, and "Mother Nature" for Chiffon.

5. Land O Lakes margarine advertising must avoid confusion with Land O Lakes butter.

Campbell-Mithun began creative development with an exploration of various strategies and positions.

Benefits and Claims Study

Previous testing already suggested that copy should borrow from the inherent appeal and heritage of Land O Lakes butter.

The next step was to examine the particular attributes within the margarine category that would be important to consumers and to evaluate a list of potential product claims and consumer benefits that would be used by Land O'Lakes in introducing the new margarine.

Personal in-home interviews were conducted among margarine users in February 1972, with 206 Atlanta housewives and 200 Indianapolis housewives. Each housewife rated alternative benefits and claims for margarine as to desirability, believability, exclusiveness, and appropriateness. The individual margarine claims were read by the respondents from flashcards. Each claim was rated on a scale of 1 to 10. Ratings of 8 or better were considered a positive response.

Here are the benefits studied:

- The margarine with the taste of butter . . .
- The margarine with no chemical additives . . .
- The completely natural margarine . . .
- The margarine from the farmer's own company—quality ingredients in all stages of processing . . .
- The margarine in reusable containers (coffee cups, flower pots, picnic dishes, etc.) . . .
- The number one margarine from the number one butter maker . . .
- The margarine in the biodegradable tub . . .
- The margarine for young, active families . . .
- The margarine made from natural soybean oil . . .
- An old-fashioned margarine . . .
- The margarine with a hint of lemon for cleaner, fresher, lighter flavor . . .
- The margarine with consistent high quality . . .
- The margarine that is high in nutrition . . .
- The margarine with the smooth creamy texture . . .
- The all-purpose margarine . . .
- The margarine that is lowest in saturated fats . . .
- The margarine best for health . . .
- The margarine that is "perfect for baking" . . .
- The margarine that is not greasy . . .
- The sunshine margarine—high in Vitamin D . . .

- The margarine with no aftertaste . . .
- The high-protein margarine . . .
- The margarine with country fresh flavor . . .
- The margarine with no oily taste . . .

The objective was to find a basic claim or theme for Land O Lakes margarine that a large proportion of margarine buyers felt embodied a very desirable promise not offered by existing brands. The findings of this study led to the development of a creative blueprint that would guide copy development.

Creative Blueprint

The next step was the creative direction—a blueprint to guide all communications execution:

What business goals must be accomplished?
Introduce a new line of margarine products from Land O'Lakes—with a share of market target of 3-plus percent in the first year, while sustaining minimal loss in butter sales.

Initial markets will be in the central United States where the Land O'Lakes name is well known, but butter consumption is only moderate compared to margarine.

What kind of person must we sell?
Women who are looking for a margarine that comes as close as possible to a real butter taste with the economy of margarine. She probably uses both margarine and butter—and can still detect the difference. She reserves butter for certain uses such as "company," frying eggs, etc. The rest of the time she uses margarine. She probably also has an understanding that margarine is lower in cholesterol. She generally buys a premium priced margarine—Imperial. She is 24 to 49 years old, has children at home, is medium upscale in income, and not a college graduate.

How does she now feel about us and competition?
She knows the Land O'Lakes name. Chances are she uses Land O Lakes butter. She knows it is more expensive than competitive butters and margarine. She also knows it is the freshest, highest quality butter she can buy. She may also be aware that there are other Land O'Lakes dairy products in her store.

She buys one or two "acceptable" brands of margarine—usually switching for price reasons. Chances are she classes these two brands as "quality" brands—and is aware that there are other, cheaper ones on the market—but that they are farther away from butter in taste.

What do we want her to feel and think and do?
To believe that Land O'Lakes has applied all its experience gained from

developing the nation's best and most popular butter to develop a new margarine. That we recognize that she'll still want to use butter for some "special" occasions, but that now she can upgrade her margarine.

What key thought can we put into her mind to make her feel that way?
Land O'Lakes, the nation's Number One butter maker, now makes a margarine that lives up to the Land O Lakes name. She can get a margarine with Land O Lakes quality.

What tone of voice will get her to hear and believe us?
Candid and newsy. One that presents this new margarine as something that is new and different in the margarine field. An approach that doesn't overpromise. One that makes a plausible case for a dairy products company developing a margarine.

To fulfill this blueprint, Campbell-Mithun pursued four approaches supported by the benefits and claims research. The concepts were based on:

1. Nutrition
2. America's number one butter maker
3. Consistent, high quality
4. No oily or greasy taste.

Success would be based on the ability to build product appeal with minimal Land O Lakes brand butter cut-in. An acceptable upper cut-in level was judgmentally felt to be 10 percent.

Execution Testing

Stimulus material for testing was developed in three 30-second TV commercial storyboards, which were converted into animatic form for the test in June 1972. They were:

1. Farmer's Own. Farmer talks about margarine, placing emphasis on "homegrown" aspect.
2. Sunshine Margarine. Emphasizes natural wholesomeness of sunshine and goodness of Land O'Lakes country.
3. From America's Number 1 Buttermaker. Features animated spokescow announcing that nation's favorite buttermaker is now making margarine. (See Figure A-3.)

The animatics were tested in Indianapolis, which was to be the initial test market.

Testing was monadic. Each respondent saw one of the test commercials in a cluttered environment of other test commercials. The "America's Number 1 Buttermaker" commercial, featuring the spokescow was most effective on all counts. Of the three viewed by more than 450 persons, it was widely preferred over the other two. (See Table A-2.)

Figure A-3
Spokescow Commercial

1. COW LEADER: Guess what, girls?

2. America's No. 1 butter maker has just introduced a margarine.

3. OTHER COWS: Gasp! Gasp! COW ONE: Oh, my! A Margarine?

4. COW TWO: They wouldn't.

5. COW LEADER: They did. New Land O Lakes Margarine is here.

6. COW ONE: But, why?

7. COW LEADER: Why? Because it takes a butter company like Land O' Lakes...

8. ...to give you the taste...

9. ...you really want in a margarine.

10. Here, try it.

11. COW ONE: M-m-m, delicious!

12. COW TWO: Oh! It's the cream of the margarines.

13. COW LEADER: New Land O Lakes Margarine is here.

14. All you other margarines...

15. ...mo-o-o-ve over!

Table A-2
Research on TV Creative Approaches

	Cows (150)	Sunshine (150)	Farmer (150)
Brand and product recall Correct (LOL Margarine)	95%	95%	96%
Copy Point Recall Tastes like butter	34%	22%	—%
Tastes good	5	8	3
High quality	37	2	28
Buying Interest Requested coupon for product (first choice)	21%	13%	14%
Total coupon requests	67	56	63
Quality Rating LOL margarine would be "better than all other margarines in over-all quality"	21%	10%	17%
Average rating (5 pt. scale)	4.1	3.9	3.9
Reasons for Quality Rating Made by butter company	71%	57%	45%
Made to taste like butter	15	10	6

Source: Land O'Lakes, Inc.

On the butter cut-in issue, only one respondent indicated a switch from Land O Lakes butter to its margarine, while almost 60 percent indicated a trial switch from the margarine brand presently used.

The spokescow approach dignified butter, borrowing from the strength of the established quality and sales leader—thus allowing the prospective consumer to make a similar inference about Land O Lakes margarine.

Packaging Graphics

The agency began working on packaging graphics with these design objectives:

1. To clearly identify the margarine as a Land O'Lakes product to capitalize on the brand's quality image.
2. To provide differentiation from the butter package, to prevent confusion or comparison.

Six designs were tested with users—and for eye appeal in the grocery dairy case.

Final design selected used the basic Land O'Lakes colors and Indian maiden logotype, with typography, background graphics, and carton construction providing the necessary differentiation from butter packages. (See Figures A-4 and A-5.)

Objectives and Strategies

The preliminary marketing and advertising strategies and objectives were refined from the comprehensive preparatory research to yield the following:

Marketing Objectives

Market share.—Obtain a market poundage share of 3-plus percent.
Cut-in (of margarine to butter sales). Hold to a maximum of 10 percent on a

Figure A-4
Forms of Land O Lakes Margarine

Regular Stick, Soft and Corn Oil—the three largest selling margarine categories.

Figure A-5
Store Planogram

national basis. (A special study by Market Potential Inc. indicated that a cut-in of 10 percent could be expected.)

Distribution.—Achieve a minimum 70 percent at the end of the first year.

Awareness. Achieve minimum 20 percent awareness of Land O Lakes brand margarine among margarine and butter/margarine users by the end of the first six months, 25 percent by the end of the first year.

Trial. Achieve minimum 25 percent sampling among all margarine users in the first year.

Image. Clearly establish a premium quality image equal to or better than the premium margarine with the highest quality image in the market (in areas where the Land O'Lakes name is already known). Also establish the idea of a "family" of margarines.

Pricing. Achieve a retail price equal to Imperial, the leading premium priced brand.

Marketing Strategy

1. Build margarine identity on Land O'Lakes' strongly established reputation as the country's Number One butter.
2. Introduce Land O Lakes margarine at a first-year spending level of double the ongoing cost for market share point.
3. Concentrate first-year spending on current margarine consumers (rather than trade) to rapidly develop awareness in the first 16 weeks after advertising begins and to help achieve initial trade acceptance.
4. Use coupons to stimulate trial, generate rapid shelf movement, aid in gaining initial placements and second chance placements.
5. Increase spending efficiency after initial introduction weight by augmenting television with magazines, which perform better in top economic quintiles.

Advertising Objectives

1. Position Land O Lakes margarine as a high-quality, premium margarine.
2. Obtain minimum 20 percent consumer awareness of Land O Lakes margarine brand in the first six months.
3. Obtain 25 percent trial by all margarine users in the first year.

Advertising Strategy

1. Help build margarine identity on Land O'Lakes' established reputation as the country's Number One butter.
2. Use television as a key medium.
3. Concentrate the first-year budget on consumer advertising to "pull" the product.
4. Emphasize couponing to gain initial trial.
5. Use consumer-oriented promotions to add value to advertising and stimulate repeat purchases.

Media Objectives

1. Use the most efficient and effective media combination possible within the budget to reach the target audience.
2. Concentrate media weight against women 18 to 49 years of age with families who are premium margarine users.
3. Recognize that reach and trial will be of primary importance during the introductory period.
4. Provide effective continuity levels against the target audience during the sustaining period.
5. Keep the trade constantly aware of the media support.

Media Strategy

1. Use prime time network television as the basic medium to reach women 18 to 49.
2. Use daytime network television for additional low-cost efficient frequency among a target of women 18 to 49.
3. Use r.o.p. newspaper to stimulate more immediate consumer response (coupon ad). This will promote product sampling and be merchandisable with the grocery trade.
4. Use magazines to provide broad reach against the target and to reach the lower viewing TV quintiles.
5. Use direct mail to concentrate on the target while promoting more sampling and retrial by the consumer, serving as a vehicle to ensure that original distribution with the key trade is maintained and increased.

(See Figure A-6 for the resulting Media Planning Chart.)

National Theoretical Plans

National theoretical spending for Year One was estimated to require $12,000,000 to meet the 3-plus percent share of market goal. This amount would be divided equally between advertising and sales promotion activities. (At the time, top national brands were spending $1,000,000 per share point on advertising and promotion to maintain share. Typically, new introductions in the category spent at least double this rate—possibly dividing the dollars 55 percent media and advertising production, 15 percent consumer promotion, 30 percent trade deals and other trade costs.)

Test Market Planning

Normally, the next step would be preparation of test market simulation—selection of projectable markets and development of plans.

Figure A-6
Media Planning Chart

	1	2	3	4	5	6	7	8	9	10	11	12
TELEVISION 70% Prime 30% Day 5,560 Points		250 Pts/Wk 8 Wks 50 Pts/Wk 2 Wks		200 Pts/Wk 10 Wks			100 Pts/Wk 22 Wks					
MAGAZINE Better Homes & Gardens Ladies Home Journal Woman's Day Good Housekeeping McCalls Pg. 4/C							☐	☐	☐	☐	☐	☐
NEWSPAPER Top 75 Markets			12¢ COUPON Page 2/C									
DIRECT MAIL 17,250,000 Homes					12¢ COUPON							
NEWSPAPER Top 25 Markets								7¢ COUPON 1,000 Li. B/W				
REFUND OFFER With Shelf Talkers											50¢ REFUND	

G-35-1

In this case, however, it was decided to take a tandem approach:

1. Institute mini-market testing, where all factors could be controlled
2. At nearly the same time, enter a single conventional test market situation

This approach provided a number of benefits for a marketer new to the category.

Mini-Market Controlled Tests

Mini-markets would allow a measurement of performance under optimum conditions, measuring consumer acceptance unencumbered by distribution or pricing aberrations. Under these conditions, the butter cut-in effects could be precisely measured. Additionally, advertising timing would exactly match the broad availability of product. With this precision, two markets were selected—one, a highly developed margarine consumption market (Albany, GA); and another (Watertown, NY), more disposed to butter, and with a slightly older and lower income population.

Benchmark studies prior to entry determined awareness and usage levels of various brands of both spread categories.

Conventional Test Markets

Indianapolis, IN, was the first of several conventionally operated and monitored test markets. It represented a medium development Land O Lakes butter market—and would be the first experience for the Land O'Lakes dairy products sales force in competing in the margarine section of the case. Until now, they had represented virtually the only well advertised broadly known butter brand—a premium product with a long and successful heritage with only modest marketing competition. Now, the sales force was up against shrewd package foods marketers with strong refrigerated case muscle.

The test markets began in the late fall 1972.

Test Market Performance—Controlled Markets

After six months, in May 1973, a survey of 200 women in each market showed that the controlled store markets were very close to their awareness and trial goals. (See Table A-3.)

After 24 weeks, actual share of market was 3.8 percent in Watertown, 2.3 percent in Albany. While this was not in excess of goal, it still demonstrated an ability to develop a successful franchise because share was building each month.

Table A-3
Awareness and Usage (Mini-Markets)

	Albany %	Watertown %
Unaided awareness	18	19
Trial among margarine users	27	28
Repeat	20	17

Test Market Performance—Conventional Market

After three months, distribution was building but still slowly. After six months, it peaked. (See Table A-4.) Retail store clerks revealed that the actual pricing was 2 to 3 cents higher than Imperial rather than at parity. After three months, market share hovered between 1.8 and 2.6 percent and was viewed as only a modest success. After three months of advertising, unaided awareness was 16 percent, trial among margarine users was 21 percent.

Table A-4
Retail Distribution (Conventional Markets)

	3 month %	6 month %
Any LOL margarine	49	77
Regular	45	73
Soft	42	45
Corn oil	18	25

Source: Land O'Lakes, Inc.

Butter Cut-In

The telephone surveys in each market also focused on the butter cut-in issue. It was found that many of Land O Lakes margarine's repeat buyers were users of Land O Lakes butter. On the other hand, it was determined that those who had bought Land O Lakes margarine only once were not very heavy butter users (and of course, did not often use Land O Lakes butter). While the information obtained was not conclusive, it was taken as an indication that the Land O Lakes label on the margarine was doing what had been hoped— attracting Land O Lakes butter users to Land O Lakes margarine, without reducing their purchases of Land O Lakes butter. (See Tables A-5 and A-6.)

Table A-5
Index of Purchases

Other Brands of Marg. Bought More Than Once	Bought LOL Marg. Once	Bought LOL Marg. More Than Once	Total
Butter Usage			
Indianapolis			
Bought butter in last 3 months	82	179	133
Bought LOL butter most recently	104	192	152
Bought LOL butter more than once	60	142	105
Albany			
Bought butter in last 3 months	105	142	132
Bought LOL most recently	117	178	165
Bought LOL more than once	90	163	143
Watertown			
Bought butter in last 3 months	101	107	104
Bought LOL most recently	83	123	106
Bought LOL more than once	100	114	108

Source: Land O'Lakes, Inc.

This indication came from tracking Land O Lakes butter sales in Indianapolis. Through June 1973, sales were up 10.3 percent versus the comparable period in 1972, while total U.S. sales of Land O Lakes butter were up less than 1 percent. This early indication provided encouragement to expand the test markets.

Rollout, Phase 1

Land O Lakes margarine had demonstrated preliminary consumer acceptance, the ability to hold distribution, and butter sales didn't appear to suffer. It was agreed Land O Lakes margarine should next be tested in areas with greater Land O Lakes butter acceptance and in areas of greater premium-priced margarine strength (e.g., higher shares for Imperial).

In September 1973, Land O Lakes entered Syracuse, Buffalo/Rochester, Terre Haute, and St. Louis. Shares in these new markets showed significant improvement. Syracuse and Buffalo, traditionally strong Land O Lakes butter markets, averaged above 4.0 share and Rochester averaged over 7.0 share, once distribution was established. (See Table A-7.)

The survey showed Land O Lakes margarine users were heavy users of every margarine. This further suggested that business would likely come from homemakers' other margarine purchases.

Table A-6

Competitive Overview

Index of LOL Margarine's Market Strength

Other Brands of Marg. Bought More Than Once	Bought LOL Marg. Once	Bought LOL Marg. More Than Once	Total
Indianapolis			
Blue Bonnet	120	132	126
Chiffon	120	223	177
Fleischmann's	135	151	144
Imperial	123	142	133
Mazola	214	177	195
Mrs. Filbert's	134	137	137
Parkay	124	112	118
Albany			
Blue Bonnet	99	119	114
Chiffon	168	115	130
Fleischmann's	114	146	137
Imperial	82	133	118
Mazola	127	111	116
Mrs. Filbert's	121	148	139
Parkay	128	97	105
Watertown			
Blue Bonnet	105	137	123
Chiffon	167	171	167
Fleischmann's	217	160	183
Imperial	107	160	136
Mazola	156	138	144
Mrs. Filbert's	110	107	110
Parkay	134	90	110

Source: Land O'Lakes, Inc.

Table A-7
LOL Margarine Market Share (%)

	ON	73/74 DJ	FM	AM	JJ	AS	ON	74/75 DJ	Eff. Dist.	Adj.* Share
Rochester Total	2.7	4.7	10.0	7.9	6.8	9.7	6.8	7.4	—	7.8
Soft	.7	1.6	2.7	2.0	1.7	2.2	1.6	2.3	74	2.5
Stick	1.8	2.9	6.8	5.5	4.6	5.2	4.1	3.9	88	3.9
Corn	.2	.2	.5	.4	.5	2.3	1.1	1.2	71	1.4
Syracuse Total	2.1	3.7	6.3	5.1	4.7	4.3	3.9	3.4	—	4.2
Soft	.4	.7	1.1	.6	.9	1.0	.7	.6	72	.7
Stick	1.6	2.5	4.3	3.5	3.1	2.5	2.4	2.1	94	2.1
Corn	.1	.5	.9	1.0	.7	.8	.8	.7	40	1.4
Buffalo Total	.5	3.6	6.9	4.9	4.7	4.9	3.8	3.9	—	6 .0
Soft	.1	.6	1.5	1.0	0.7	1.1	.8	.7	58	1.0
Stick	.3	2.1	3.5	2.0	2.1	2.4	1.5	1.4	63	1.8
Corn	.1	.9	1.9	1.9	1.9	1.4	1.5	1.8	45	3.2
St. Louis Total	.8	2.7	3.7	2.9	3.1	3.1	3.1	2.5	—	12.5
Soft	.2	.6	1.4	1.0	1.0	1.1	1.1	.6	9	5.3
Stick	.6	2.0	2.2	1.9	2.1	2.0	1.9	1.8	32	4.5
Corn	—	.1	.1	—	—	—	.1	.1	3	2.7

*Adjusted for expected distribution goal of 80%.

Source: A.C. Nielsen Co.

Land O Lakes had now demonstrated the ability to successfully enter the margarine market.

1975–1982

A number of developments occurred over the next seven years.

1. **Pricing**. In 1976, Land O'Lakes reduced its price to establish parity with Parkay and Blue Bonnet. Share of market increased by 0.7 percent almost immediately.

2. **Copy**. In 1980, the advertising campaign was replaced with a new high-scoring campaign that retained the "From America's Number One Buttermaker" theme but changed the focus away from the animated cows to real farm people.

3. **Volume/Share Projections**. A thorough analysis of current markets was done to determine if any variables might correlate to the performance of Land O Lakes margarine in the marketplace—margarine consumption in pounds per capita, competition, advertising impact, and Land O Lakes butter sales per capita. The latter proved to be a good, consistent indicator. By applying the correlation between butter and margarine sales per capita in current markets to possible rollout markets, it was possible to project margarine volume in new markets. The system proved to be totally consistent, and led to more accurate forecasting.

5. **Major Expansion**. In 1981, Land O Lakes margarine was introduced in 85 percent of the country with a strong acceptance. At the same time, a 40 percent butter/60 percent margarine, Land O Lakes brand Country Morning Blend, entered several major markets.

Land O Lakes Butter's Future Prologue

Since the first years of Land O Lakes margarine introduction, the total U.S. butter market has stabilized at a relatively low level. In spite of this, Land O Lakes butter sales from the mid-1970s through 1982 are similar to the sales of the early '70s. Share has grown and Land O Lakes margarine does not appear to hurt butter sales. In fact, butter is more likely aided by the stronger support margarine provides to the Land O Lakes brand name.

Conclusions

The margarine experience for Land O'Lakes was a bold move with lasting effects on the corporation. It redefined their business from being "butter marketers" to becoming "spread marketers."

The margarine success helped provide today's Land O'Lakes management commitment and confidence in a more aggressive future program of new products development.

And this experience has demonstrated to Land O'Lakes the tremendous consumer franchise embodied in their brand name. This has caused them to not only recognize the opportunities this represents, but to also place more stringent guidelines on the use of this valuable equity.

Fisher-Price Children's Phonograph

We are not entering the toy business to copy ideas, but to contribute new, advanced creative thoughts.
—*Fisher-Price Toys Inc., 1931*

Background

In 1930, Herman G. Fisher, Irving L. Price, and Helen M. Schelle founded a toy company in East Aurora, NY (20 miles southeast of Buffalo), called Fisher-Price Toys Inc. Small manufacturing facilities were established in the first year of operation and 16 new toys, largely made of wood, were produced and marketed in 1931.

In 1931, a "Fisher-Price Creed of Toy Making" was drafted by the founders. This same policy guides Fisher-Price's toy development today:

We are not entering the toy business to copy ideas, but to contribute new, advanced, creative thoughts, guided by these five sound principles of toy making:

1. Intrinsic play value
2. Ingenuity
3. Strong construction
4. Good value for the money
5. Action

A successful toy for the modern selective buyer must pay its way on the counter every day in the year. It must be in demand for birthdays, parties, and week-end trips, and meet the daily need for good cheer and recreation, for amusement and education. It must contribute to the toy counter and volume to the sales.

Fisher-Price case history information was provided by courtesy of James R. Tindall, vice president and general manager, U.S. Fisher-Price Toys Inc.

Fisher-Price's sales growth was strong and steady from the period 1930 until 1969 when Fisher-Price, the leading manufacturer of preschool toys (toys appropriate for children ages 2 to 5), was acquired by The Quaker Oats Company of Chicago. In the decade since the acquisition, Fisher-Price sales and profits have grown at a compounded growth rate of 20-plus percent a year. (See Figure B-1.) This growth was made possible as a result of product line diversification, geographic expansion, and a significant infusion of capital investment from the parent company.

Figure B-1
Fisher-Price Sales Growth 1930–1980

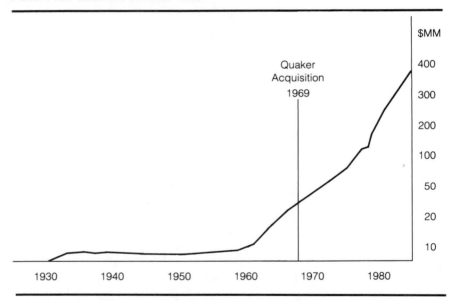

Source: Fisher-Price Toys, Div. The Quaker Oats Company

Today, Fisher-Price toys are retailed in more than 150 countries around the world. The product line consists of more than 200-plus toy products covering a wide variety of play needs, prices, ages, and technologies. Fisher-Price operates nine manufacturing locations around the world and maintains its headquarters in East Aurora, NY.

One of Fisher-Price's fastest growing lines of business is its group of audio visual products. The audio visual product line was established in 1973 when Fisher-Price introduced a hand-held, manually operated Movie Viewer, which allowed a preschool child to view licensed cartoon films available in an assortment of interchangeable plastic cartridges. This toy product was developed and produced for Fisher-Price by the Montron Corporation of Mountain View, CA.

In 1977, Fisher-Price expanded its audio visual toy line by introducing a table-top version of the Movie Viewer called the Fisher-Price Movie Viewer Theater. This was Fisher-Price's first electrically powered product and allowed children to view the same cartoon film in two modes: rear screen projection or wall projection. In the same year, Fisher-Price acquired the assets of Montron Corporation.

A third audio visual product, called the Talk-To-Me Player and Book, was introduced to the toy trade in 1978. The product consists of a small ($3'' \times 5'' \times 3''$), battery-powered, hand-held phonograph that plays a plastic record mounted to each page of a 16-page book. When operated, the phonograph "reads" a story to the child complete with sound effects. The Talk-To-Me Player was completely "sold out" in its first two years of production. Based on the strength of consumer and trade response, Fisher-Price continued to investigate new product concepts to broaden its Audio Visual line. (See Figure B-2.)

Figure B-2
Fisher-Price Product Lineup

By 1981, the Fisher-Price line of easy-to-operate child entertainment items included The Movie Viewer (introduced in 1975), The Movie Viewer (introduced in 1977), the Talk-To-Me-Player (introduced in 1978), the Phonograph (introduced in 1979) and the new Fisher-Price Tape Recorder for children.

Source: 1981–82 advertisement prepared by Waring & LaRosa, Inc., New York, advertising agency.

Project Analysis

Opportunity Investigation

Among the audio visual product opportunities investigated by Fisher-Price was that of a children's phonograph. An analysis of secondary source information generated the following information:

- Phonographs were the second largest category of audio visual products for children (see Table B-1).

Table B-1
Children's Audio Visual Products

Audio visual sub-category	Category market share
Viewmasters/viewers	28
Phonographs	24
Radios	14
Theaters	7
Walkie-talkies	6
Tape recorders	2
Other	19
Total	100

Source: Syndicated diary panel service

- Almost 700,000 children's phonographs were sold in the United States in 1976. Unit sales grew 25 percent per year for the next two years, reaching 1,100,000 units in 1978.
- No single manufacturer dominated the market.
- Children's phonographs were generally low quality, causing a great deal of frustration among consumers. Consumers complained of phonographs breaking shortly after purchase. This problem was especially serious because of the relatively high price point of phonographs.
- Character licensing was commonly used to differentiate phonograph products.
- Focus groups conducted among mothers of boys and girls ages 6 to 9 indicated a dissatisfaction with the durability and audio quality of competitive phonograph products currently on the market. At the extreme, a few mothers characterized these products as "disposable."

Decision

The phonograph project (including further commitment of design, engineering, and market research resources) was accelerated at this point for several reasons:

- The Audio Visual category was exceeding its sales projections.
- The development of a child's phonograph was consistent with Fisher-Price's long-range product line strategy.
- The phonograph market was large and growing.
- The high-quality segment in the market was a "natural" for Fisher-Price, whose reputation for safety and durability was very strong.
- Fisher-Price's franchise was extremely strong among mothers, the most frequent purchaser of children's phonographs.
- Fisher-Price was already selling other toy products to the most important channels of distribution of children's phonographs.
- Fisher-Price had the necessary in-house technical expertise to produce a superior children's phonograph.

Development

A wide array of phonograph models and features were developed by R&D. After sorting a number of variables, based on judgment and experience, several different prototypes were consumer-tested. These test results yielded the following profile for the product:

- Quality solid-state phonograph with a 4-inch speaker and simplified controls.
- Genuine diamond needle that allows five times the play of the commonly used sapphire needle.
- Tone arm designed to withstand abnormal abuse (in fact the entire phonograph can be held up by the tone arm without sustaining damage).
- As an added precaution, the tone arm will automatically lock securely into place when case is closed.
- Molded removable case cover with convenient carrying handle.
- Plays at 33⅓ or 45 RPM speed and has a built-in adapter for playing 45s.
- Operation on normal household 120 volt, 60 cycle current.
- 64-inch electrical cord that neatly winds into recessed area beneath the unit.
- 1-year limited warranty against defects in material or workmanship.
- UL listed.

Marketing Plan

The 1979 marketing plan was as follows:

- Advertising was directed to mothers because they were the primary purchaser of children's phonographs. Print advertising (see Figure B-3)

Figure B-3
Introductory Ad

Fisher-Price 1979 introductory advertisement run in women's service magazines for its children's phonograph, directed to mothers, the primary purchasers of children's phonographs.

placed in women's service magazines was used to communicate the idea that this was a dependable piece of audio equipment designed especially for children.

- Distribution. The Fisher-Price phonograph was merchandised in the Fisher-Price section of the toy department rather than with stereo systems in the electronics department.
- Pricing. The introductory wholesale price of $21.95 represented a significant premium over competitive products which averaged $14.95 and ranged from approximately $8.95 to $17.95. Retail prices ranged from $24.95 to $39.95 depending on the channel of distribution.
- Package. Because other Fisher-Price audio visual products were already in preschool packaging (blue box with red scallops) and because the age appropriateness of the product was 4 and up, the Fisher-Price phonograph was also packaged with preschool graphics.

Sales Results

The Fisher-Price phonograph was introduced at the American Toy Fair in New York City in February 1979. Dollar sales have grown in each subsequent year since then. In 1981, the Fisher-Price phonograph had an estimated 30 percent of the children's phonograph market and was the largest dollar volume item in the Fisher-Price line.

Toro Power Shovel

As a leader, Toro places primacy not only on quality of product and a strong distribution and service network—but also on innovation, the creation of all new need-fulfillment products in the outdoor consumer and commercial maintenance fields.
—Kendrick Melrose
  President,
  The Toro Company

Background

The Toro Company began in the early 1900s as the Bull Tractor Company. The Toro Motor Company, a tractor engine subsidiary, was created in 1914.

Toro first turned away from its agricultural orientation in 1922 when the golf course superintendent of a Minneapolis, MN, country club suggested that the company design a tractor-towed gang mower unit for fairway maintenance. By 1925, Toro turf maintenance machines were in service on nearly every major golf course in the country and on parks and large estates as well.

Toro produced its first power mower for residential use in 1939, but it was not until 1945, when a group of World War II veterans took over the management of the company, that Toro began to move aggressively into the home lawn market.

Through a combination of acquisitions and innovative research and development, Toro began a program of expansion in 1948 that has served as the basic business strategy of the company for over three decades.

Toro entered the snowthrower market in 1951. It was a major step in transforming the company from a seasonal business into a year-round one.

In the snowthrower market, Toro pioneered the development of compact, lightweight snowthrowers, first with the Snow Pup in 1964. The subject of this case history, the Toro Power Shovel, was introduced in 1979.

Toro Today

Today, the Toro Company is the nation's leading independent manufacturer and marketer of equipment offering labor-saving, resource-conserving solutions to the problems of outdoor maintenance for both residential and commercial use. Toro is the leading independent producer of consumer lawn equipment, a category that includes walk power mowers, riding mowers, trimmers, hoses, and other lightweight appliance products.

Toro also is the worldwide leader in the snow removal equipment market, a category that includes a full line of products ranging in price from under $100 for the Toro Power Shovel to well over $1,000 for heavy-duty, two-stage Toro snowthrowers.

Toro is also a world leader in automatic underground irrigation systems and in professional turf equipment for the commercial and golf course markets.

Toro products are distributed through a network of distributors; approximately 50 in the United States and over 50 in the rest of the world.

Toro sales exceeded $50,000,000 in 1959; $100,000,000 in 1973; $200,000,000 in 1978; and $400,000,000 in 1980. Due to two years of light snowfall, a downturn in consumer economy, and inventory build-up throughout the distribution system, sales of $247,000,000 were reported in 1981.

Toro has supported its products and distribution partners with consistently high-quality marketing programs and advertising over the years. This, combined with a high-quality product offering, has made Toro the Number One brand name in the lawn and garden market.

Snowthrower Market

Toro entered the snowthrower market to gain a seasonal counter-balance to its growing summer yard care business. Toro's first products were two-stage* snowthrowers, then the mainstay of the industry. These machines were large, heavy, cumbersome to operate, and expensive. As a result, the market was limited to very heavy snow areas, primarily in the Northeast.

Toro completely changed the snowthrower market in 1964 when the company introduced the first single-stage* snowthrower. This machine, called the Snow Pup, was much lighter, more compact, easier to operate, and less expensive than the traditional two-stage snowthrower.

Following a successful test market effort, Toro launched a major marketing campaign behind its single-stage snowthrower, including heavy television advertising. The market responded and snowthrower sales took off.

---

*Two-stage snowthrowers employ an auger to meter the snow into the machine and a high-speed impeller to actually throw the snow. Single-stage snowthrowers utilize a single rotating mechanism to both lift and throw the snow in one continuous operation.

Fueled by above-average snowfalls and a strong economy, the snowthrower market nearly doubled in size each year in the late 1970s. Homeowners in snowbelt markets found the Toro Snow Master, a later version of the Snow Pup, an irreplaceable partner in the battle against winter. The market expanded, sales outstripped production, and Toro firmly established itself as the market leader. Toro snowthrower sales jumped from $13,600,000 in 1975, to $30,400,000 in 1977, $119,300,000 in 1979, and peaked at $129,900,000 in 1980.

Toro Power Shovel

It was in this period of sales growth and market expansion that the Toro Power Shovel was developed and prepared for market introduction. Since its introduction, a series of market factors, including two successive years of light snowfall and a sharp decline in the consumer economy, have resulted in sharp declines in the total snowthrower market.

Market Opportunity

The key to the tremendous growth of the snowthrower market in the late '70s was above-average snowfalls and a product designed to meet consumer needs. Toro led the way in innovative product designs, shifting the market from big two-stage to compact, consumer-designed, single-stage machines.

By 1978, 72 percent of the industry volume was single-stage units, yet penetration was only 20 percent of the snowbelt households. Price was the primary buying deterrent. Toro saw this situation as an opportunity to further expand the market through the introduction of an even more compact, lower-cost unit—the Toro Power Shovel.

General consumer exploration of the snowthrower market had suggested the need for such a product. Many snowthrower prospects had a need for light snow removal—but many felt that even the smaller single-stage snowthrowers were too large and inappropriate for their snow removal problem.

Toro conceived the Power Shovel to fill this need. It was to be a smaller, lightweight, electric-powered unit that would work like a manual snow shovel except that the Power Shovel, not the shoveler, would lift and throw the snow.

First Product Concept

The Power Shovel marketing concept was transformed into a product concept. Additional consumer research was conducted. Respondents said that snow removal was a difficult chore, often undertaken in adverse conditions. They listed *bulk snow removal*, *snow directional control*, and *convenience* as important buying considerations for a snowthrower. *Price* was the reason most often cited for not owning a snowthrower.

Based on this research, the original Power Shovel product design was modified to enhance its actual and perceived performance. Directional vane controls were added to the unit along with a double bar handle and wheels.

The program moved rapidly through the remaining developmental stages, and in March 1978, a final prototype unit was presented to Toro management for approval. Concern was expressed that while the prototype presented looked excellent, it did not truly represent the original Power Shovel concept. As a result, two key decisions were made at this point:

1. Introduce this unit as a more compact, light-weight, modestly priced electric *snowthrower*. It was to become known as the "S-120."
2. Continue to pursue product development of a true Power Shovel.

The Toro S-120 was introduced in 1979 as the most compact, easiest to use, and easiest to afford snowthrower on the market. The unit was positioned as an extension of the Toro single-stage line and retailed for $129 to $149. It was sold primarily through Toro's two-step distribution system, but there was increased emphasis on expanding mass merchandiser outlets.

New, Refined Product Concept Development

To put the Power Shovel project back on track, a tight product concept statement was drafted. This "Reason for Being" concluded that the Power Shovel device "is offered for the prospect who currently removes snow with a snow shovel and is willing to pay as much as $75 to clear small areas of shallow snow with a minimum of strain and maximum of ease in less than 20 minutes."

Power Shovel developmental efforts at Toro proceeded at an accelerated rate. Several outside consultant groups collaborated on the project. Booz Allen & Hamilton of Cleveland, OH, worked primarily in motor design and selection. BKM, Inc., of Bonita, CA, was charged with primary efforts in the rotor system. King Casey, of New Canaan, CT, was given responsibility for the final prototype development and styling efforts.

The product progressed through design development, including numerous design review meetings, cost reviews, and tooling releases. Manufacturing drawings and a final engineering release culminated in an Underwriters Laboratories' product listing. (Figure C-1 traces Toro's moves to develop a smaller, lightweight snow remover.)

Consumer research confirmed the appeal of the redesigned Toro Power Shovel. The unit was perceived as "easy to operate." Two-thirds of the target market felt it would meet their snow removal needs; over a third indicated a high buying probability. Consumer estimates of the price were very close to the proposed $75 to $80.

Figure C-1a & b
Toro Snow Removers

Toro expanded the consumer snowthrower market by innovating and introducing smaller, lighter, easier to use and more affordable snow removal equipment. The progression of each new item reveals this development.
Source: The Toro Company

Initial production began in October 1979 after late tool deliveries were overcome. By the end of January 1980, total units produced had reached 220,000.

Market Plan

The Toro Power Shovel was recognized as an opportunity to create an entirely new snow market with tremendous growth potential. The product was believed appropriate for almost half the homeowners in the snowbelt, or a segment of 7,000,000 households.

The basic introductory strategy was to position the product as an all-new household convenience item, not a snowthrower, and to generate massive consumer impact through heavy advertising.

The Power Shovel was introduced in 1979 throughout the entire snowbelt. The objective was to achieve major first year sales volume and establish a strong position in this new category before lower-priced competitive entries could be introduced.

Figure C-1c & d
Toro Snow Removers

Product Description

The Toro Power Shovel is a highly-engineered snow removal product incorporating advanced technology in rotor, drive system, and electrical design. The versatility and performance of the unit makes it suitable for a wide range of applications, almost anywhere a manual shovel can be used.

Weighing only eleven pounds, the Power Shovel is operated basically like a push snow shovel. (See Figure C-2.) The operator slides the unit along any hard surface on its polyethylene scraper blade. Snow is pushed into the unit and thrown out at the rate of up to a hundred pounds a minute. Directional control of the snow being thrown is achieved by simply angling the Power Shovel to one side or the other as it's pushed forward.

The Power Shovel was introduced with a full one-year limited warranty, with a Toro option of over-the-counter exchange or repair. Toro also provided additional discounts for service distributors and dealers to encourage development of a service network and responsive consumer service.

Pricing

Toro's pricing objectives were to provide the trade with a standard 40 percent gross margin and a discount structure to support a volume sell-in. At the same

Figure C-2
Toro Power Shovel

The new Toro Power Shovel was unique: Weighs less than 12 pounds, but throws snow up to 20 feet.

Source: The Toro Company

time, Toro set its price to generate sufficient internal funds to afford a heavy marketing investment in the product.

The objectives were accomplished through the combination of premium price points with long discounts to encourage retail promotional activity. Toro also utilized a multiple discount structure based on functions performed and a strong early-order incentive to gain fast distribution.

With a suggested manufacturer's retail price of $89.99, the Power Shovel was significantly less expensive than any snowthrower on the market. This low price point would encourage impulse buying and gift purchasing.

Product Position Development

In the spring of 1978, Toro and its advertising agency, Campbell-Mithun Inc., developed six positioning statements for the Power Shovel. Two of the positions keyed on labor saving, two on time saving, and two on price. (See Figure C-3.)

Figure C-3a & b
Ad Positioning Test

Introducing the Power Snow Shovel. For people who are tired of lifting snow.

The Power Snow Shovel lifts and throws snow so you don't have to. Throws a hundred pounds of snow a minute. It ends the exhausting labor of digging in, scraping, pushing, lifting and trying to heave wet snow. Spare yourself the strain with this easy way to take the load off.

Introducing a quicker way in from the cold.

In just 10 minutes, the Power Snow Shovel clears two inches of snow from a 3 ft. x 50 ft. sidewalk. And gets you back indoors faster than shoveling. Out of the wind-chill weather that numbs bone deep. Why suffer it any longer than necessary?

Posterboards, used as stimulus material in appeal testing, focused on labor saving, time saving and price. The poster on the left had preferred appeal. Indications from this led to successful print and television executions featuring the best scoring appeals.
Source: Campbell-Mithun, Inc.

Consumer testing indicated that the labor saving appeal was the strongest. The winning position statement was headlined, "For people who are tired of lifting snow" and showed a weary shoveler, snow shovel in hand.

As a result of this work, the Toro Power Shovel was positioned as an *all new product for people who don't like to shovel snow.* The position underscored two key elements:

1. The Toro Power Shovel is all new—an innovation from Toro.
2. The Toro Power Shovel is for anyone with appropriate snow conditions who doesn't like to shovel snow.

New Product Category Created

The Toro Power Shovel was not positioned as a small snowthrower or an extension of the single-stage product line. Instead, the over-all objective of

Figure C-3c & d
Ad Positioning Test

For $70, you can stop shoveling snow.

Introducing the Power Snow Shovel. It removes snow at the rate of 100 pounds a minute. Yet it costs just $70. Where else can you find a less expensive way to put an end to hand shoveling this winter and the winters to come.

Introducing the Power Snow Shovel. For people who don't need a snowthrower.

The Power Snow Shovel is just the right size snow remover if you have only small areas to clear. Like short walkways, porches, steps or balconies. It's a labor saver that's ideal for places where a snowthrower is more than you need.

the product introduction was to create, and become the market leader in, a whole new product category—the power shovel category.

The strategy was based on the need to appeal to consumers who had already determined that a snowthrower was not appropriate for their needs, because of insufficient snowfall, too small an area to clear, or price. Clearly differentiating the Power Shovel would also minimize cannibalization of the highly profitable Toro single-stage business and help Toro more clearly position the new product with the trade.

Product Name Decision

The Toro snowthrower marketing group and advertising agency explored many product name candidates before deciding on *Toro Power Shovel*. However, after this name was considered, it was felt to be so appropriate and the rationale for it so sound that the name was adopted without consumer research.

Some of the supporting points for use of the name Toro Power Shovel were:

Figure C-3e & f
Ad Positioning Test

Fast getaway to what you'd rather do this winter.

The new Power Snow Shovel makes quick work of snow removal. In just 10 minutes, it clears two inches of snow from a 3 ft. x 50 ft. sidewalk. And saves you time getting to the ski slopes, ice rink, snowmobile trail, winter camp, bobsled or pipe and slippers by the fire. Whatever you'd rather do with winter.

Introducing the snowthrower for people who think snowthrowers are too expensive.

At $70, the Power Snow Shovel costs less than half as much as any other snowthrower. Which makes it not so much of a luxury, but more of a plain old, practical, economical labor saver. And that, in turn, makes it all the more attractive. Right?

1. The buying prospect is currently using a snow *shovel*.
2. The product to be replaced is the *shovel*.
3. The motion used with the product is like a push snow *shovel*.
4. The name is unique and memorable.
5. The name helps differentiate the product from Toro's single-stage line.
6. The name capitalizes on the strong Toro awareness and quality image and works to further build the Toro consumer brand franchise.

Distribution

Historically, Toro had sold its snow equipment through its distributors and network of outdoor power equipment and hardware store dealers. While these dealers provided strong sales and quality service, they had a limited ability to generate a high volume of consumer traffic.

The Toro Power Shovel required a strategic shift in this distribution pattern. This change was supported by consumer research. While only 13 percent of all Toro buyers purchased at mass merchandisers in 1977–78, 77 percent of the Power Shovel prospects indicated they would shop for this product at mass merchant outlets. Toro's historical snow distribution channel did not adequately cover the indicated shopping habits of the primary market.

Broad distribution through mass merchants, as well as traditional power equipment and hardware dealers, was required to achieve strong consumer impact and major first-year sales volume. It also provided Toro's distributors with an opportunity to develop a profitable relationship with mass merchants.

Toro supplemented the distributors' effort with a direct sales program. This national account program was designed for direct quantity sales from Toro to national accounts with distributor support on reorders, stock fill-ins, parts and service, and merchandising assistance. The single most important account sold through this program was J. C. Penney.

By the end of the first season, the Toro Power Shovel was stocked in over 3,500 outlets, including 2,100 traditional independent dealers, 600 discount, 400 department, and 400 home center stores.

Target Market

The primary target market for the Toro Power Shovel consisted of single-family households in areas averaging a 20 to 49-inch annual snowfall. A majority of the target market was concentrated in the large industrial centers in the central and lower snowbelt, such as New York, Chicago, Philadelphia, Detroit, Cleveland, and Boston. A secondary market was the fringe snowbelt area averaging 10 to 19 inches of snowfall.

Market research indicated a large potential demand for the Power Shovel. Using a screen of "high intent to buy," the prime Power Shovel market potential was calculated at over two million households.

Compared to Toro snowthrower buyers, the Power Shovel prospects were younger, lower income, had sidewalks instead of driveways, and there was greater female interest in the product. (See Table C-1).

Table C-1
Prospects for Power Shovel

	Power Shovel	Toro S-120	Toro Snowthrower
Age: Under 35	47%	24%	19%
Income: $10,000–20,000	56	47	31
No Driveway	74	8	3
Sex: Female	41	24	20

Source: The Toro Company

Consumer attitude was determined to be just as important as demographics. The Power Shovel attracted people who had a need for snow removal but did not consider a snowthrower appropriate. They appreciated not having to shovel but considered snowthrowers too big and expensive for their situation.

It was also determined that the Power Shovel was seen as an appropriate gift, particularly for an older person.

Advertising

The early positioning work on the Power Shovel revealed that buying prospects for this product tended not to be very knowledgeable about snowthrower operation and pricing. This suggested the need for a strong creative concept and product demonstration to stimulate initial interest.

The advertising agency recommended that the introductory advertising be *highly impactful* for several other reasons:

1. The Power Shovel was a new concept, a new category. They didn't want prospects relating the Toro Power Shovel to snowthrowers.
2. Prospects needed to be jolted into recognizing the value of the Toro Power Shovel. They'd already determined they didn't want or couldn't afford a snowthrower. There was a need to break through this mind set.
3. The Power Shovel faced a short selling season; there were just 12 weeks during which time it was necessary to gain high awareness and move the prospect towards a buying decision.
4. Mass merchandisers were to become an important retail outlet. Prospects were not accustomed to seeing and buying Toro products at these outlets.

It was also believed that the advertising needed to be action-oriented, show the product at work, and capitalize on the fun and enjoyment of operating the Toro Power Shovel. The advertising needed to build talk value for the product.

The introductory television execution utilized the manual snow shovel as a foil. The commercial opened with an on-camera presenter holding up a shovel, while asking the viewers if they still had one. The presenter then abruptly broke the shovel handle over his knee. This opening not only grabbed the viewers' attention, but created interest and talk value by relating directly to their feelings about shoveling and the snow shovel. The presenter then introduced and demonstrated the new Toro Power Shovel. The demonstration so intrigued his watchful neighbors that they broke their snow shovels in favor of the new Toro Power Shovel. (See Figure C-4.)

The commercial proved highly effective. Copy testing generated a recall score 70 percent above the category norm and a brand preference change 60 percent above the norm. More importantly, the commercial generated consumer awareness, store traffic, and consumer sales.

Figure C-4
Introductory TV Commercial

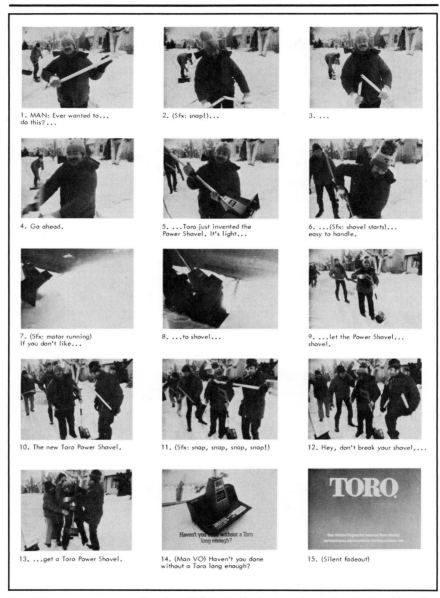

1. MAN: Ever wanted to... do this?...

2. (Sfx: snap!)...

3. ...

4. Go ahead.

5. ...Toro just invented the Power Shovel. It's light...

6. ...(Sfx: shovel starts)... easy to handle.

7. (Sfx: motor running) If you don't like...

8. ...to shovel...

9. ...let the Power Shovel... shovel.

10. The new Toro Power Shovel.

11. (Sfx: snap, snap, snap, snap!)

12. Hey, don't break your shovel,...

13. ...get a Toro Power Shovel.

14. (Man VO) Haven't you done without a Toro long enough?

15. (Silent fadeout)

Dramatic opening of conventional snowshovel being broken immediately captures attention and symbolizes the analogy of the light new Toro Power Shovel benefits vs. back-breaking hand shoveling in this introductory commercial. (Dealer identification is superimposed on closing frame.)

Media

The basic objective of the Toro Power Shovel introductory media plan was to build fast awareness and communicate the product concept. This supported the trade sell-in program and was designed to ensure fast sell-through and minimum end-of-season inventory.

Toro made a major investment in consumer media. The company allocated and spent about $2,000,000 for advertising in 1979, or 18 percent of planned net sales.

The basic media strategy was concentration. The media mix was concentrated in television, with 90 percent of the budget going into this medium. Spending was concentrated in key market ADIs: 2,000 GRPs in markets representing the top 50 percent of potential and 1,500 GRPs in markets representing the next 30 percent of potential. Scheduling was concentrated in a 12-week period to create maximum impact during the early winter and pre-Christmas periods. Communication was concentrated in one strong introductory television commercial, with dealer and Christmas gift five-second tags.

Toro funded 100 percent of the television advertising. A 75/25 percent Toro-funded co-op advertising allowance was also provided to help stimulate strong retail promotion advertising.

Promotion

The Toro Power Shovel was not included in the traditional Toro Red Tag pre-season dollars-off promotion for other items in the Toro snowthrower line. Instead, distributors participated in an extension cord promotion that encouraged retailer displays, promotion, and tie-in advertising. The suggested consumer offer consisted of a free cord with purchase of a Power Shovel.

National and direct accounts were given a 100 percent Toro-paid advertising/merchandising allowance to support their Power Shovel purchases.

Toro also supported the introduction with a complete Power Shovel point-of-sale kit. The primary fixture was a product display stand with a built-in Fairchild projector and a two-minute concept-sell point-of-sale film. The display unit picked up the broken snow shovel visual idea from the television commercial and carried the "Hate shoveling? Try the new Toro Power Shovel" proposition right to the store.

When early winter snow failed to develop, Toro continued to support the product with a "Mid-Winter Clean-Up" promotion. Geared to stimulate retail activity, the event was supported with spot TV, including a Super Bowl announcement, newspaper, and radio.

Results

The recommended build quantity for the introductory year was 175,000 pieces. This was based on 7 percent first year penetration of the total estimated potential power shovel market. That market potential was calculated to be 2,846,000 households, or the percent of total snowbelt households that indicated a high buying interest in the product. The projections were based on the assumptions of distribution through direct and distributor sales, average snowfall, and moderate economic growth.

Toro sold 207,000 units and moved them into the distribution pipeline. However, by the end of the first season, only 110,000 units had been sold at retail.

Consumer sales were hampered by a delayed introduction due to late tooling and a mild winter. Following record-setting snowfalls the two preceding seasons, the winter of 1979–80 almost didn't happen. Many key Power Shovel markets strolled through the season with mild temperatures and without a trace of snow.

Toro did succeed in creating a unique and innovative product. The Toro Power Shovel proved to be an excellent performing unit that met the needs of a potentially large segment of the snow market. However, it also became apparent that accurately forecasting sales volumes for snow products, including the Toro Power Shovel, was almost as difficult as predicting the very snowfall on which those sales depended.

Appendix

A

New Products Checklist

By permission, Campbell-Mithun Inc., Chicago and Minneapolis.

Loosely chronological organization of new products operational considerations.

Broad areas of major functions as follows:

Research & Development
All product and consumer research except for that directly related to development and evaluation of communications. This category includes technical, engineering, styling, and market research.

Production
Purchasing, manufacturing, warehousing, shipping, quality control, labor.

Finance
Budgeting, cost analysis, pricing, profitability.

Legal

Distribution
Sales operations, trade practices and policies.

Communications
Advertising, promotion, merchandising, product publicity, advertising research.

Whenever action is required by the major operational officer responsible for the company activity, an asterisk (*) is indicated.

New Product Checklist

	Research and Development	Finance	Production	Distribution	Legal	Communications
I. EXPLORATION						
*Statement of company objective	Policy Objective					
Initial exploratory and creative activities						X
Statement of product idea	Originator					
Judgment evaluation of merit	New Product Committee					
*Plan to investigate approved	Operations Executive					
Profile of products known on the market	X					
Survey of product ingredients, design standards, general technology of the field	X					
Analysis of competitive product claims	X					X
Analysis of competitive media use						X
Analysis of competitive advertising expenditures						X
Areas of brand share/volume history	X					
Survey of trade information regarding CGS, wholesale discounts, distribution costs	X			X		X
Survey of traditional channels of distribution and other distribution opportunities	X			X		X

		New Product Committee				
Survey of general selling practices, promotional allowances, buying standards				X		X
Survey of specific federal and state legal problems in reference to ingredients, sales practices, controls				X	X	
Survey to determine marketing opportunity area	X					
Cyclical, seasonal, and long term marketing considerations	X					
Product class profile study	X					
Survey of potential consumer interest in new product	X					
Definition of the selected market	X					
Preliminary opportunity estimate		X				

II. SCREENING

*Appointment of project coordinating executive						
Estimation of period of product exclusivity	X		X	X		X
Research of consumer satisfaction and use habits of current products	X					
Consumer motivation research in area of advertised brand claims, etc.	X					X
Product concept screening	X					X
Analysis of sizes, colors, shapes, textures, types required	X					
Isolation of CGS/price opportunities in distribution mix	X	X				

New Product Checklist

	Research and Development	Finance	Production	Distribution	Legal	Communications
Investigation of additional sales outlets—government, export, institutional, premiums				X		
Report of findings and indicated opportunities	X			X		X
III. PROPOSAL						
*Request for Planned Development Program, with estimated investment and timeable	New Product Committee					
Approval of research and development budget	Operations Executive					
Initial design/formulation of product	X		X			
Copyrights or patents	X				X	
Preparation of product platform	X			X		X
Securement of required government clearances					X	
Initial costing based on optimum manufacturing levels	X	X	X			
Determination of local tax, licensing, and other financial considerations		X			X	
Life and fatigue tests of materials and finishes	X		X			
Performance and efficiency tests	X		X			

*Independent laboratory/engineering analysis of prototypes					X
Preparation of copy platform	X				
Social science evaluation of consumers relative to the new product area	X				X
Panel evaluation of prototype product					X
Forecast of volume potential	X		X		X
Determination of plant capacity and facilities availability				X	
Consumer blind test comparison					X
IV. DEVELOPMENT					
Large scale research of prototype product					X
Plant location and transportation considerations				X	
*Basis of appropriation	New Product Committee				
Development of national media plan	X				
Decision on manufacturer association-identification on/with product	X		X		X
Creation of brand name possibilities	X				
Creation of/or agreement on established generic descriptive name	X				
Legal search of brand name possibilities		X			

New Product Checklist

	Research and Development	Finance	Production	Distribution	Legal	Communications
Registration of trademark, copyright brand name					X	
Development of basic consumer selling theme						X
Test of consumer selling theme						X
Labeling requirements					X	
Initial packaging	X					X
Packaging testing	X					
Approval of package design (and inserts)						X
Preparation of instructions/directions to conform					X	X
Adoption of media philosophy, based on selling theme, budgetary consideration, coverage of prospects, and availability						X
Test of advertising execution (in form of basic media)						X
Creation of total national campaign concept						X
Determination of labor availability			X			
Study of labor or union regulations			X		X	

Determination of raw material commitments and availability			X		
Determination of special tooling and equipment			X		
Packaging and components commitments			X		
Prediction of competitive reaction to new product	X	X			X
V. SALES TESTING					
Assignment of product manager to work with project executive				Operations Executive	
Setting of test area sales goals—share, penetration, unit, and dollar volume				New Product Committee	
Determination of introductory test area timing	X				X
Determination of service and repair problems and facilities		X			
*Sales representative recruitment		X		X	
Sales training		X			
*Manufacturing pilot run			X		
*Approval of test area production			X		Operations Executive
Shipping, storage, and packing tests			X		
Definition of all aspects of available test areas, including demographic, media patterns, trade outlet patterns, and distribution centers	X				X
Plan to meet competitive reaction	X	X			X

New Product Checklist

	Research and Development	Finance	Production	Distribution	Legal	Communications
Finalization of test areas	X					X
Forecast of test area unit and dollar volume (goals)	X			X		
*Forecast of P/L limits of successful venture and of unsuccessful write-off	X	X		X		
Test area simulation of national campaign concept						X
Development of test area media plan (in line with expansion objectives)						X
*Determination of test area total appropriation	New Product Committee					
Approval of test area consumer advertising materials						X
Approval of trade advertising materials				X		X
Determination of merchandising plan and appropriation				X		X
Preparation of media merchandising				X		X
Preparation of trade selling sheets				X		X
Determination of educational plan and appropriation						X
Preparation of consumer educational materials						X

	1	2	3	4
Determination of publicity plan and appropriation	X			
Preparation of introductory publicity materials	X			
Determination of sales promotion plan and appropriation	X		X	
Devising of consumer incentives, if required—premiums, contests, price offers, couponing, etc.	X		X	
Consideration of multiple product tie-ins	X		X	
Determination of cooperative advertising policies	X		X	
Preparation of cooperative ads	X		X	
Preparation of point of purchase materials	X		X	
Preparation of product hang tags, boots, self-displays	X		X	X
Decision on trade sampling appropriation	X		X	X
Approval of test area commercial plan and insertion schedule	X			
Determination of product indemnity for field test		X		
Setting of sales quotas			X	
Establishment of sales force incentives, bonuses, premiums			X	
Establishment of trade incentives—buying allowances, contests			X	
Commission of product printed material				X

New Product Checklist

	Research and Development	Finance	Production	Distribution	Legal	Communications
Setting up of test area consumer sales audit panel	X			X		
Trade sales kick-off				X		
Pre-introductory measurement of brand name awareness in test area	X					X
Advertising kick-off						X
Survey of trade performance in test area					X	
Research on test area users	X					
Media coverage and intensity progress reports in test area—adjust to meet standards						X
Post-introduction measurements of brand name awareness in test area	X					X
Post-introductory new product profile study in test area	X					
Analysis of factory sales data from test area	X					
Program performance reports in test area—adjust to meet standards						X
Competitive media trend report of test area						X

					New Product Committee
Evaluation of sales and advertising, via progress reports throughout area test timetable	X			X	X
Test area evaluation	X			X	X
*Definition of special line management attention or policy changes required in large scale marketing	X	X	X	X	X
*Recommendation for major expansion					

VI. MARKETING

Turn over to appropriate product manager and revenue division

B

New Products Responsibility Checklist

By permission of 3M Company, from its internal policy publication "Guidelines for Planned Policy Responsibility."

1. NAME OF PRODUCT

    Brand name or trademark clearance with the secretary of the corporate trademark screening committee.

2. PRODUCT CHARACTERISTICS AND FUNCTION

    Summary of the general physical composition or design of the product.

    Identification of the customers who will use the product, and where and how they will use it.

3. PATENTS

    Patent clearances.

    Determination by patent counsel of the patentability of the product and its use by customers before any divulgation outside 3M.

    Filing of appropriate patent applications.

    Investigation of possible infringement of patents owned by others.

4. MARKETING

    Legal approval of merchandising plans (pricing, discounts, proportionately equal treatment, terms and conditions of sale, etc.)

    Instructions, technical, and product literature to delineate product purpose, intended use, use instructions, and caution as to serious health and/or property hazards from reasonably foreseeable misuse.

    Warranty statements in conformance with warranty disclosure requirements.

Labeling in conformance with corporate policy.

Labeling in conformance with federal, state, and local laws.

Advertising and promotional messages including press releases and commercials in conformance with corporate policy.

Information on product claims and limitations to sales force, agents, brokers, and distributors.

5. PRODUCT ASSURANCE
   A. Reliability

   Conformance to applicable government or industry standards.

   If there is no government or industry standard, evaluation against a "guideline" standard or a similar product of proven reliability.

   Product evaluation assessment considering, but not limited to, its description and performance under normal storage conditions as well as after extended storage life in the warehouse and within production facilities.

   A periodic program to verify and document reliability procedures.

   Tests with extremes of reasonably foreseeable customer use environment (i.e., temperature, humidity, altitude, input voltage, etc.).

   B. Quality

   Establishment of quality requirements as determined by the user.

   Comparison of optional methods of achieving quality requirements.

   Establishment of quality monitoring procedure.

   Periodic analysis of results-progress toward goal.

   C. Maintenance (where applicable)

   Definition of training and skill requirements for maintenance personnel and procedures for service and efficient maintenance.

   Replacement parts system.

   Information program on warranties for sales, distribution, and maintenance.

6. PRODUCT SAFETY
   A. Health hazard evaluation

   Evaluation of any adverse effect on human health of any component under conditions of recommended use or reasonably foreseeable misuse in these situations:

   (1) If swallowed, ingested or inhaled.

   (2) With single or repeated eye or skin contact, the occurrence of irritation, toxic absorption, or future sensitization.

   B. Product chemical substance regulatory evaluation

   If the product contains a "new 3M" chemical substance; and it is subject to Premanufacturing Notification (PMN), to be considered six months prior to planned manufacture.

C. Physical safety evaluation

Evaluation of the following under recommended conditions of use or reasonably foreseeable misuse:

(1) Flammability/explosivity
(2) Static electricity
(3) Other electrical effects
(4) Thermal extremes
(5) Mechanical failures
(6) Muscle injury because of weight or design
(7) Noise, color, odor, brightness, etc., effects
(8) Potential injury from sharp corners or edges or "pinching" fingers
(9) Potential injury from unprotected moving parts

Appropriate measures—warning labels, advisory literature—for risks.

D. General safety considerations

Government safety regulations, approvals, or certification requirements for:

(1) Special safety warning labeling
(2) Disclosure of the product's ingredients
(3) Specific handling instructions, safety data sheets, etc.
(4) Special instructions regarding packaging, transportation, and/or storage
(5) Language requirements

E. Evaluation of the product safety characteristics for insurability and claims exposure as follows:

(1) Availability of product insurance in corporate program
(2) Claims exposure level
(3) Cost of insurance in relation to normal coverage

7. ENVIRONMENTAL IMPACT ASSESSMENT

A. Evaluation of the reasonably foreseeable impact of the product and its package on the atmosphere and on the aquatic and terrestrial ecosystems for applicable regulations, including registration and labeling, in all areas where sale is contemplated.

B. Evaluation of the product or material resulting during and from its manufacture, use or disposal for effects on environment regarding:

(1) Effect on human, plant and animal life
(2) Persistence in the environment and the effects of any degradation products
(3) Effect on air quality
(4) Effect on any aquatic ecosystem into which product or its wastes are discharged

    C.   Efforts in products and packaging development to minimize waste and eliminate adverse environmental effects

    D.   Noise considerations; acceptable levels for noise in manufacture and/or use of product

    E.   Acceptable methods of treatment disposal to recommend to customers

    F.   Determination of resource recovery potential from this product

    G.   Acceptable clean-up and disposal procedure for accidental spills

8.   INTERNATIONAL DISTRIBUTION

Outside United States requirements for product responsibility

Legal Clearance for Inventions

By permission, 3M Company

Introduction

We understand you have an idea that you think may be of interest to 3M.

At the outset, let us say that 3M is committed to growth, and much of our past growth can be traced to new ideas. We appreciate the fact that you thought of 3M when you had your idea.

However, you must understand that it is only on rare occasions that we actually utilize an idea submitted to us by a person outside of the company.

With this fact in mind, you may, if you choose to do so, submit your idea to us. However, it will have to be according to the procedures set out in the following pages.

Also you must understand that it is 3M's policy not to accept ideas from the outside on any kind of confidential basis. If you decide to submit your idea to 3M you must keep this policy in mind.

Markets 3M Serves

3M is a large and growing company whose success has been based on the development of new and useful products for the home and industry. The vast majority of these products are developed by our laboratories.

3M currently sells products in the following marketing areas:

- Health care
- Transportation equipment manufacturing and maintenance

- Electronics/electrical manufacturing
- Safety and security
- Voice, video, and data communications
- Office, training, and business
- Consumer
- Communication arts
- Industrial production
- Construction and maintenance

Even though 3M sells over 40 thousand products, our markets are confined primarily to the ten listed. Also, history indicates that while 3M receives many ideas, few are truly new. For these reasons and others, the chances of acceptance of an idea are low . . . usually because the idea does not fit with 3M's overall goals even though it may have apparent value.

This booklet will tell you the basis on which we can consider your idea.

If Your Idea is Already Patented*

We prefer to consider an idea after it has been described and claimed in a patent, since we are then in a position to know exactly what is considered new. If you already have an ISSUED PATENT covering your invention, just send a copy to us; nothing else is required.

On occasion patents have been ruled invalid by courts after being challenged. Invalidity usually results because an earlier publication or products were already in use that were not discovered until after the grant of the patent. There are many other reasons why a patent can be invalid, and 3M has had patents held invalid in the past. Thus any individual or company—including 3M—must retain the right to challenge a patent it considers invalid, and that right extends to any patent submitted for our consideration.

If You Have No Patent and Seek No Compensation For Your Idea—

Just complete the Idea Submission Agreement, check the box adjacent to "3M may use my idea freely. I neither expect nor seek compensation," and send us the information requested.

If You Have No Patent but Hope To Be Paid For Your Idea—

3M will consider your idea only under certain conditions.

Your idea must fall in one of the classes of subject matter which could lead to the development of a product. (It must not, for instance, be concerned with advertising, slogans, selling, or how to run a business.)

You must complete and return to us the original of the Idea Submission Agreement form which is part of this booklet. Make certain you check the box adjacent to "If 3M uses my idea, I hope to receive compensation." If you have already sent us a description about your idea, we will keep it sealed in a locked file unavailable to 3M employees for evaluation until the signed form is returned.

You must accompany the completed Idea Submission Agreement form with a detailed written description of your idea, illustrating it with drawings or photographs, if you can. If you have a patent application pending before the U.S. Patent & Trademark Office, a copy of the specification and drawings will be satisfactory. Please do not send bulky models: We'll ask for them if we need them.

You must agree to let us keep whatever material you submit for our records. To be certain that our files correspond, be sure to keep a copy of everything you send us.

3M Requirements

If 3M considers your idea, we do so with the understanding that it may not be new to us. Please also understand that any disclosure of your idea to a 3M officer or employee cannot establish any obligation to you on behalf of 3M.

We can't assume any obligation to act in a consulting capacity in regard to the patentability of your idea, the desirability of a patent, the commercial possibilities of your idea, or your rights against others.

Nor can we consider any idea you submit unless you are its sole owner. If anyone else has any rights to your idea, you must tell us the name of each such person and the nature of his/her interest.

If you are not at least 18 years old, we must have the signature of your parent or guardian on the Idea Submission Agreement.

You may, of course, appoint an attorney or agent to submit your idea; if you do, however, he should also submit proof of his appointment.

If you are employed, we will need a release from your employer if your employer has any right or equity in your idea.

In Addition, Your Idea Must Pass Some Tests

3M will be interested in your idea only if it passes these tests:

1. It is concerned with a working device, product, process or formula and is not a sales promotion idea.
2. It is an idea for a new product, process, working device or formula which was not in existence when you thought of it. By "in existence" we mean:

- shown or described in a patent, catalog, magazine, encyclopedia, or some other printed publication
- commonly known to the public or trade
- already known to 3M

3. 3M believes the idea has attractive possibilities of becoming a useful product.
4. It fits the markets 3M serves.

Your Idea May Warrant Legal Advice

Unless your invention is already patented or is the subject of a pending patent application, your agreement to the conditions set forth in this booklet may cause you to lose the opportunity to obtain a valid patent in many foreign countries. Consequently, before subscribing to the terms of the agreement set forth in this booklet, we strongly urge you to see a lawyer specializing in patents.

What 3M Will Do

After you have sent us either (1) a copy of your issued patent, or (2) the completed Idea Submission Agreement form accompanied by the information you have checked and noted on the form, here's what we'll do:

We will submit your idea to those people in 3M best able to evaluate it.

If we have an interest in your idea, we will notify you as soon as we can—but this will probably take more time than you would suppose because we may want to have your idea fairly evaluated by several divisions of 3M. We'll try to write you within six weeks; but some ideas require more time than this to evaluate.

Meanwhile, you are free to submit your idea to other companies should you desire to do so.

After Our Evaluation

If we are interested in your idea after our evaluation, we may wish to enter into a formal written agreement which may, among other things, grant patent rights to 3M and provide for compensation. We will not conduct any negotiations before we receive an issued patent or a signed Idea Submission Agreement. A meeting may be arranged after our evaluation of the idea, if both you and 3M are interested in pursuing the matter further.

Until we have evaluated your idea, we can assume no obligation to you whatsoever other than to tell you whether or not we are interested in it. Further, we are not obligated to tell you anything we previously knew or have discovered since you submitted your idea.

In Summary, Here Is What We've Tried To Say:

- Although 3M does not solicit ideas, we will consider your idea at your request provided it is submitted on the enclosed form.
- You must assure us that to the best of your knowledge you are the one who originated the idea, that you own the idea, and that you have the legal right to negotiate with 3M concerning it.
- By submitting your idea to 3M you are not giving us any rights under a patent you now have or may obtain in the future.
- By considering your idea, we are not necessarily admitting that it is new.
- No confidential relationship between us is established when you submit your idea. 3M does not promise to keep it secret.
- After we have studied your idea, we will tell you in writing whether we are interested in it. We assume no obligation to tell you anything we previously knew or have discovered since you submitted your idea.
- Until we have evaluated your idea, we can assume no obligation to you whatsoever. If the evaluation of the idea is promising, 3M may enter into a formal written agreement with you.
- We suggest that you consult with an attorney before proceeding with the submission of your idea.
- Remember, the odds are very low that any idea will be one which will qualify as a new product possibility in which 3M will invest.

It's Your Move

If the rules for submitting your idea sound harsh, it's only because we're trying not to mislead you. We congratulate you for your creativity and thank you again for associating 3M with new ideas.

Now with these conditions in mind—if you would like to have 3M consider your idea, please complete the Idea Submission Agreement which follows. Make sure you describe your idea on the top line of the agreement. A duplicate form is included for your records. Tear out the original and mail it to:

Corporate Technical Planning and Coordination/3M
223-5S 02, 3M Center
St. Paul, Minnesota 55144
Attn: External Ideas Correspondent

If your idea is described and claimed in your issued patent, you do not need to complete the Idea Submission Agreement—just send a copy of the patent to us at the address mentioned.

If you have more than one idea, each must be accompanied by an Idea Submission Agreement. Please note that in signing the agreement, you agree that any related ideas you send us will be subject to the same conditions as the present idea.

Idea Submission Agreement

Minnesota Mining and Manufacturing Company
Idea Submission Agreement

3M

My idea relates to _____
_____
_____

Check all
appropriate boxes
and fill in all
pertinent blanks.

☐ I have sent to you   ☐ I am enclosing
☐ I am sending under separate cover information on this idea
This information is in the form of:
☐ Patent Application (include serial number and filing date)
☐ Other (specify)_____
☐ Written description
☐ Photographs, Drawings, or sketches
Please indicate the number of pages of any of the above materials you send
us on this line

_____ pages

☐ 3M may use my idea
freely. I neither
expect nor seek
compensation

☐ If 3M uses my idea I hope to receive
compensation

☐ I am keeping a copy of this agreement
and the other information sent to you
as indicated above

☐ I am less than 18 years old
☐ I am at least 18 years old

Name and address of present employer_____

Name and address of employer when you first got the idea_____

Does either of above employers have any right or equity in the idea?   ☐ Yes   ☐ No

List the names, addreses and interests of
others having any rights in this idea and
ask them to sign this agreement.

(If none, write "None")

_____

_____

_____

_____

I have read the 3M "ABOUT YOUR IDEA" booklet, and particularly the conditions set forth on Pages 12 and 13, immediately preceding this agreement. I agree to each of the conditions contained in the 3M "ABOUT YOUR IDEA" booklet with regard to the presently submitted idea and all ideas I send 3M in the future.

_____ _____ _____
Signature of submitter   Date   Name (please print)

                     Address (please print)
_____ _____
Signature of parent or guardian if submitter   Date
is not at least 18 years old

                   City, State and Zip (please print)

If this idea is submitted by an agent of the originator, the agent should sign and submit written proof of his authority.

_____ _____
Signature of Agent   Date

D

Checklist for Written Agreements With New Products Services

By permission, American Association of Advertising Agencies

This checklist represents some of the many considerations that must be taken into account in new product assignments.

1. Agency service
    A. Scope of agency work, including research, package design, sampling, etc.
2. General provisions
    A. Mutually exclusive arrangement
    B. Mutual cooperation
    C. Approval of expenditures by client
    D. Care of client's property
    E. Cancellation of plans
3. Charges for agency service
    A. Method of compensation
    B. Amount of compensation (fee, retainer, etc.)
4. Charges for materials and services purchased (including handling of cash discount from suppliers)
5. Reimbursement for out-of-pocket costs
    A. Telephone and telegraph
    B. Shipping costs

Reproduced by permission from American Association of Advertising Agencies, New York, NY, from its private membership publication, "Agency Compensation and Written Agreements with Clients for New Products Assignments," October 1981.

6. Terms of payment
    A. Client agreement to pay
    B. Mailing date of agency's invoices
    C. Agency right to change terms if client's credit impaired
7. Termination of agreement
    A. Period of agreement
    B. Notice of termination
    C. Payment for materials purchased and work done
    D. Disposition of client's property
    E. Agency title to unused plans and ideas
8. Examination of records
9. Client's acceptance

E

Sample New Products Agreements With Advertising Agencies

By permission, American Association of Advertising Agencies

Reproduced by permission from American Association of Advertising Agencies, New York, NY from its private membership publication, "Agency Compensation and Written Agreements with Clients for New Products Assignments," October 1981.

<u>COPY</u>

<u>Agency-Client New Product Agreement</u>
<u>Sample "A"</u>

(DATE)

(NAME OF CLIENT)

Gentlemen:

This letter represents an amendment to the basic agreement in existence between your company and the agency and is intended to outline the method of compensation which is to prevail in connection with <u>new product development assignments</u> which we may be requested to perform on your behalf from time to time.

These new product assignments may include such work as brand name and concept development, creative concept development, product and creative concept testing, package design development, introductory and prototype advertising campaign development and production.

It is agreed that over and above the compensation provided for in our basic contract, you will reimburse us for the services of all agency personnel devoted to these assignments at hourly rates which recover the basic salaries of these persons and include a factor for overhead and normal profit. These hourly rates and the overhead-profit factor are detailed later in this letter.

These charges will be based on the agency's computer cost-accounting. Time sheets are kept by all agency personnel on a daily basis by quarter-hour units. These time sheets, as well as job jackets and other cost information related to these assignments, are available for client examination.

To the extent that charges other than those mentioned above are incurred in connection with new product development assignments, including charges in connection with production and creation of advertising materials and the placement of same, research, travel and cable expenses, etc., the provisions of our basic agreement will apply.

Billing for these services will be rendered on a monthly basis including documentation of all charges. (See prototype invoice attached.) The hourly rates will be billed according to our standard hourly rate schedule (attached). Rates on this schedule are based on actual annual salary costs, including benefits, divided by _____ hours and multiplied by a factor for overhead and profit. This factor is _____ for personnel in the agency's U.S. offices; _____ for offices in other countries.

Hourly charges will be billed by the 10th of the month following from time sheets for the month and are payable ten days from the date of invoice.

This agreement will apply to each product as long as it continues in the development, test and introductory campaign stages. It will terminate for each product at such time as regular commissionable media billing is in effect for the product. Thereafter, when advertising developed by the agency is placed by the agency or one of its associated offices throughout the world, the agency will continue to service the advertising of the new product in accordance with the terms and conditions set forth in our basic agreement. However, in those cases where the advertising developed by the agency is placed by one or more of (Client's Name) other agencies, (Name of Agency) will be entitled to a commission of _____ percent of the gross billing of such advertising.

If advertising for the product developed by the agency is placed domestically in media in the U.S.A. through the agency, _____ percent of media commissions on such advertising will be credited against the original development fees, up to _____ percent of such fees.

You may, of course, discontinue the development of a new product and our assignment in connection with it at any time by notifying us to such effect on ninety days' written notice. Termination of a new product assignment for any one product will not affect other product assignments or our basic contract agreement.

If the above meets with your approval, please sign both copies of this letter, retain one for your files and return the other to us.

                        Cordially,

                        _____

Approved for

                        _____

_____

By_____Title_____

Date_____

Attachments: Hourly rate schedule
             Prototype invoice

<u>COPY</u>

<u>Agency-Client New Product Agreement</u>
<u>Sample "A"</u>
(Supplementary Letter)

(DATE)

(NAME OF CLIENT)

Dear _____:

Attached is our supplementary agreement letter outlining the terms under which we handle new product assignments. I think you will find it in order.

Specifically, for the handling of the new product assignment you outlined to us, we will, of course, assign an account group to the project. The group will include an account supervisor, account executive, a creative copy-art team under supervision of the agency creative director, a research supervisor, media supervisor and international estimator, plus the necessary secretarial, administrative and traffic personnel.

We estimate the time charges for this group for the project outlined will average approximately $_____ per month over the period of the assignment. Advertising preparation and mechanical production costs, of course, are not included in this figure nor is research.

Research in the three markets, _____, _____, and _____ will cost approximately $_____ to $_____ plus travel for the basic creative concept testing. To this you must add about _____ per country for the advertising pre-testing, plus production of animatics. An outline of the research proposal is attached.

In total, our services on the project will include brand name and product concept development, creative concept development (both including basic package design), creative concept testing (including package concept) and advertising development and testing. Advertising testing would include preliminary concept and copy evaluation and communications effectiveness and response evaluation.

In addition, we will develop, prepare and place introductory advertising campaigns for the various markets involved.

We appreciate this assignment. It's an exciting and interesting opportunity.

Cordially,

COPY

Agency-Client New Product Agreement
Sample "B"

·

(DATE)

(NAME OF CLIENT)

AGREEMENT made between (Company) having an office at (address) (herein called the "Advertiser"), and (Agency), a _____ corporation having an office at _____ _____ (herein called the "Agency").

WITNESSETH:

The parties have entered into an agreement dated (date) (herein referred to as "The Advertiser-Agency agreement) wherein the Advertiser has retained Agency in connection with the advertising of certain existing products of Advertiser, and the parties now desire to extend these arrangements to cover the terms and conditions under which Agency will service and develop advertising and marketing plans for (such) new product or products developed by Advertiser as may be assigned in writing by Advertiser to Agency (these new products that may be so assigned to Agency hereunder are hereinafter individually referred to as "new product"). Accordingly, the parties hereby agree as follows:

1. The Agency will bill Advertiser for Agency's services on each new product in the following manner:

    (a) Except for the preparation of copy and layout for collateral material, Agency will bill Advertiser monthly in a lump sum for the actual salaries paid to Agency personnel for the time which they have spent in the preparation of advertising and the development of advertising and marketing plans for the new product, plus _____ percent (_____%) to cover profit-sharing, vacations, social security, Christmas bonus and insurance, and _____ percent (_____%) of the above two amounts to cover secretarial costs. The basis for computing salary costs will be the time sheets of individuals who work on the new product. At Advertiser's request, this basis will be subject to review of an independent firm of Certified Public Accountants designated by Advertiser.

    (b) For the preparation of copy and layout for collateral material, Agency will bill Advertiser monthly in a lump sum, at Agency's then prevailing hourly rate, for the entire time spent by art and copy creative personnel of the agency.

    (c)   Costs incurred by Agency on Advertiser's behalf for materials and services purchased from outside vendors and other expenses incurred by Agency on Advertiser's behalf in connection with each new product, and Agency's commissions on the foregoing costs and expenses, will be charged in accordance with and to the extent authorized by the Advertiser-Agency agreement.

2.   This agreement will terminate as to each new product at such time as regular commissionable media billing is in effect for such new product. Thereafter, Agency will continue to service the advertising of the new product in accordance with the terms and conditions set forth in the Advertiser-Agency agreement. This agreement will also terminate simultaneously with the termination of the Advertiser-Agency agreement.

IN WITNESS WHEREOF, the parties hereto, each duly authorized, have set their hands this   day of   , 19   .

              (ADVERTISER)

              By _____

              Title:

              (AGENCY)

              By _____

              Title:

COPY

Agency-Client New Product Agreement
Sample "C"

(DATE)

(NAME OF AGENCY)

Gentlemen:

This letter states the arrangements under which your organization is to provide services to the _____ Company in connection with specific new product developmental work as described in Paragraph 1, below, and subject to the terms of the remaining numbered paragraphs in this letter:

1. Assignment

    You will provide us with consultation, advice, analysis, reports, general planning and work assistance as required to complete all work pertaining to defining and evaluating new product opportunities in the specific areas of _____ _____

2. Compensation
    a. Basis

        For your work in connection with the foregoing specifications, we agree to pay you monthly fees as follows:
        1) Part I: $____ per month. This will purchase a month total of "Y" hours of supervisory staff time;
            or "Z" hours of internal staff time.
    b. Special Conditions

        1) It is agreed that the monthly charge for _____ will be $_____ but that if analysis reveals considerably less than the scheduled amount of time charges scheduled above, the amount deemed excessive will be returned to the _____ Company.

            If considerably more than the scheduled man hours are incurred, you will bill us for this extra time at per man hour charges consistent with the above schedule.
        2) General travel expenses and out-of pocket costs for special activities requested by the _____ Company will be reimbursed by the _____ Company upon submission of itemized statements. Such statements shall be independent of and in addition to monthly retainer fee statements.
    c. Billing Procedure

        Monthly service fees and all other approved expense submissions will be billed on the last working day of each month and will be payable not later than the tenth working day of the following month.

3. <u>Protection</u>

    a.   <u>Service Exclusivity</u>

        During the period covered by this letter of agreement, you will not assist in the marketing of physically developed products that compete with products of ours to which we have assigned your services unless prior approval is granted by us.

4. <u>Period of Agreement</u>

    a.   All work pertaining to this agreement described will be accomplished between _____ and _____.

    b.   <u>Option to Terminate Agreement</u>

        Written notice from either party may terminate this agreement at the end of a calendar month, provided that such notice is given at least one hundred and twenty days (120) in advance of the effective date of termination.

If the above meets with your approval, please sign both copies, retain one copy for your files, and return the other copy to us.

                          The _____ Company

                          By _____

                          Title_____

                          Date_____

Accepted by _____

_____

Date _____

<u>COPY</u>

<u>Agency-Client New Product Agreement</u>
<u>Sample "D"</u>

(DATE)

(NAME OF CLIENT)

Gentlemen:

Effective _____ your company and our Agency have entered into an agreement pursuant to which we are to serve as your advertising agency for _____.

The nature of this product assignment is such that during the initial period of our relationship our cost of handling your account will exceed the amount of the commissions we will be able to earn from media billings.

Accordingly, in addition to our receiving a _____ percent Media Commission and _____ percent commission on non-media costs, you have agreed to reimburse us for all of our Direct Payroll and other Direct Costs, plus _____ percent of our Overhead incurred in handling the _____ account from and after _____. The combined total payroll and other direct costs are referred to in this letter as "Direct Costs." For this purpose, the Direct Costs include, but are not limited to, necessary travel, lodging and meals incurred in servicing your account, but do not include entertainment costs. In all other respects, the elements of reimbursable Direct Costs and Overhead will be in accordance with the standard (Agency Name) accounting procedures.

We will bill you monthly on an estimated basis for all Direct Costs and Overhead to be incurred in the month. One month after the end of each calendar quarter, we will adjust the estimated reimbursable costs to the actual Direct Costs and Overhead incurred within the quarter. Any Media Commissions earned will be applied against the Direct Costs and Overhead. However, commissions on non-media costs shall be retained by the Agency and will not be utilized for the purpose of crediting costs.

In addition, either party may terminate this arrangement at any time by giving the other party at least 90 days written notice of such termination.

If the foregoing accurately reflects the understanding and agreement between us, will you please sign and return to us the enclosed copy of this letter.

Very truly yours,

<u>COPY</u>

<u>Agency-Client New Product Agreement</u>
<u>Sample "E"</u>

(DATE)

(NAME OF CLIENT)

Gentlemen:

This will confirm our Agreement with you, pursuant to which Agreement you have appointed us, and we accepted such appointment, to act as your advertising agency for various "new products" of the _____ on the following terms and conditions:

1. You retain us and we agree to act as your advertising agency for all advertising you may do on designated "new products" in any type of media.

    Definition of "new products": A "new product" is any product not already in test market or general distribution that requires separate marketing and advertising plans. (This distinguishes it from products which vary in only minor respects from products now in general distribution). You and we will agree in advance what products shall be treated as "new products".

2. You shall have the sole right to designate which "new products" shall be handled by us. Our Agreement shall in no way be interpreted as granting us the exclusive right to act as your advertising agency on all "new products".

3. No advertising is to be contracted for in your behalf by us nor are we to undertake work or order work or material chargeable to you, unless it has been authorized by you. You agree to pay promptly any bills rendered on account of advertising work or material.

4. This agreement may be terminated at any time by either party having given the other party no less than ninety (90) days' prior written notice of its intention to terminate. In the event of termination, you will reimburse us for any commitments or expenditures authorized by you and made by us prior to the effective date of such termination.

5. Our compensation for commissionable advertising will be determined as follows:
    a. On media that allow agency commission of _____ percent, we are to retain these commissions. On media that allow agency commission of less than _____ percent, we are to charge you the net amount, plus an amount which will yield the agency _____ percent of agency's total charge before cash discount.

    All cash discounts allowed by media are offered to you predicated on the understanding that your funds are in the hands of the agency at the time the agency is required to make payment. In cases where media allows rebates or lower contractual rates to us, the amount of such reductions in cost shall be allowed in turn to you. You agree to pay us for all short rate payments made on your behalf.

    b.   We shall be entitled to a commission of _____ net cost on all other services and materials purchased by us for you, including but not limited to, art work, engraving and other production costs.

6.   We will be reimbursed monthly for all work on new products, except at the management level, at the rate of _____ per hour. The _____ per hour fee will apply to only those "new products" which have not as yet been committed to entering a test market. You will not be charged for any work done at the account management level. We will also be reimbursed monthly for all out-of-pocket expenses at cost.

We agree to forego the above mentioned _____ per hour fee on a new product, after the time you designate that a specific "new product" will enter one or more test markets. Compensation, if any, will be derived from normal commissions earned in the test market(s) and in future national programs if you decide to use us as your advertising agency for such new product.

A letter will be sent by you to us each time a "new product" is designated and approved by you to enter a test market.

7.   Any notices required or given hereunder shall be deemed adequately given if by Certified Mail, postage prepaid, and addressed as follows:
TO
        (NAME AND ADDRESS OF AGENCY)

8.   This Agreement and the rights and obligations of the parties hereunder shall be construed in accordance with the laws of the State of _____.

If this letter correctly states our understanding with regard to this matter, please sign the enclosed copy and return it to us.

        (NAME OF AGENCY)

        By _____
        Date _____

Accepted:

By _____
Date _____

F

Decision Considerations

By permission, Schrello Associates

Decision Considerations

Decision Factors

Is It *Real*?	Is The *Market* Real?	Is There A *Need/Want*?
		Can The Customer Buy?
		Will The Customer Buy?
	Is The *Product* Real?	Is There A *Product Idea*?
		Can It Be *Made*?
		Will It *Satisfy The Market*?
Can We *Win*?	Can *Our Product* Be Competitive?	On *Design/Performance* Features?
		On *Promotion*?
		Is The *Price* Right?
		Is The *Timing* Right?
	Can *Our Company* Be Competitive?	In *Engineering/Production*?
		In *Sales/Distribution*?
		In *Management*?
		In *Other Considerations*?
Is It *Worth* It?	Will It Be *Profitable*?	Can We *Afford It*?
		Is The *Return* Adequate?
		Is The *Risk* Acceptable?
	Does It Satisfy Other *Company Needs*?	Does It Support *Company Objectives*?
		Are *External Relations* Improved?
		Is There An *Overriding* Factor?

Considerations

[Developed and Specialized for Each Company, Product Area and Market by Their Experts]

Kind of need/want; Timing of need/want; Alternate ways to define need/want

Structure of the market; Market size & potential; Availability of funds

Priority; Product awareness; Perceived benefits/risks; Future expectations; Price vs. benefits

---

Ways to satisfy identified market; Feasibility; Acceptability; State-of-the-art

Designed; Developed; Tested; Produced; Inspected; Distributed; Installed; Serviced

Design/Performance features; Cost; Unit cost vs. Volume; Availability

---

Quality; Utility; Convenience; Reliability; Serviceability; Style; Color; Safety; Uniqueness

Customer & trade advertising; Packaging; Technical Services; Sales promotion

Cost; Pricing policies; Terms & conditions; Competition; Other price considerations

Introduction; Design changes; Sales campaigns; Price changes; Competitor reaction

---

Experience; Capabilities; Plant locations; Processes/Patents; Unique ideas

Relation to present customers; Distributor/Dealer network; New marketing techniques

Experience; Organization; Financial strength; New management approaches; Commitment

Past performance; General reputation; Present market position; Geopolitical

---

Cash flow; Investment & timing; Sales & timing; Net cash flow

Absolute profit; Relative return on investment; Compared to other investments

What can go wrong; How likely; How serious; What can be done; Uncertainties

---

Future business; Relation to present products/markets; Use of resources; Company desires

Distributors; Dealers; Customers; Local communities; General public; Governments

Labor; Legal; Political; Stockholders/owners; Company image; Executive judgment

---

Bibliography

Banning, Douglas, *Techniques for Marketing New Products*, McGraw-Hill Book Company Inc., 1957.

Clark, Charles H., *Idea Management: How to Motivate Creativity and Innovation*, AMACOM, a division of American Marketing Association, 1980.

deBono, Edward, *Lateral Thinking*, Harper Colophon Books, New York, 1970.

Douglas, Gordon; Kemp, Phillip, and Cash, Gordon, *Systematic New Product Development*, Halsted Press, John Wiley & Sons, New York, 1978.

Drucker, Peter F., *Management, Tasks, Responsibilities, Practices*, Harper & Row, 1973.

Drucker, Peter F., *Managing in Turbulent Times*, Harper & Row, New York, 1980.

Engel, James F.; Blackwell, Roger D., and Kollat, David T., *Consumer Behavior*, The Dryden Press, Hinsdale, IL, 1978.

Fuller, R. Buckminster, *Critical Path*, St. Martin's Press, New York, 1981.

Gregory, James, and Mulligan, Kevin, *The Patent Book*, A & W Publishers Inc., New York, 1979.

Hafer, W. Keith, and White, Gordon E., *Advertising Writing*, West Publishing Co., St. Paul, MN, 1982.

Hambidge, Jay, *The Elements of Dynamic Symmetry*, Dover Publications Inc., New York, 1967.

Harvard Business Review, On Management, Harper & Row, New York, 1976.

Hilton, Peter, *Handbook of New Product Development*, Prentice-Hall, Inc., Englewood Cliffs, NJ, 1961.

Kepner, Charles H., and Tregoe, Benjamin B., *The Rational Manager*, McGraw-Hill Book Company, 1965.

Kinnear, Thomas C., and Taylor, James R., *Marketing Research—An Applied Approach*, McGraw-Hill Book Company, 1979.

Kraushar, Peter M., *New Products & Diversification*, Business Books Limited, London, 1969.

Larson, Gustav E., *Developing & Selling New Products*, U.S. Department of Commerce, Washington, D.C., 1955.

Marting, Elizabeth, Editor, *New Products, New Profits*, American Management Association, New York, 1964.

Peters, Thomas J., and Waterman, Jr., Robert H., *In Search of Excellence*, Harper & Row, Publishers, 1982.

Porter, Michael E., *Competitive Strategy*, The Free Press, division Macmillan Publishing Co., New York, 1980.

Rothberg, Robert R., *Corporate Strategy and Product Innovation*, The Free Press, division of Macmillan Publishing Co., New York, 1976.

Schultz, Don E., and Martin, Dennis G., *Strategic Advertising Campaigns*, Crain Books, Crain Communications Inc., Chicago, 1979.

Shanks, Bob, *The Cool Fire*, Vintage Books, Random House, New York, 1977.

Tregoe, Benjamin B., and Zimmerman, John W., *Top Management Strategy*, Simon and Schuster, New York, 1980.

Urban, Glen L., and Hauser, John R., *Design and Marketing of New Products*, Prentice Hall, New York, 1980.

Wind, Yoram; Mahajan, Vijay, and Cardozo, Richard N., *New-Product Forecasting*, Lexington Books, D. C. Heath and Company, Lexington, MA, 1981.

Wind, Yoram J., *Product Policy: Concepts, Methods, and Strategy*, Addison-Wesley Publishing Company, Reading, MA, 1982.

Yankelovich, Daniel, *New Rules*, Random House, New York, 1981.

Index

About the Author

George Gruenwald is a corporate growth and development consultant specializing in the identification and hands-on implementation of new business and new products opportunities for his clients, which include some of the largest consumer products companies in the world. From 1972 to 1984, Mr. Gruenwald was successively president, chairman, chief executive and chief creative officer of Campbell-Mithun, Inc., Chicago and Minneapolis, a $300 million billings advertising agency with an international reputation for successful new products marketing development. He has worked in the subject field of this book with more than 20 Fortune 500 corporations.

Mr. Gruenwald frequently writes, speaks and consults on the subject of new products development for private industry, trade groups and universities. Prior to joining Campbell-Mithun in 1971, he was a founder and chief executive of Pilot Products Incorporated, a new products marketing development service, Advance Brands, Inc., a sales and distribution firm, and a founder and executive vice president of North Advertising Incorporated (now Grey Chicago). Prior to this, he was a New Products Brand and Advertising Manager at The Toni Company (now Gillette's Personal Care Division). Earlier in his career, he was successively Educational Director and Assistant to the President of Uarco Incorporated, and Creative Director and Director of Merchandising Aids at Willys-Overland Motors (now American Motors). In the '50's and '60's, he also provided marketing communications services and consulting to major automotive and publishing firms.

For the past 17 years, Mr. Gruenwald has been deeply involved with the development of public broadcasting. At the 1983 PBS annual meeting, he reported on Future Service Opportunities for the system and its member stations, based on the findings of a task force he headed. His emphasis has been on new products and services as a member of the Public Broadcasting Service Executive Committee, its Board of Directors and as chairman of several of its committees. In 1980–81, he chaired the Joint PBS-NAPTS (National Association of Public Television Stations) Committee on Technology Applications, which recommended the program for further development of the system's full satellite and cable signal delivery capabilities. In 1984, his interests in new developments in nutrition and health led to his election as a trustee of The Linus Pauling Institute of Science and Medicine, Palo Alto, California.

He is a graduate of Northwestern University's Medill School of Journalism (Bachelor of Science) and attended the Chicago Academy of Fine Arts.